BELONGING TO LIFE
THE JOURNEY OF AWAKENING

By Mary O'Malley

Awaken Publications
Seattle, Washington
©2002

Awaken Publications
Seattle, Washington 98033

ISBN 0-9720848-0-0

9 780972 084802

Dedication

"Sometimes our light goes out, but it is blown again into instant flame by an encounter with another human being. Each of us owes the deepest thanks to those who have rekindled this inner life."

Albert Schweitzer

This book is dedicated to

Christy Magnuson,

A wise mentor, and the best "parent" I ever had.

Because you were the "midwife" for my true nature,

you played a huge part in giving this book to the world.

Words can never speak the depth of my gratitude.

May my life be a mirror of my appreciation.

The Intention of the Book

To belong to Life, to belong to your own life, to trust the activity of Love.

To belong to Life, to belong to your own life, to know the activity of Love.

To belong to Life, to belong to your own life, to become the activity of Love

Preface

I am still. My mind is centered and my heart is as big as the universe. The mind that believes it is separate has fallen away and I am completely here, steeped in the beauty of my favorite park. In my heightened awareness, I see that nothing is ordinary. A blade of grass is not just a blade of grass. It is a creative, intelligent community that is permeated with the Sacred essence of life. As I fully open to the moment, rather than seeing the wind in the trees, I feel it inside of me. Rather than hearing the sounds of the children playing, I experience the joy of their voices in every cell of my body. Colors are vibrant. Smells are delicious and I am awake. Being so present I know everything, including myself, as an alive, pulsating and unfolding miracle. All that has gone before me has brought me here to this park, to this moment and to this breath. Being this present, I finally belong to the awesome adventure that is my life.

I have not always known this. As my personality was developing in childhood, it contracted around a core of self-hatred and mistrust of life. This led me into the maze of isolation, separateness and deep (but usually hidden) despair that we all experience. I didn't belong to Life; I didn't belong to my own life and I didn't belong to myself.

But every step of my journey, including the most challenging of times, was a necessary part of my awakening that brought me to this day, to this moment, to this full and deep connection with Life. Even though the journey from isolation into connection was long and at times very difficult, in this moment of truly belonging I could now see that I had been supported all along the way. Step by step I was brought into the clarity, the courage and the compassion it takes to show up for the living process that is Life.

Being so fully present, I recognize that probably all of the people here with me in the park are lost in the maze of struggle, disconnected from themselves and disconnected from life. A moment of grief moves through but is immediately replaced by clarity. Even though I am only one human being, my awakening is evidence of the shift in human perception that is showing up all over our planet.

Remembering that life is a journey, I envision the Earth from space, enfolded completely in darkness. For thousands of years there had been only a few pinpricks of light, coming from the awakening beings that were living in the sanctuary of monasteries or secluded in high mountain retreats. All of a sudden, like fireflies flickering in the velvety black of the night, I can see a multitude of lights beginning to shine out from the dark and those lights connecting with other lights until there is a web of awakening all around the world. I know that this moment of being fully present in the park is one of those flickers of light. And I know that as more and more people have moments such as these—moments beyond the struggling mind where they are fully engaged with life as it appears out of mystery—humanity itself will be shifted into the next step of evolution, the step of intimately belonging to the Sacred adventure that is life.

This awareness fades as I continue throughout my day. But even though ordinary consciousness takes over again, it isn't able to ensnare me into the illusion of struggle and disconnection like it used to. I know that in recognizing myself as a part of a grand and mysterious unfolding, I can now show up over and over again for the living process that is my life. Rather than being an endless stream of problems to be solved, I perceive life as an adventure of awakening with absolutely everything—every single experience, person, thought and feeling—here to awaken me out of the illusion of separation, inviting me back into the whole. I finally belong to my own life and know the joy and healing of being awake!

It is my hope that in reading this book, you will come to experience this joy for yourself.

ACKNOWLEDGMENTS

A book such as this does not evolve through the contributions of just one person. Even though it was born out of the crucible of my own journey, it was clarified and supported through the wisdom and the efforts of many people. To all of the Godparents of this book, I thank you for your support, your vision, your insight and your patience. I especially want to thank the weekly groups and the many people I have had the good fortune to engage with in a counseling framework. I hope I have given to you as much as I have received. I also want to acknowledge my family and friends who, each in their own way, were an integral part of my own journey and thus an integral part of this book. And heartfelt appreciation goes to Mary Sue Phillips, who not only skillfully and lovingly edited this book, but who also has been and will continue to be the deepest of friends and a true companion with whom I joyfully, curiously and gratefully walk the walk of awakening.

Table of Contents

Introduction

What you are holding in your hands is an invitation, an invitation to know again the joy, the wonder and the peace of truly belonging to Life and belonging to your own life. Let us explore what I mean by this:

*Take a moment and lift your eyes from this book. Receive Life, right here, right now. Rather than drifting off into a conversation **about** life, be **here**, fully available to the moment life appears out of mystery. Notice colors, shapes, the space between things, the dance of shadow and light. Feel the symphony of sensations that is your body. Hear the music of life as it swells and recedes all around you.*

THIS IS IT.

*This is the living moment of your life. Every single experience you have ever had has brought you here to this day, to this moment and to this breath. Recognize that this is the only moment that matters for it is the only place that is totally brand new, truly vibrant and completely alive. Let it in. Allow yourself to simply **be**.*

As your mind drifts off—and it will—bring it back into deep curiosity about what is happening right now. The past will come flooding in. Gently release it and return. The future will try to grab your attention. Let it go and return. For just these few moments drink from the nectar of being present for your own Life.

*When you go back to reading again, pause for a moment here and a moment there and be fully **here**. Recognize the preciousness of each and every moment. Life is not a given. It is a gift and one day it will be gone. For these moments be truly and fully alive. Know that moments such as these will transform your life and the life of all beings in ways you cannot even imagine.*

As soon as our focused attention leaves the living moment of our lives, the vibrancy of being fully present may fade but it never goes away. Right here, underneath all of our ideas *about* Life *is* Life in all of its wonder and glory. This book is about how to be present for Life again. It is about how to clear a pathway through all of the thoughts in our head so that we may be fully *here*, in this moment, with Life.

To cultivate the art of being present for Life is one of the most healing things a human being can do. For *here* is a doorway. There is something *here* that can only be found *here*. As we relearn how to be present for Life again, we discover a deep safety, the joy of curiosity, a wellspring of creativity, the healing balm of compassion and the ecstasy of communion with the whole that we are.

And yet, rather than being present, for most of our existence we live in afterthoughts, a dream laid over the magic, wonder and mystery of the living moment. We are like sleeping Beauty who, after pricking her finger on the spindle, fell asleep for 100 years. It is time for us to awaken – to awaken back into the experience of being fully present for Life.

In this book we will explore ideas and techniques that will invite you to free your attention from the mind that feels it needs to *do* Life so you can *be* Life again. Through *being*, you will discover yourself again as a part of a vast and sacred process, one that is working tirelessly to bring you into full consciousness of Life. In this awakening of your mind, body and heart, you will know again the awe, wonder and reverence that is your birthright. That is belonging to Life.

You will learn how to not be seduced by fear, self hatred, resistance and despair so that you can stay fully connected to Life. Rather than struggling, you will find out how to engage with Life, *using* your mind rather than having it *use you*.

You will also discover how to trust all of Life again, even the difficult. In this trust, you can let go of trying to create a Life and instead be here for creation. And it is safe. In fact the safest thing you can do is be present for your life. That is belonging to your own Life.

The healing that we will be exploring together isn't just for you. By cultivating Sacred moments of being fully present for life, allowing them to become like a precious string of pearls woven throughout your day, your whole experience of life is transformed. As you learn how to live in a mind that is alert and receptive to the present, discovering a reverence for all moments, beings and things, you will be able to give to Life one the most powerful gifts any human being can, the gift of your undivided attention.

You then become a place of healing on our planet, for all that you touch and every being you meet is then transformed by the inclusion of your consciousness. Therein lies the possibility of heaven on Earth. As Vaclav Havel, President of the Czech Republic said, "The basis of a new-world order must be grounded in an environment that respects the Sacred dimension: the miracle of Being, the miracle of the universe and the miracle of our own existence."

When you are done reading this paragraph, lift your eyes. Notice the quality of the light in the space where you are – the air surrounding you, the river of breath as it moves through you. It is different than when you began reading this introduction for the river of life has continued to flow. Drink from the nectar of this living moment. For this moment, belong to this moment. For this moment, belong to your life. For this moment heal yourself and heal the world.

AUTHOR'S NOTE

There will be a statement at the end of each chapter summing up the core intention of the chapter. These statements are intended to be used as helpful reminders in the midst of your daily life.

Some chapters in this book may be more helpful to you at this time in your awakening than others. Feel free to focus on those that are most helpful and skim through, or even put aside until later, those which don't feel as relevant to your journey at this time.

The word *life* is used throughout this book in two different ways. The first way uses it in a finite sense, as in "your life" or "human life." The second way refers to it in a nonspecific or all-inclusive sense, such as "the wisdom of Life." I have chosen to make this distinction apparent by capitalizing the word Life whenever it is used in the latter sense. I have also capitalized words such as Universe, Presence and Awareness when using them in a nonspecific or all-inclusive sense.

Chapter 1
The Extraordinary Ordinary

Be Now..... Be Here

Be here in your now, Be now in your here.

Be in your here now, Be in your now here.

Now, be in your here, Here, be in your now.

Be your now, here-in, Be your here, now-in.

Here in, be your now.   Now in, be your here.

In our now, be here. In your here, be now.

Here, now your be'in! Now here, your be'in!

You're in here, be now! You're in now, be here!

In here, be your now, In now, be your here.

You're here now, be in! You're now here, be in!

You're be'in here now, You're be'in now here.

You're in here, now be, You're in now, here be.

Now you're be'in here! Here you're be'in now!

Now you're here, be in, Here, you're now, be in.

Now you're in, be here, Here, you're in, be now.

Here, now be, you're in! Now, here be, you're

Now you're here, be'in

Here, you're now, be'in.

Be your now, in here, Be your here, in now.

Now your in here, be! Here, your in, now be!

Jim Ayala

THIS IS IT

*People say what we're all seeking is a meaning for life. I don't think that's what
we're really seeking. I think that what we're seeking is an experience of being
alive so that our lives experiences on the purely physical plane will have
resonances within our innermost being and reality so that we actually feel the
rapture of being alive.*

Joseph Campbell

The drive had been both tiring and exhilarating. In the last ten days I had
been at Breitenbush Hot Springs with Stephen Levine, a skilled teacher of
consciousness and author of many books on how to be truly awake for Life.
The workshop had opened my Awareness in ways that had been atrophied
since childhood. He taught me how to lovingly watch the workings of my
mind so that my attention could become free from struggle and again engage
with the living moment of Life. After many long, confusing and grief-filled
years, I was able to reconnect during that retreat—for moments—with the joy
and nourishment of belonging to Life that I had briefly known as a child.

Back home again, standing in my kitchen, I was beginning to feel the anxiety
of nothing to do. The retreat was over, the driving was done, and my children
hadn't yet arrived home. Seeking to relieve this anxiety, I found myself going
out to the back yard and lying down under the oak tree's protective arms.
Suddenly I let go. For the next few moments of my life I wasn't trying to go
anywhere, understand anything, or be anybody. I let go by allowing my life to
be exactly as it was. Not needing anything to be different, I was enough. Life
was enough.

In a flash, I was *here,* making contact with the only moment that matters—*now*.
I felt the Earth holding me and the wind caressing my cheek. I could see the
veins in the leaves and was deeply moved by the wonder of it all. I completely
opened to Life and received the Love that radiated from everything. In this
opening I belonged to Life and I belonged to my own life, reconnecting with
the rapture of being alive.

I began to sob from the depths of my being. These tears came not only
because I had been disconnected for so long, but also because I knew, in the
marrow of my bones, that I had just discovered the safest place I would ever
know—the moment that Life appears out of Mystery. In that moment, I
recognized that I was I being breathed by Love, and I *was* this Love.

Recognizing the radiance that poured forth from every single leaf, rock and
blade of grass as being myself, a thread of trust was rewoven. I knew that my
perception of where to find safety, connection and joy beyond anything I had

ever known was radically altered. It wasn't *out there* in somebody else's perception of me or in some idea I hadn't yet figured out or in some healing that hadn't yet happened. It was *here*. It had been *here* all along, and it would always be *here*.

After a few moments, the vibrancy began to fade and grief began to take over as the many filters in my mind that separated me from the incandescent moment began to reassert themselves. Then I remembered grief was just another filter, and I was able to let it go. Again I was fully present for Life!

When my children came back, bringing with them all the myriad duties that come with being a single parent, the clarity, immediacy, safety and joy I experienced under the oak tree faded. My attention was again seduced back into the narrow realm of struggle that so often envelopes us. But the essence of that gift has stayed with me, fueling the core intention of my life.

I could now see that I would not find lasting healing in the realm of thought. My job was to learn how to clear a pathway through the story in my mind so I could make contact with Life—right here, right now. I needed to relearn how to let go into the adventure while curiously and compassionately paying attention to what was unfolding in the moment.

THE RAPTURE OF BEING ALIVE

Our way out of our difficulties is the journey into the Universe as sacred. Our way out is activating the sensitivities of the human that respond to the sacred dimensions of the Universe. It is a regeneration of the human spirit, enabling it to once again tremble with awe before these naked mysteries. What awaits us is the unfurnished eye, meaning seeing what is before us.

Brian Swimme

It has been said that after his enlightenment, the Buddha was met on the road by a man who noticed his extraordinary Presence. This man asked, "Who are you? Are you a god?" "No," the Buddha replied. "Well then, are you some kind of magician?" the man queried. "No," the Buddha replied again. "Are you a man?" "No." "Well, what then are you?" the man asked. "*I am awake,*" the Buddha said.

Do you remember the magic of childhood when you saw—deeply saw—your mother's face, really tasted your food and were able to let go to the flow of Life? Whether you remember it or not, you knew a time in your life that you were fully connected to Life. Before you grew up and contracted your focus into a narrow band of wants, fears and learning how to struggle with Life, you loved yourself; you loved Life; and you were present for the moment it all appeared out of Mystery. In other words, you were *awake*. You weren't yet fully *aware*, but you were *here*.

I invite you right now to place your finger on the side of your neck and find the spot where you can feel your heartbeat. Rest your finger there for a few moments, feeling how steady and rhythmic the pulse is.

Now sense that same pulse in the people living in the buildings surrounding you and driving the cars that are going by.

Now become aware that this rhythm is in the birds and animals that live in your neighborhood.

Expand your Awareness and find it in the pulse of sap through the trees, the dance of night and day and the music of the tides. Experience Life as rhythm.

Now come back to the pulse in your neck and realize that you are a part of this great rhythm and that every cell in your being vibrates in tune with this cosmic dance.

As we feel the pulse of Life in our own bodies, we begin to get glimmers of what it is like to be awake for Life. It invites us to soar on the winds of awe, reverence and trust in this majestic and creative dance that is our lives.

But most of us sleep walk through our lives. Even when we slumber in a mind that thinks it is separate from Life, the living adventure of our lives is calling to us. Breath by breath, step by step, it is inviting us to intimately and immediately connect with Life the moment it appears out of Mystery.

This process is spoken about in practically every myth that has ever been written. Intimate connection with Life is the pot of gold at the end of the rainbow, the sleeping princess who awakens with a kiss, the Golden Fleece. This sense of connection we are yearning for is to be found *here* in this living moment. And yet we look everywhere else except *here* for our peace, for our joy and for our sense of belonging.

Let us take a moment to experience what it feels like to be here.

When you are done reading this section, put down the book, and explore the space you are sitting in. See it.; really see it. If your mind isn't curious, pretend you are an alien who has come to inhabit a human body for just a few moments and need to describe what the Earth is like when you go home. Pay keen attention to what is. See lines and curves, colors and shadows. Feel the temperature of the air and hear the sounds that surround you.

This is it. This is the living moment of your life. *Touch it with your attention. Feel it; experience it. Notice that the mind will want to think about what it is experiencing. Over and over again, with deep curiosity, simply return to what is here.*

This living moment is the birth place of creativity, safety and unlimited support, and it holds all that you have been yearning for. For just a moment, let this moment be enough. Let go of wanting, fearing, grasping and resisting and instead simply connect with Life.

Now bring your attention into your body, and find your breath. There it is, rising and falling, rising and falling as you read this book. Watch your next breath arise out of the heart of mystery, and then watch it fade away. That breath is now in the past, never to be again. Now watch the next one arise and pass away. Each of these breaths now belongs to the 'already lived'—to the land of dinosaurs, ancient Egypt and second grade. They are gone, never to be experienced again. Fully be with the next breath for this is the living moment of your life—the only place that truly matters. You will again drift off into the mind, back into a conversation about Life rather than the real thing. But that's okay. Just keep on returning and know that each moment of connection is a moment of healing.

Being *here* is a doorway back into Life. Moments such as these, sprinkled throughout our day, bring us into immediate connection with Life. As we cultivate them, we can discover how to *be* Life rather than *doing* Life. Being Life is where true and lasting healing happens.

There is a wonderful parable from Peter Russell's book *White Hole in Time* that tells about the power in opening into Life and rediscovering the safety of *being*.

There once was a man who was holding onto a piece of rope for dear life, knowing that if he were to let go, he would fall to his death. His parents, teachers and friends had all told him this was so, and when he looked around, he could see everyone else believed this too. So he held on.

Along came a wise person. She knew that contracting brings pain and suffering and the security it offers is illusory. She talked to him of real security, deeper joy and true happiness. She told him this is available if he would release just one finger from the rope.

5

*"One finger," thought the man. "That is not too much to risk for greater peace."
So he agreed to take this first initiation, and he discovered that it was safe.*

*"Even greater happiness and peace can be experienced," she said, "if you will
release a second finger."*

*"This feels more difficult. Can I do it? Will it be safe? Do I have the
courage?" He hesitated. Then, flexing his finger, he felt how it would be to let go
a little more and took the risk. Not only did he not fall, but he discovered
greater happiness and inner peace.*

*But could more be possible? "Trust me," she said. "Have I failed you so far? I
know your fears. I know your mind is telling you that this is crazy, going against
everything you have ever learned. But it's safe."*

*"Do I really want happiness and inner peace so much," he wondered, "that I am
prepared to fully let go?" With a little coaxing he began to look at his fears and
to consider their basis. Slowly he felt his fingers soften and relax. He is then
hanging by one finger. Reason told him he should have fallen a finger or two ago,
but he hadn't. "Is there really something here beyond my controlling mind?
Maybe it is truly safe to let go." Trusting his inner knowing he gradually
released the last finger…and nothing happened! Then he realized why. He had
been standing on the ground all along!*

The ground beneath our feet—the *here and now* of our lives—holds all of the
safety, clarity, peace, wisdom and communion we long for. And it is safe to
open to Life. It is not only safe, it is our home.

So how did we get so far away, lost in the maze of a mind that feels separate
from Life? How do we open back into Life when we've been gone for so
long, with only vague memories of what is *here*? How do we cut through the
shoulds and *oughts* of our educational and religious training that say that what
we long for is in some far off place and that we'll only get there if we do it
right? How do we discover the wisdom, support and Love that is always with
us and is accessed in living moment of Life?

The key is to cultivate a curious mind and an inclusive heart so that we can
not only make contact with Life—here and now—but also learn how to see
the stories that flow through our heads all day long— stories that keep us cut
off from Life. Let us begin the journey of quieting our mind and opening
our hearts by intriguing ourselves with what we miss when our attention is
ensnared in the mind that believes it is separate from Life. This will bring us
to the place where we can again engage with Life in a deeply curious and
merciful way.

NOTHING IS ORDINARY

Unknowingly, we plow the dust of stars, blown around us by the wind, and drink the Universe in a glass of rain.

Thah Hassah

You and I are so much more than we think we are; and Life is, too. It is about something so much deeper than just laughing and crying, living and dying. Let us go on a journey together in order to open up our perception so that we can taste the true nectar of Life:

I invite you to travel to the moon in your mind's eye and settle down in a comfortable spot. As you look across the vast expanse of space, there is the Earth before you, a blue-green jewel floating in a dark embrace. Such beauty!

Look out past this astounding creation and notice the stars twinkling in the velvety black of space. You are only seeing a small smattering of the totality of stars that are in our galaxy—10,000 at most. If all of the stars you see became grains of sand, you would be able to hold them in the palm of your hand, but there are more stars than there are grains of sand on every beach of the Earth!

Look back at this beautiful planet. Can you see the sand on your favorite beach? Now add to that the sand on all of the beaches around your city. Expand that into every river, lake, creek and pond of your country and finally into all of the beaches of the great oceans of the world! There are more stars in the Universe than there are grains of sand on the Earth! We are a part of such an immense and awesome unfolding.

Take a look to your right and there is Mars – rocks, rocks and more rocks. Now look back at the Earth and see the myriad blues that make up the oceans, the variety of browns and greens that make up the continents and the dancing swirls of the white clouds that veil and unveil her in an endless dance.

Look again at Mars and see the barrenness of crystallized creativity. Compare that again to the extravagant expression of life on the Earth. See the towering waves of a tropical storm in the Pacific, the breathtaking beauty of wild flowers cascading across mountain ranges, the sleek and fierce movement of a wild jaguar, the lush vegetation around the Amazon, and the exuberant curiosity of babies of all species.

Look off to your left to the whirling, swirling mass that is Venus. Imagine what this cauldron of heat and gas would smell like. Now smell the Earth—fresh baked bread, rich loamy dirt, gardenias growing in the wild, the skin of a newborn baby. Our home is a veritable treasure box of scents, each one radiating the essence of its owner.

Listen to the stillness of space around you, and then listen to the Earth. She is music personified. Hear the gentle lapping of the waves in inland seas, the cascading symphony of racing rivers, the rhythmic beat of every heart in the world, the musical composition of the songbirds, the different tones of the wind and the beauty of an opera. Realize that this is just the music that we can hear. Every atom, every cell and every being, including the Earth, creates music of its own, becoming notes in the symphony of Life.

This is our home, a place of incredible beauty, awesome intelligence and astounding creativity. Move beyond the idea that you are looking at a solid, fixed, inert planet filled with animate and inanimate things. Realize that she is a living process—a being that has been on a long journey to get to this point in her unfolding. She was much, much different in her infancy. Out of her gaseous and molten beginning, she wove herself into ever more complex communities that have now shown up as the awesome and extravagant dance we find ourselves a part of.

Now weave yourself into this cosmic dance. Lift your hand so you can see it. Move beyond the idea of hand and see Life, in all of its glory, expressing itself right in front of you. Realize that it took the Universe billions of years to figure out how to bring star stuff together into this form.

Find the creation of the first fin in your hand. Connected with this hand are also the first webbed feet that allowed amphibians to venture out onto the land. But Life wanted to be able to explore rocky terrain and vast plains, so the hoof and paw showed up. They, too, are the ancestors of this hand.

Life then wanted to experiment with reaching out, touching, holding and actually picking itself up. This didn't happen until it figured out how to create the thumb. Move your thumb around and comprehend the vast expanse of time that was needed for its evolution. It is such a complex creation that it takes a greater portion of your brain to orchestrate the movements of your thumb than it does to orchestrate the entire thoracic and abdominal cavities!

Your hand would not be here without the entire chain of experimentation and exploration that has been going on for billions of years —all of the trial and error of evolution which came out of Life's longing to unfold into the fullness of its possibility.

The same is true for your whole being. You are a unique facet of the Earth that has arisen out of the web of Life. You are not an isolated, disconnected person. Just like your hand you are the result of the billions of years of creativity that preceded you and your very existence is dependent upon absolutely everything throughout space and time.

And the life you are living is an essential thread in the whole tapestry. It is not a series of random events that you have either done "correctly" or "incorrectly." It is a living adventure specifically designed to awaken you back into Life. Through all your experiences you are being ripened just as a peach is ripened on a tree. The ripening of a human being is about becoming conscious., —learning how to see and be with what is.

Move beyond the idea that you are a man or a woman – even that you are a human being. You are Life waking up to itself. Through your mind and heart the sacred beauty of everything can finally be recognized.

In your Awakening also lies the possibility of the essence of Life becoming aware of itself. Lift your gaze again to the panorama before you, and shift your lens of perception. Rather than objects, beings and things, see the activity of Love everywhere. Love is what made all of this possible for Love is the essence of Life. It is the allurement at the heart of creation that keeps electrons dancing around the nucleus of every atom, that brings forth stars out of the heart of mystery, and keeps the planets spinning as they do in a love affair with the sun.

Love brought the "stuff" of creation first into communities called atoms and then drew them together into communities called molecules. But Life longed to know and express itself at its fullest so it then brought molecules into the astounding community of a cell and finally onto the multicelled beings that now populate the Earth.

Love, this activity of allurement, permeates absolutely everything on the Earth. All things – animate and inanimate – are alive, pulsating miracles. Rather than separate objects, it is all the activity of Love. Pebbles in a parking lot, the astounding creativity of the raisin in your breakfast cereal, and even the presence of the wind are all brought forth out of the longing of Love to express itself.

Now bring your Awareness back into the place you are sitting. For a moment move beyond the struggling mind, and see Love. It's in the air, the light, the walls, the furniture and even in the pages of this book. It radiates from every single atom that makes up every thing in this space. Breathe it in, and allow yourself to be loved. Life is longing for you to receive its Love.

Bring your Awareness into your body and feel the rising and falling of your breath. For a moment, move beyond the idea that your body is a solid object. It is a field of energy and Love is at the heart of every cell of your being. Let go of the holding in your belly, your shoulders and your jaw and allow Love to shine. Be radiance. This is your destiny; this is your birthright; this is home.

The part in each one of us that knows that we are so much more than we think we are, soars on the wings of remembering when we are invited to shift our perception out of the struggling mind, back into intimate, immediate connection with the essence of Life. Yet it is so easy to fall back into *ordinary mind*. When we see Life as ordinary, we see ourselves as separate, cut off from the Love that we are.

We are now living at the zenith of our species' disconnection from Life and from Love. We live in little boxes and travel in metal containers that cut us off from the experience of wind and gentle, soothing rain. With electric lights, we seldom allow ourselves to be bathed by the moonlight and moved by the stars. Buying our food in plastic packaging and paper boxes, we have no idea that we are the Earth eating the Earth. The deeper we fall into the illusion of separation, the more we lose our ability to connect with Life, to feel it, to be moved by it, to let go to it.

In our alienation, we have also lost sight of the sacredness of it all. We live in ideas about Life—afterthoughts that look like they carry the taste and feel of Life, and yet turn to dust before our very eyes when closely examined. We try to be nourished by pictures on the movie screen of our minds and wonder why we are so hungry. In our disconnection we pollute the Earth, not knowing that it is our own body that we are destroying.

Lost in the story in our heads that feels it needs to *do* Life rather than *be* Life, we learn to *work at Life*. We struggle with everything that comes our way, hoping this struggle will bring us the peace that we long for. Most of our struggles are small—the stoplight is too long, or our hair isn't right, or our car is too old, or our friends and loved ones irritate us. But we also have big struggles—illness, betrayal, deep loss. Our propensity to struggle spills out into the world and we pit skin color against skin color, ideology against ideology, country against country, and good against evil.

Whether it is small or big, within us or outside of us, our addiction to struggling with Life causes such heartache, keeping us away from the *here and now* of our lives. We've lived inside the struggling mind for so long that we rarely tap into the joy, vision and communion with Life that are our birthright. Our destiny is not to be cut off. No matter how deep our contraction becomes, Life in all of its magical splendor is continuously unfolding, inviting us back into the ultimate adventure, our own lives and back into the Love that permeates everything.

Lynn Andrews, author of *Medicine Woman*, tells a story about a time that speaks to this Awakening into Life that is beginning to spread across the planet.

> *Lynn and her teacher, Agnus Whistling Elk, are sitting in a booth at a diner in the wilds of Manitoba. Placing a glass of ice water between them, Agnus says,*

"Lynn, take a good look at this glass and describe it to me."

"Well," responds Lynn, "it is a clear glass of water with ice cubes in it."

"Suppose this glass of water is you and the life you are living," Agnus said.

"How do you mean, Agnus?"

"You are like an ice cube floating on the water. Imagine you're the ice cube in the glass now. Let's say the water in this glass represents the all-surrounding ocean of enlightenment. And you're floating on it like an ice cube. As an ice cube, you look down at the primeval sea and you know a great truth—that you are made out of the same substance. You are made out of water. There is only one difference. Do you know what that is?"

"I am frozen," responds Lynn.

"Correct. The only difference is temperature. We come to this Earthwalk for only one reason. This turtle island is a great schoolhouse. We have chosen to come here only to become one with the Great Spirit. In your words, to become enlightened. Yet it's the one thing we're most afraid of. You come here like everyone else, like an ice cube trying to melt into the all-surrounding ocean of enlightenment."

We have come here to melt, to become one with the all-pervading sea of Love that is Life. This happens in a moment here and a moment there when we wake up to the sacredness of Life right here, right now.

THE GIFTS OF SPACIOUS CONNECTION

The same stream of Life that runs through my veins, runs through the world and dances in rhythmic measure.
It is the same Life that shoots in joy through the dust of the Earth.... into numberless blades of grass and breaks into tumultuous waves of leaves and flowers.
It is the same Life that is rocked in the ocean cradle, of birth and death.....ebb and flow.
My limbs are made glorious by the touch of this world of Life, and my pride is from the Life throb of ages dancing in my blood in this moment.

Rabindranath Tagore

Even though we may be cut off from the sea of Love that we really are, like ice cubes floating in a bowl of water, it is time now for us to awaken. It is time for us to *melt* back into the full experience of Life. This Awakening of humanity is a moment in the unfolding of this planet that is as important as when living organisms) came out of the sea and onto land.

Everything human beings have done up to this point has prepared us for this time. We have explored the depth and breadth of this beautiful planet all the way from the freezing cold of the Antarctic to the blazing heat of the Gobi desert. We have gone from the heights of mountains to the depths of the oceans and we have explored every nook and cranny in the human body. We have also gone into the world of the mind and the ever changing ocean of the human psyche.

All of this exploration has brought us to the place where we are the first generation to unearth information from billions of years ago, to enter the heart of the atom, to travel through radio telescopes to the beginning of time, and to be able to grasp that we are simply one planet, revolving around one star, that is situated on one arm of a small spiral galaxy which is dancing with myriad other galaxies. And we only discovered galaxies 100 years ago!

We are the first generation that can see the journey of Life from particles to matter to the living cell to multicell beings to consciousness and now into conscious recognition of the interrelatedness and sacredness of everything. These discoveries are changing our perception, inviting us into a more spacious view that can recognize the sacred essence of Life. This is the view that we explored while sitting on the moon—a view that can see the interconnectedness of everything.

Cultivating a spacious view of our lives brings us a treasure box of gifts that crack open our perception, engaging us with the sea of Love that is Life. The first gift is the understanding that we are not an isolated, separated being who has randomly shown up on an already completed planet. *We have evolved from the Process itself.* The threads of our lives are intimately interwoven in the tapestry of the Universe throughout all time and space.

We can see this by recognizing there is an unbroken line stretching from the moment the Universe followed the call of allurement to make atoms, to the birth of the Earth and our early ancestors, and finally to the appearance of us. All that has gone before was absolutely essential in giving us bodies and minds and allowing us the wondrous skill of reading this book.

Without Life's willingness to continually explore unknown territory and create the absolutely rare gift of water, animated life could not exist. Without the process painstakingly discovering how to digest sunlight through the exquisite creation of the chlorophyll molecule, plants would not exist. Without the first plants willingness to follow the call to explore land, we would not exist.

12

Without those first multicell beings who figured out how all their parts could communicate with one another, the nervous system would not have been born, along with our ability to hold and comprehend what we are reading. Without those forerunner cells that painstakingly figured out how to differentiate between dark and light, we would not be able to see this book.

The astounding thing to realize is that everything needs everything to exist. But this is not the only gift of spaciousness. It also allows us to see *we are all kin*. We are joined at the very core of our being with everything in the Universe. The chlorophyll molecule that makes up plants is identical to the molecule that makes up our red blood cells, except that in our cells, the magnesium atom is replaced by iron.

To be lifted out of our very narrow self-absorption and be awe inspired by the Mystery that we are a part of, is to also realize that *we are the Earth*. We may not have roots like trees nor the ability of mountains to rise from the heart of the land, but we are the Earth nonetheless. The same atoms that make up our bodies were once a part of the cooling Earth, were on hand when Life made the atmosphere and were a part of the seething creativity of the primal seas. The same Intelligence that orchestrates our bodies flowed across the land in the form of plants and went through the vast experimentation of amphibians, reptiles, mammals and then the human being.

The strength of the minerals in our teeth once helped to create huge granite slabs in pristine mountain ranges. The air that is moving through us has molecules that once moved through the breath of every living species that has ever been. The same salt water that makes up the great oceans of the world is bathing every cell of our bodies. We can take this back even to the beginning of the Universe and say that we are stars that have learned how to think. Human beings are not necessarily the pinnacle of evolution or the "end all-be all" of Life. Our mental-physical-emotional selves are simply matter grown curious, a conglomeration of star stuff that carries the ability to explore Life.

As we become unlocked from our narrow perception of Life, it can then begin to press in upon our Awareness that *we live in a sea of Intelligence*. This Intelligence is not just in the domain of the human mind, no matter how much thought tries to convince us of this. It resides in the molecules of air that we breathe, in the atoms of the paper these words are printed on, in the photons from the sun that fill our rooms with light.

Take a look now at your hand. Imagine your attention is a microscope that can magnify it a multitude of times. First observe your skin, and then go underneath it to the nerves, muscles and blood vessels. Allow your imagination to go inside of one of these and find one individual cell. Explore it, seeing the astounding creativity that lives there. Go to the elegant spiral of DNA that resides in the heart of the nucleus. Recognize that all of the information that Life has ever gathered about human beings resides in these sacred spirals, and that this is just one single cell! See that all of the cells surrounding this one also contain this vast network of information.

This wisdom is imprinted in every single cell of your being—in your eyelashes, the skin on your knee, the walls of your lungs. But it isn't only in your body. It permeates and penetrates all of Life. It orchestrates the rhythm of the seasons and the waves of your breath. It heals the cuts on your skin and brings forth mighty Sequoia trees from a seed no bigger than a flea. This Guiding Presence—the Intelligence that resides behind the scene—exists everywhere, in everything, throughout all time and space.

The most profound gift we receive from a spacious view is the recognition that we are a part of a living, evolving process, one that has been brought forth by Love, is permeated and penetrated by Love, and is finally waking up to this truth about itself. Gently, persistently, firmly and benevolently we are being pulled back into Life so that we can discover the healing truth that Love is the glue that holds it all together and that we have never ever been separate from its Presence. We just thought we were.

All of these gifts of a spacious view are changing the way we look at ourselves and at our world. No matter how crazy it looks, we are not dying. We are being birthed into a healing that has never happened before on our planet. There is now the possibility of moving into the radical experience of trusting this process, both the dark and the light. It may not always be pleasant or joyful, but we are beginning to understand that whatever it is that has brought forth galaxies and dewdrops is weaving the entire dance of Life. This includes the entire dance of humanity, which is so full of joy and sorrow, chaos and clarity, and pleasure and pain.

This creative unfolding that we call evolution has not ended now that humans have showed up on the scene. It is living us right here, right now—as I write this book, as you read it. Connecting with a spacious view brings a deep trust in the process, a keen curiosity for what the living moment is presenting and the healing balm of compassion for all beings, including ourselves. It also allows us to become bigger than our own individual stories so that we can connect with the sacredness of it all—every particle, every being, every moment of our lives.

DISCOVERING SPACIOUSNESS

From a distance the Earth looks blue and green and the snow-capped mountains white.

From a distance the ocean meets the stream,
  and the eagle takes to flight.

From a distance there is harmony, and it echoes through the land.

It is the voice of hope. It's the voice of peace.

It's the voice of every man.

Julie Gold

If we look closely, Life speaks to us over and over again about the essential nature of space. If there were no space between the notes of music, there would be no music. If there were no space in a potter's bowl, there would be no bowl. The next galaxy is 2.2 million light years away from us! The Universe loves space. Artists will tell you that space is more important than the contents of their creation.

Space is even an integral part of our own existence. If we took all of the space out of our body, we would be left with the elementary particles our bodies are made up of. And if we brought all of those particles close enough together that they touched, the resulting mass would be smaller than a grain of sand. So we are mainly space!

The truth is that Life thrives in spaciousness. It is also true that spaciousness is trustworthy. Let us experience this:

Take your attention, and bring it to whatever you are sitting on and realize it is holding you. If it weren't there, you would fall. Take a few breaths and let go of 'sitting on top of' and allow yourself to be held. Now recognize that whatever you are sitting on is also being held by something else (a floor, the bottom of a bus, a slab of concrete under a park bench). With your imagination, go through every layer of support that lies between you and the Earth and discover both you and what you are sitting on are being held by the Earth.

Now enter the crust of the Earth, this paper-thin skin of creativity out of which life as we know it arises. Keep on traveling downward, through the dense rock mantle and finally into the hot molten cauldron of the core. Who could ever imagine that right now we are sitting on such heat?

Keep on traveling in your mind's eye until you find yourself emerging on the other side of the Earth. There to greet you is a vast expanse of space. Recognize that the Earth is being held by nothing more substantial than the openness of the Universe! Take a moment, and allow this to sink in. This is not just a flight of imagination. This is the literal truth. As you are sitting here reading this book, you, and everything around you, are being held by space.

Now take this one step further. At the same time you are being held by space, you are also spinning around the sun at the amazing speed of 66,000 M.P.H.. As the Earth spins and dances, she is responding to a call of rhythm and order so finely tuned that its movement around the sun can be predicted to a millisecond. Let go to being a part of this great and rhythmic dance.

Expand your Awareness out through our galaxy and beyond. All of the celestial bodies in the Universe are also responding to this same call of harmony. Myriad galaxies—these grand creations of the Universe—are all silently and with great elegance dancing the ballet of Life. Now bring your Awareness back here. Experience yourself sitting here and reading at the same time that you are a part of this universal ballet.

A human mind that can look at Life from a spacious view is a mind that can heal the world. It is a mind that can remember that we are a part of an astoundingly creative, hugely immense and ultimately trustable process. But anyone who has tasted the heart-soaring connection with spaciousness will tell you that the door to an open perspective can close in a flash. The mind, being familiar with contraction and struggle, is resistive to the openness of spaciousness. Yet it is not our destiny to stay lost in the maze of a struggling mind. Our destiny is to know the connection and communion that comes from belonging to Life and belonging to our own lives.

Consciously cultivating spaciousness is a skillful tool and can help us immensely on the journey of reconnecting with Life. There are many ways to bring our minds back to a more spacious perspective as we move throughout our day. One of my favorites, and one that works well when I am caught, is to imagine myself sitting on the moon (as we did on Page 7). As I look at the Earth from a much bigger perspective, I remember that I am watching an evolving being, one that has gone through very specific growth phases on the journey to this moment.

From this spacious place, I recognize myself as a part of the Earth, born from the heart of her creativity. My Awareness then says, "This is it. This is the living moment of my life" and I become very curious about what is happening right now—what is appearing in my body, in my mind and in my life that is a part of the Earth's unfolding. This allows the full power of my attention to engage with Life.

To stay connected to spaciousness, Brian Swimme, a mathematical cosmologist, recommends in his video *The Hidden Heart of the Cosmos* using the experience of sunrise and sunset. Even those words hint at the depth of our contraction. Most people, when looking at a sunset, still experience the sun going down below the horizon of a fixed planet. We live and walk upon the Earth as if it were set on a concrete slab in a fixed place in the Universe. To watch the sun rising from the perspective that the Earth is turning *toward* the sun and observe the sun setting from the perspective that it is turning *away* from the sun can open us for a moment to the realization that we are spinning in space. For that moment, our narrow vision of ourselves as separate and isolated individuals disappears, and we find ourselves standing in the middle of an awesome process. After a time the door closes and the box of static perception reassembles itself, but the more we cultivate this perspective, the more our lives become oriented around the experience of spaciousness and connection.

A number of years ago, Jack Kornfield, meditation teacher and author of *A Path With Heart*, shared a wonderful way to shift our perspective out of the narrow and back into the spacious. He invited us to go out under the stars at night (preferably beyond the dim stars of a "city night") and to lie down upon the Earth. He suggested that as we gaze up at the stars, we imagine that the Earth is a big magnet and that we are affixed to *the bottom of the world, looking down into space.* It took me a while before I could shift my perception, but once I did it was exhilarating. It moved me out of the linear mind that says there is *up* and *down, left* and *right, north* and *south.* The old narrow mental constructs melted away, and I was actually experiencing the dance of the Universe.

Eating, something we do all day, everyday, can also awaken a spacious connection with Life. Let us take the raisin in your breakfast cereal. Where did it come from? A mother plant. But where did that come from—a grape that was connected to another plant that came from another and another and another down through time. But where does it end? There is an unbroken line from your raisin to the first grape plants, back to algae, back to the creativity of the seas and onto the cauldron of gas and dust that was the beginning of our Earth. But it doesn't stop there. The Earth was created out of elements that were born in the heart of stars. So yes, you are eating a raisin. But it is also true that you are eating stars, for every single atom in every single raisin in your cereal was once a part of a star!

Water can evoke the same spaciousness of awe and reverence. We have not found running water anywhere else in our solar system except on the Earth. It is a very precious creation of Life, one that took enormous creativity to bring forth. And of all the water on the planet, only 2% of it is fresh water, with most of it being locked in the polar ice caps. The other astounding thing is that the Earth isn't making any new water. The water it created in the beginning is recycled over and over again. At moments, when I am taking a shower or drinking a cup of tea, I realize I am being touched by particles that were once a part of a rainbow, a baby's tear or the early morning dew. In those moments, I am out of the narrow box of struggle and back into a spacious, alive and reverent perspective.

Anything looked at from this widened perspective can deepen our sense of connection. That pebble in the grocery store parking lot was once a part of a boulder in the mountains or the bottom of a sea. Our coffee cup is made up of particles that were once a part of almost everything on the Earth. That breath that is moving through us is a part of a river of breath that moves through all beings. It is also astounding to realize that every single thing in the Universe is unique. It's never been seen before and never will be seen again (think of human thumbprints). This is also true of each hair on our body and every leaf, rock and mosquito.

Having cultivated spaciousness for a number of years now, it has become a thread throughout my daily life. These moments of moving back into spaciousness—of recognizing that we are a part of an endlessly creative and awesomely intelligent process—are deeply nourishing and enlivening. Oftentimes this shift seems to happen at transition points. I will be exiting a social situation where there has been much noise and movement and in the doorway my perception will change. Rather than just being in a room and walking through a door, I experience myself as the Earth unfolding. In the next moment, ordinary consciousness may take over, but those moments, so rare and precious, are very nourishing and healing.

Bathrooms seem to have become a holy sanctuary, too. When I am alone in the stall and sitting still for those few moments, or washing my hands with water that has come from clouds over China, my attention becomes focused and my Awareness says, "This is it. All of the vast experimentation of Life that wove humanity out of the creativity of the Earth and that has birthed my body out of the elements has brought me to this moment, this experience. Be *here*." That connection is ecstasy. It is discovering myself as a part of a living process and at the same time becoming intimately, safely and completely present with it. It is the experience of belonging to Life and belonging to my own life.

Spaciousness allows us to relax from the deepest of levels. To live outside of the box of struggle is to discover ourselves as an integral part of an interconnected web of Being. There are many other ways to claim spaciousness. Use your own life as your practice field. Take little steps into the vastness of the process that you are. And be gentle. We have been in a very deep sleep, completely unavailable to Life, but now it is time to awaken.

WHAT IS UNFOLDING?

Spirit that hears each one of us, hears all that is...
listens, listens, hears us out...
Inspire us now!
Our own pulse beats in every stranger's throat,
and also within the flowered ground beneath our feet.
And....teach us to listen!...
We can hear it in water, in wood and even in stone.
We are Earth of this Earth, and we are bone of this bone.
This is a prayer I sing, for we have forgotten this,
and so the Earth is perishing.

Barbara Deming

As we comprehend ourselves as a part of a vast unfolding that is interconnected throughout all time and space, an interesting question to ask is "What is Life about at this moment of its unfolding?" The key to that question is in Life's propensity for coming together in ever increasing communities. We went from atoms to molecules to cells. We then moved onto multicelled beings with a nervous system capable of thought and self-reflection so that Life could perceive itself. In order to do this we had to step back into separation and use thinking to see and label what we were perceiving. And since thought has showed up on the scene, we have known both the soaring joy of being able to comprehend the parts of the whole and the unbearable sorrow of being separate.

Now it is time for us to rejoin the whole. Before this point in evolution, shifts into greater communities happened on the physical level. Now at this place in the unfolding, the community that is being created is happening in human perception, *in our ability to recognize the interdependent whole that is Life so that we can weave ourselves back into the fabric of existence.* Thich Nhat Hahn, Zen master and author of *Being Peace*, calls this perception of Life *Interbeing.* The cultural historian Thomas Berry describes it as a shift from the idea that Life is a collection of objects to the understanding that it is a communion of subjects.

This shift in perception is causing us to rethink our very definition of what Life is about and what humanity's place is. This transformation evokes what I call *the ethics of the Sacred,* an understanding that everything is our kin. This recognition of the Sacred brings forth a sense of stewardship, an up welling of deep compassion for how fully caught in the web of disconnection most people are and a deep commitment to allow our lives to be used for the Awakening of all beings.

It is now time to come out of our deep sleep and consciously return to the whole, *connecting with the Mystery that lies within the ordinary and recognizing the sacredness of absolutely everything.* Our healing and the healing of the planet lie in our returning to the memory of our wholeness. We can no longer afford the view of separation, the exclusivity of the human that divides Life into human against human and human against Life and causes us to live at the expense of everything else. We were able to sustain this old view as long as we believed that the Sacred was someplace else. We are now recognizing that the Sacred is right *here*, right *now*, in this breath, in this moment.

To rediscover the *here and now* of our lives and to be fully present for whatever we are experiencing is one of the greatest gifts we can give to our collective Awakening. It nourishes ourselves; it nourishes our friends and loved ones; and it nourishes all living beings. Learning how to be with *what is* will teach us how to show up for the living adventure that is our lives so that we can discover the Love that resides there. When the Dalai Lama was asked why anyone should cultivate an Awareness of the present moment he said, "It is the only place where you will know Love."

To cultivate the art of paying attention to Life is challenging, but it is also much simpler than it may seem. Let us begin by looking at how we can discover these sacred moments throughout our day, moments when we step off the conveyor belt of thought and connect, intimately and immediately, with the living moment of Life.

May each of us be touched, moved and blessed by the awe-some mystery that is Life.

May we come to know the healing of reconnecting with the living moment of Life, discovering the joy of belonging.

And in this discovery, may each one of us give back to the world an undivided attention and an inclusive heart.

Core Intention: This is it!

Chapter 2
Reconnecting With Life

LIFE IS A LOVE MAKING

Life is a love making.

Run your hands over it, gently though, lovingly.

No need to rush, there's no where to go.

Listen to your very own breath, this very moment.

The thought of it is intoxicating.

Life is a love making,

water falling from beginning to end,

all hearts falling towards You in Love, always towards You, the
Beloved.

If this seems too much like a dream you can't quite remember,

let it go, it doesn't matter.

Look out your window though,

the Earth is suspended in empty space, and the Sun feeds us all.

And do you ever wonder, who do they dance with?

Life is a lovemaking.

We are the fruit in Your orchard.

You plant, nurture your little ones, make us fertile, ripen and harvest.

The ovens in Your kitchen are always hot and ready,

baking all throughout the night.

The aroma is everywhere, sweet, spicy, ecstatic.

And these words? What are they?

The quiet

……..swish,

……….swish,

…………swish,

of a single leaf plucked by the wind

turning in gentle circles as it falls into the arms of the Earth.

Jim Ayala

21

THE MYTHICAL JOURNEY

We're so engaged in doing things to achieve purposes of outer value that we forget that the inner value, the rapture that is associated with being alive, is what it's all about.

Joseph Campbell

Sesame Street was a core staple of our family's TV diet when my children were young. I would often find myself sitting on the floor, watching in pure joy. I deeply appreciated Jim Henson (the creator of the Muppets) as the products of his exquisite imagination danced across the screen. In addition to his productions involving the Muppets, he made a movie titled *Labyrinth* which had a profound effect on my life.

It begins with Sarah, a beautiful young woman in a long, white, flowing dress, reciting a poem to a majestic owl while walking through an idyllic park. The scene evokes the imagined peace and magic of a time long ago. As Sarah beings talking, she says in a voice full of strength, "Through dangers untold and hardships unnumbered, I have fought my way here to the castle beyond the Goblin City to take back the child that you have stolen. For my will is as strong as yours, and my kingdom is as great." She then forgets the last line. In frustration she takes out a book and reads, without much vigor, "You have no power over me." As she finishes, the town clock strikes 7:00 PM. She is late! In horror, she lifts up her skirt (which has been hiding her jeans), and begins to run home in a panic as a torrential downpour begins.

Arriving home soaking wet, her very angry stepmother is awaiting her with words of shaming. Sarah was to have returned earlier in order to baby-sit her new half-brother while the adults went out for the evening. All of the classic feelings of shame, anger and self pity come rushing through her. She finally ends up in the baby's room where he is fussing and crying up a storm. In her frustration she leaves, wishing aloud that the Goblin King would take away this annoying child. As she closes the door she hears a great ruckus and when opening it again, discovers the child is gone.

Through the window comes the Goblin King (David Bowie in tights!), and she asks him where her brother is. He responds by saying, "Forget about the baby, I have taken him to the Goblin City and in return I offer you this crystal. If you turn it this way and look into it, it will show you all of your dreams. Do you want it? Then forget about the baby." When she refuses, he warns her not to defy him, for she is no match for his power. He then goes to the window and points out the labyrinth that lies between her and her brother. "If you insist on getting the child back, you must travel through the labyrinth to the castle beyond the Goblin City," he says with a voice that evokes trepidation. Without a moment's hesitation, she chooses the journey.

The night I first saw this movie, I experienced it as a metaphor for the journey of Awakening. It begins with a beautiful young woman and a mysterious owl in an idyllic, lush, green park. When we first arrived here out of mystery, we also knew this idyllic place of innocence where our mind, our body and our heart were all in the same place at the same time. Whether our lives were like *Leave It To Beaver* or were more traumatic, we all lived for a while deeply connected to ourselves and to Life. But each of us is destined to make the journey into the labyrinth (the maze of the mind), taking on a belief in separation and becoming lost in the illusions of isolation, struggle and fear ("Through dangers untold and hardships unnumbered...").

Our wanderings can last for decades, possibly our whole lives. Rarely, if ever, do we see that the journey is one through and then beyond the maze of the struggling mind. This place "beyond" is the place of being available to Life the moment it appears out of Mystery. It is in sacred moments such as these that we know deep love and respect for ourselves, an abiding trust in Life and the joy of being alive.

From the moment she forgets the last line of the poem in the park, until the moment she is confronted by the Goblin King, Sarah is at the mercy of many of the facets of the struggling self—fear, shame, confusion, boredom, judgement, anger, self pity, hopelessness and finally rage at her own vulnerability (the crying child). She meets this child in exactly the way we meet our own vulnerable parts—with judgement and rejection, abandoning ourselves when we most need ourselves. We rage at Life, but most importantly, we rage at ourselves. In frustration she leaves the bedroom and shuts the door saying, "I wish the Goblin King would take you!"

When she opens the door again and finds the child (her innocence) gone, the King of the Labyrinth gives her the choice that we all are invited to make. We can choose the crystal ball of the mind that believes it is separate from Life and which will give us endless ideas about Life, but which keeps us cut off from the real thing. Or we can choose to brave the journey through the labyrinth/maze of our mind, becoming conscious in the process. The Goblin King reminds Sarah not to defy him, for he believes his power is greater than her Awareness. Without a moment's hesitation, she chooses the journey through the labyrinth in order to become conscious and reclaim the living moment of her Life.

In Sarah's journey through the Goblin King's labyrinth, she experiences many of the core beliefs of the struggling mind that keep us seduced into struggle. But she finally arrives at "the castle beyond the Goblin City to take back the child whom you (the Goblin King of the separate mind) have stolen." When she confronts him and asks for the child, he says, "Sarah beware." As he is listing all of the generous things he has done for her, she begins to recite the poem that she spoke in the park. "Through dangers untold and hardships unnumbered, I have fought my way here to the castle beyond the Goblin City to take back the child that you have stolen." You can feel the strength flood her being as she says to the separate, struggling mind, "My will (Awareness) is as strong as yours and my kingdom (mercy) is as great." But just as she did in the park she forgets the last line, the most important piece of the poem.

As she is struggling to remember, the Goblin King offers her the crystal again and says, "Stop. Wait. Look what I am offering you (the crystal ball of the mind)—your dreams. I ask for so little, just let me rule you, and you can have everything you want. Just fear me, love me and do as I say and I will be your slave." The mind will remind us over and over again that it will create a reality for us, allowing us to think our way through our lives, rather than experiencing the real thing. It doesn't remind us that this throws us into a maze of struggle, disconnecting us from ourselves and from Life.

The joy is that Sarah suddenly remembers the last line, and empowerment washes over her as she says in joy and in amazement, "You have no power over me." In that moment, the separate mind looses its ability to seduce her, becoming what it truly is, a passing show moving through the space of her Awareness.

Through his film *Labyrinth*, Jim Henson is calling us forth out of a deep sleep, reminding us that our lives are a mythical journey of Awakening, one in which we become bigger than the struggling mind that believes it is separate from Life.

In infancy, we found ourselves in primal connection with the living moment. Slowly and surely we begin to think our way through our lives, pulling ourselves up and out of our bodies and beginning to live in the narrow room of our minds. *Lost in conversations about Life and about who we should be, we became cut off from the living experience.*

The image I often use in my basic class is of a beautiful mansion with exquisite gardens, full of flowers and birds. The house and the grounds represent the beauty and wonder of the living moment. But we don't walk the grounds nor live in the main part of the house. If you look way up you will see a tiny room at the very top of the attic. This is the room of the struggling mind. It is entirely enclosed with no windows to look out upon Life. But it does have a VCR and a TV that allow us to watch the movies in our mind. There we sit, inside our heads, cut off from the rest of Life, absorbed in thought. The walls are lined with shelves, stocked with any videotape we would desire, each filled with memories from the past projected onto the future. Every once in a while we can hear the rain on the roof, or become aware of the call of a bird and we feel a funny longing deep inside. But then we flip in another video, feeding ourselves with more ideas.

But ideas *about* Life and Life itself are two different things. In order to reconnect with the living experience, we need to learn how to use thought rather than being lost in its content all day long. Awakening back into Life is not about stopping thought, it is about becoming conscious around what thought is doing so that we have the choice as to what we will pay attention to. And Awakening isn't about judging thought. Thought is an exquisite tool , but that is exactly what it is —a tool. It is not the entirety of who we are. When we think we are thought, we become caught, following it wherever it goes and staying unconscious in the process.

There is a way out of the seemingly endless maze of the struggling mind. It involves the simple and basic art of paying attention—the ability to see, without judgement or expectation, *what is* right now. In this seeing, we are birthed back into the living process that is Life. But the journey from separation to connection is just that—a journey. The first step is to recognize that most of the day we live in a conversation *about* Life rather than experiencing the real thing. The second step is to learn how to use our senses to groove a pathway back into Life.

RETURNING FROM FAR, FAR AWAY

This Love between us goes back to the first humans.
True Love has no beginning; it has no end.
Deeply, look deeply, at this great Love.
It cannot be annihilated; it is the river giving itself to the sea.
What's inside of you, moves inside of me.

Kabir

In order to learn the art of showing up for Life, we first need to see how often we go unconscious, how often our attention is caught in the maze of the struggling mind. When we first arrived on this planet as infants, we didn't *do* Life—always trying to make it better or different than what it is. Instead, we *were* Life. Being at one with our environment, we unfolded moment to moment. We lived as immediately as a fish in a mountain stream or a rose bush growing in our garden. In other words, we paid attention to Life. We used touch, taste, smell, listening and seeing to connect with the world. We experienced insatiable curiosity and delighted fascination throughout our bodies. No great explorer of any new territory, whether it was the first human being on the Australian continent or Neil Armstrong on the moon, has ever experienced so many strange and fascinating things as we did in our first two or three years on Earth.

While we were discovering the world, something else was being developed that is not present in any other creature—the ability to reflect on and language what we experience. Slowly and surely, as the neural synapses of our brains began to link up, ideas about Life began to encroach upon our intimate connection, and we learned to think our way through our days. Our natural, spontaneous trust of ourselves and of Life began to give way to molding ourselves to what was expected and appropriate.

We became human *doings* rather than human *beings*, adapting to outer authorities and losing sight of trusting our inner knowing. As we repressed our natural exuberance and curiosity, we lost sight of the radiance of openness. Our senses began to shut down, and the division between experiencing Life and thinking about Life became greater every year.

It is important to see how far removed from Life we are. Imagine that a woman is sitting in a car at a stoplight next to you and suddenly you have the ability to overhear her internal conversation. It might go something like this.

"Why is this light still red? I'm already late and now I'm going to be later, and my boss will get mad at me. This stoplight is going to ruin my whole day! The boss will probably pour extra work on me, and I'll have to skip lunch... The girls were going to go to Freddy's to eat, and they have the most divine chocolate cheesecake. Maybe I could even buy an extra one to help me get through the afternoon... So what if my clothes don't fit any more. Joe is always nagging me so much about my diet that I just don't care. My only joy is chocolate anyway, so why shouldn't I have some?... But we are going to Hawaii, and I can't fit into my swimsuit. Oh why don't I have any will power? Joe is right. I'll go to the gym and work out tonight. Oh my god, the light is green, and I didn't even notice."

Conversations like this are where most of us live, most of the time. It's much like being in a theater, totally reactive to the images on the screen, forgetting that it is just a movie. No matter how scary or enthralling it is, it isn't the real experience.

If Life does capture our attention—usually through pain or something that startles us—it only lasts for a moment before the conversation about the experience interjects its opinion. So we miss most of Life and the subtle invitations it is giving us—the smell of the morning air, the blue of the sky, the beauty of our loved one's face, the exquisiteness of silk on bare skin, the

26

touch of another's hand, the sound of children playing in the yard next door or the taste of a fresh, crisp fall apple. We rush by these experiences, always on the train of becoming, constantly trying to get our lives and ourselves 'together'. Underneath all of this becoming, we are hungry for *now,* hungry for the place of again belonging to and trusting our own lives.

How do we reconnect? We can use our senses. No matter what the mind is doing, the living moment is always full of sounds, sensations, smells, colors and, many times throughout the day, tastes. The field of sensations that is Life can become a sanctuary from the ever-struggling mind, a place we can rest and reconnect. There is no accident that when something is right, we say it makes sense, or if someone is out of control, we invite them to come to their senses. In order to use our senses to reconnect with Life, we first need to make friends with our bodies.

MAKING FRIENDS WITH OUR BODIES

You do not have to be good.
You do not have to walk on your knees for a hundred miles through the desert, repenting.
You only have to let the soft animal of your body love what it loves.
Tell me about despair, yours, and I will tell you mine.
Meanwhile, the world goes on;
Meanwhile the sun and the clear pebbles of the rain are moving across the land-scapes,
over the prairies and the deep trees, the mountains and the rivers.
Meanwhile the wild geese, high in the clean blue air, are heading home again.
Whoever you are, no matter how lonely, the world offers itself to your imagination, calls to you like the wild geese, harsh and exciting —
over and over again announcing your place in the family of things.

Mary Oliver

To uncover the living experience of Life does take time. We have buried our openness to Life under layers of doing, controlling and contraction. Deep and painful experiences have desensitized us to Life, causing us to retreat into the maze of the mind. To step out of our addiction to being lost in thought requires that we make friends with our bodies and that we learn to feel again—both the wonderful feelings and the unpleasant ones.

For most of us this is a scary thing to do. Our bodies felt feelings when we were young that were both terrifying (rage, longing, sadness and fear) and socially inappropriate (exuberance and sexuality, to name a couple). So we learned to live from the forehead up, freezing these feelings in the nether world of our bodies. In order to stay unconscious, we only give our bodies fleeting attention and then abuse them with extremes of food, inactivity, overwork and the social drugs of alcohol, caffeine, nicotine and sugar. When our bodies give us the feedback that all is not in balance, we rail at these demands. In our unconsciousness, we've called this gift of a body an alien object that resides in the realms below who we really are.

Usually we only listen to our bodies when they call out in pain. Because we're not *at home*, the body is a repository for our emotional pain, becoming the enemy and a scapegoat for all sorts of problems. Many religions see it as something *less than*, a defilement of the spirit. It is interesting to note that most of our swear words are a judgment about some function of this exquisite creation. No wonder we move through our lives in such a disconnected way.

To come back into our bodies is to come back into our wholeness and into a deeper experience of Life. To be present in our bodies is to access the health and energy we have yearned for, allowing us to consciously engage with the reservoir of wisdom that is always there.

After you read this paragraph, close your eyes and take a few deep breaths. Now begin to shake your hand vigorously. Allow it to move back and forth through space, working up to a fast pace. Stop suddenly, and bring your full attention to the sensations in your hand. Feel the pulsating energy of Life moving through your entire hand. Stay with it as it slowly fades away. Be adventurous, and shake your whole body. Stop suddenly, and bring deep curiosity to what is happening. Experience the wonderful feeling of energy flowing freely.

This simple shaking exercise allows us a glimpse into the possibility of radiance. When we are lost in our heads, absent from our lives, our bodies hold on. They also mirror the struggle of our minds (the furrow in the brow, the clenched shoulders, the tight fist in our stomach). To come back into our body is to soften and melt these ancient patterns of contraction, freeing up the flow of energy that we are.

Free flowing energy is the experience of joy and radiance. Shaking our hand is an artificial way to open into it. This can also be experienced through our whole body and into the depths of our being by *paying attention*—by simply being *here*. When we are *here*, it is safe to let go of our guard. Our muscles soften and our bodies open. This brings about the free flow of energy that is radiance—the essence of our true being. It is best to rekindle this relationship slowly, taking brief journeys into actually experiencing the dance of sensations and wisdom that is our body.

There is a growing resource of people skilled at inviting us back into our bodies: massage therapists, Akido instructors, T'ai Chi teachers and Chi Kung artists, to name a few. To give ourselves the gift of an ongoing body practice brings treasures that can barely be understood when we are lost in our heads.

When looking for the most appropriate way for you to connect with your body, it is skillful to engage with a system that not only brings greater health and harmony, but also one that invites you, as you are participating in it, to over and over again be present with your body exactly as it is.

Whatever you do to reconnect with your body, have moments when you ask yourself, "What am I experiencing right now?" Because we are usually so far away from our physical experience, to ask ourselves to pay attention to what is going on inside ourselves may be like stepping into a fog bank. At the beginning you can't see anything, but as you practice being aware of your body, the sensations will reveal themselves.

After you read this section, close your eyes and bring your attention to your body. Allow your attention to settle so that the sensations can reveal themselves. Be curious.

Notice what you notice first. Once you've connected with the more obvious sensations (hungry stomach, sore neck, pain in your back), move to the more subtle. What is the experience of your left foot? Is your skin warm, cool or neutral? If there is a feeling that captures your attention, stay with it and ask your body, "What are you communicating?" Don't look for an answer; simply be willing to be present and curious about the feeling exactly as it is.

Stay with this as long and only as long as your curiosity is engaged.

The key to connecting is to suspend all judgment and expectation and simply be curious about *what is*. We can do this at any time of the day. The sound of a beeping watch can be very helpful to remind us to take just a moment to drop into our bodies and discover what is there.

It is also glorious to allow ourselves to have fun with our bodies again. Find a grassy area and do log rolls, somersaults or even cartwheels if your body allows that. Cartwheels are beyond my scope now, but give me a gradual slope, and I revel in the joy of rolling over and over again down the hill. You can also find a pool that has a slide into the water or maybe a river with a rope swing.

Watch children and see how natural they are in their bodies. When I am speaking away from home, I look for a park so that I can reconnect with being in my body through the joy of swinging. The children playing there also remind me what it is like to be truly alive. But we don't have to have a park. We can simply drop into our body throughout our day, whether we're in line at the grocery store, washing dishes in our kitchen or waiting for the bus to come. In those moments of being fully *embodied,* we discover that whatever we pay attention to becomes more alive.

Another wonderful way to access the wisdom of the body is to ask it how it wants to move and to stand quietly until the movement begins of its own accord. The glorious dancer Bill T. Jones, when interviewed by Bill Moyers said, "I think that movement is liberating...that it is good for you. The body is a reservoir of all sorts of tensions and dark forces, and it is also a potential source of amazing energy. Movement begins to negotiate the distance between the brain and the body, and it can be surprising what we can learn." Through movement we can discover how to live in our bodies again.

I have found that when a heavy emotional state is on the verge of engulfing my Awareness, if I take a few moments and allow the body to express the feeling, the process becomes fluid and waves of insight and mercy begin to flood my being. For example, when anger begins to move to the surface of my Awareness, I often find myself very restless, easily distracted and uncomfortable. At the point Awareness kicks in and I realize that something is asking to be met, I find it safe and even enjoyable to open to the feeling, simply being present for the experience. I now know the joy of anger freed up from fear. It is a passionate, alive, sensual feeling, and the more I am present with it, the more skillfully I am able to work with it in my daily life.

In order to truly listen to the body, it is necessary to know the truth—that it is a storehouse of hidden knowledge with a richness beyond our wildest imagining. It is *for us* and it is *for Life,* even with all of its aches and pains. Nestled in the heart of every communication from our bodies, whether these feelings are pleasant or unpleasant, is great wisdom.

We have gotten lost in the idea of pathology—thinking that if the body is experiencing anything that is uncomfortable, something is wrong and must be exorcised by denial, drugs or surgery. If we observe the body carefully, however, we will notice that it is committed to maintaining a balance that promotes health. We can see this in its adjustments around temperature. If its too cold, it will shiver to create heat, and if it too hot, it sweats in order to cool down. This can also be seen in the acid/alkaline balance of the whole body and in fluctuations of the heart rate.

The fruits of this reconnection with our bodies can enrich our lives in so many ways. The body is wisdom itself—a source of insight, support and clarity that comes from the heart of Life. We've been gone so long that we have bought into the illusion that with all of its disturbances and discomforts, it is the enemy. Nothing is further from the truth. The Intelligence that orchestrates Life communicates to us through the sensations, the ecstasies *and* the difficulties of our bodies.

Not only is the body a sea of intelligence that is constantly working towards balance and order, but it is also a most skillful partner in the dance of Life. As we learn to listen to it, it will tell us more quickly than the mind will whether a situation is safe or not. It will also tell us what is the best course of action among the many choices we have to make in any given situation. Our job is to learn how to pay attention—responding rather than reacting, listening rather than trying to fix, making friends with this exquisite creation of Life.

COMING TO OUR SENSES

Keep your mind in the present...Then it will become quieter and quieter in any surroundings and will become still like a clear forest pool. And all kinds of wonderful and rare animals will come to drink at the pool. You will see clearly the nature of all things in the world. Many wonderful and strange things come and go, but you'll be still. This is the happiness of the Buddha.

Achaan Chah

After my Mother had taken her last breath, it was evident that what lay there on the bed was just a shell, a former home for her spirit. I was amazed at how quickly her body became cold, and eventually stiff, when the Life Force was no longer present. I was also stunned at how deeply I take my life for granted, forgetting that someday it will end.

Lift your hand to your cheek and feel the warmth. At this moment you are being given the gift of Life, a gift that is yours to treasure for however long it is here. The amazing thing is that none of us knows when it will be taken away. It could be seven decades from now or this afternoon. We have very little control over that. But we do have the opportunity to become consciously and creatively engaged with this wondrous gift we have been given. It doesn't matter if we're caught in a traffic jam, late for an important meeting, or are struggling with the fear of being fired. We are still *here*, *alive* in this moment. Our mind may be somewhere else, but the rest of us is engaged in the only moment that truly matters. It makes no difference if we've gained 10 pounds and can't fit into the dress for the party, we are still *here*. It doesn't matter if our partner left us and we're deep in the throws of a broken heart. We are still *here*.

Are you ready to live in this moment, to actually be *here* for your life? Are you ready to free your attention from the maze of struggle and use it instead to connect with Life? In order to do this, you need to groove a pathway from the struggling, controlling, fearing mind back into the living experience of your own life.

Our senses are the doorway. No matter what the mind is doing, they can reconnect us with *here* and *now*. Is there any accident that the phrase, *coming to our senses* means getting clear again? Our senses are a wonderful place to learn the art of engaging with Life. Each of these exquisite gifts can, in their own way, invite us back into the magic and wonder of Life. There is almost no greater joy I know of than to be lost in an old pattern of struggle and suddenly be awakened by the sound of a bird, the smell of a camp fire, or the sensation of my breath moving in and out.

When my children were little, I was washing dishes one day with my attention firmly ensconced in a maze of struggle. The struggle crystallized around a challenge in one of my children's lives. I was slowly and surely tumbling down the steep slope of overwhelm when, all of a sudden, Awareness kicked in. "Ahh, I am lost in thought again, and what is happening is that I am washing dishes." I brought my attention to the sensations I was experiencing in that moment—warm water, the smell of the soap, the sounds of a pan against the sink and a utensil against a pan. At first my mind wanted to go back into the struggle, but I gently and persistently kept on bringing it back to the actual experience. Soon my mind began to settle and my Awareness could see (rather than being lost in) this old and very familiar pattern of overwhelm. With my Awareness freed up from the struggle, I could now make skillful choices around this challenge.

I was able to pull myself out of struggle because I have cultivated Awareness of my senses, using them as a place to rest from the ever forward tumbling of the mind. As one of my teachers once said, "Where there is Awareness, there is choice, and where there is choice, there is freedom."

Now let us take a journey through the mysterious workings of our senses, learning how to connect with them so that we can become more alive.

I invite you to *experience* as much as you can while you are exploring each of the senses in the following sections. The invitation is to not just read, but to *feel* what is being evoked. All of the information presented in each section is intended to awaken your senses so that they can become a doorway back into your life.

Seeing

Take a moment and recognize that right now you are using your eyes to see. It took a long time for eyes to evolve. In the Earth's youth there were no eyes. At the beginning of Life's ability to see itself, it figured out how to create cells that could tell the difference between dark and light. These specialized cells evolved to the point that they could perceive motion, then form, and finally a wide spectrum of the details and colors that Life is capable of. Your ability to read this book is possible because of all of the eyes that have come before.

At this point, seeing has become the king of the senses for the human being and has a tendency to dominate all of the others. 70% of the body's sense receptors are clustered in the eyes. It is the sense that can extend the furthest. To taste or touch something, it has to be very close. To smell or hear it, there can be more distance. But our eyes can take us almost anywhere, being able to receive information from as far away as the Pleiades and in the next moment to explore the heart of a flower.

Seeing is really receiving. Sight is the experience of actual particles of an object, in the form of photons, flooding our retina. They are then translated into electrical impulses that travel along the optic nerve to the brain. Seeing is not so much an *extending out* as it is a *letting in* of what is before us. The only reason we can even see any object is because it is flooding us with a celebration of itself.

To stop the restless searching of the eyes and to really focus on what is before us connects us with *here* and opens us to a facet of our destiny—the ability to bear witness to Life. To see brings us out of the wanderings of past and future back into the immediacy of the moment, back into the magic and mystery we have lost sight of. Seeing can open us into deep reverence.

After you read these paragraphs, lift up your hand, and begin to explore it with your eyes. There are a variety of colors and shades, the dance of shadows and light, and all sorts of lines and edges, bumps and valleys. Be fascinated. Pretend you have never seen a hand before. Move it all around, seeing spots and scars, the swirling art of your fingertips. Become intrigued by the creation called a hand, this map of the history of your life.

Now move one finger and be stunned by its ability to do so—words seen on a page, translated into a thought in your brain and finally into movement. How does that happen? Become aware that in receiving your hand with your eyes, actual particles that were once a part of your hand are now flooding your retina. Allow sight to open you up into worlds you have not visited for a long time.

Realize you are experiencing your hand at one moment of its life. See it when it was tiny and new—soft, plump and curious. Comprehend all the variety of tasks it has performed throughout your life. It has played in the dirt, held the handlebars of a tricycle, and has prepared food for you in order to live. It has also hit and caressed other human beings. It has brought to you the things you needed and desired and has let go of or pushed away what you disliked or no longer needed.

This hand has touched many of the experiences of your life. Acknowledge the different feelings it is capable of expressing, from the belligerent gesture of a raised middle finger, to the welcoming of an outstretched hand, to the fear inherent in a tightly closed fist. See it growing older, the skin wrinkling and spotting, and imagine the moment that it will merge again into the void of mystery. Lift your eyes and take in the entirety of this moment of your life. This moment is it...the only place where your life is truly lived.

Our relationships with friends and loved ones are also a wonderful place for reconnecting with *here*. To begin, ask one of them to sit quietly in front of you.

Both of you close your eyes. In a moment you will open your eyes while theirs remain closed. Take a moment to tense and relax the muscles around your eyes. We are very used to perceiving sight as an experience of going out to an object. Relaxing these muscles can foster the experience of having Life come to you. When you are ready, open your eyes and allow this person's Presence to flood you.

Very rarely do we have the experience of intimately seeing a fellow human being. Be awed by the beauty before you. See colors and shades, lines and valleys, shadows and light. Know that your attention is a tangible gift you are giving them. The very cells in this person in front of you are responding to the power of your gaze.

Allow a sense of wonder to open in order to create an even more healing form of attention. Realize that what is before you is a unique manifestation of Life, one that has never showed up this way before and will never show up this way again. They arrived out of Mystery as one cell, and now they are made up of trillions of these intelligent beings all working together!

Allow your heart to open, too. See that on their journey from one cell to this moment, they have experienced the same highs and lows you have. They have known the deep grief of separation, the agony of self-judgment, the shattering experience of despair, the heaviness of rage and the hopelessness of doubt. They also have had moments of great exhilaration when they thought joy would never end and deep waves of gratitude for simply being alive. Include them in the gaze of compassion that understands we are all in this together.

Before you invite them to open their eyes, know that one of the greatest gifts we can give to our fellow human beings is this act of truly being present with them in wonder and compassion.

If they are willing, switch places. As they are gazing at you, notice what your experience is like when you are seen in this way. You have waited for this kind of undivided attention your whole life. The fears you have about people seeing your imagined defects are the same fears we all have. Move beyond them, and allow yourself to be like a dry sponge, drinking up this healing attention.

When you are done reading this section, give this gift to yourself too. Take a tour through your house. Pretend that in one hour the house and everything in it will evaporate back into Mystery. Really see what is there. Be awed by how much you miss, even in your own home. Exploring through new eyes can bring you to deep gratitude for all of the gifts you have been given and for all of the beauty that surrounds you. It can also invite you into awestruck wonder at the gift of sight.

Now find a mirror, and explore your own face. Move beyond our very limited viewpoint of beauty and even beyond the fear of aging and receive yourself for exactly who you are. You are totally unique in the universal scheme of things. Nobody has ever looked like this, and nobody ever will again. Meet yourself as the divine made manifest.

Touching

Right now as you sit here reading this book, a symphony of sensations is dancing throughout your body. There is the pressure of the book on your hands, tingles somewhere in your legs, warmth in the small of your back, the caress of air on your cheeks, the gentle feeling of clothes moving against your body as you breathe, and maybe a hint of tension in your neck. You are always touching and being touched, whether it is the pressure from the back of the chair, the caress of a loved one's hand on your skin, or the softness of a baby's cheek.

Touch is the mother of all of the other senses, for each of them is simply a highly refined expression of touch—air molecules touching our ear drums and turning into a song, atoms that were once part of a pot of home made soup wafting through our nose and bumping up against the taste sensors of our tongue, and photons of light bouncing off the retina of our eyes.

We define ourselves more by touch than any other sense. It is the first sense to awaken—being caressed by the amniotic fluid in the womb—and the last to leave, long after hearing, sight, taste and smell have faded away.

We can get along without taste, sight, hearing and smell, but to be cut off from touch means certain death. We would not be able to orient ourselves physically, experiencing either traumatic injuries or simply withering away as the children did in the orphanages of the 19th century. Premature babies who were touched rather than being left in the isolation of their incubators were found to gain weight 50% faster than those who were not touched. They also were more alert and responsive. Children who are touched a lot when they are young literally connect more neural synapses in their brains.

One of the main reasons this happens is that when we were just embryos, we came in three layers, each of them turning into two or three of the major systems of the body. The outer layer of the embryo turned into only the skin and the nervous system. So the brain could be said to be the inner part of the skin or the skin the outer part of the brain! To touch and be touched is to enhance and enliven our whole experience of being alive.

Close your eyes and bring your finger very slowly to your cheek—so slowly that you are completely aware of the moment that finger and cheek connect. Keeping the touch very light, move it around. Feel how your cheek becomes alive with this simple touch. Know that you are evoking activity throughout your entire nervous system and even into the deeper regions of your brain, all with one very light and very basic touch. Explore your face, experiencing the myriad of sensations. Feel the difference between your lip's experience of being touched and the tip of your nose. This is the intelligence of fifteen billion years of creativity responding to itself touching itself.

No matter what the mind is doing, we can return to the sensation of touch in order to become centered again, giving ourselves a sanctuary when we are caught in the maze of the mind. Whether it is the actual experience of a chair against our back or the tender, compassionate touch of a hand on our cheek, touch has the ability to bring us back into the living moment of our lives.

The extraordinary thing is that even though there is a symphony of sensations happening right now, there is no touch that is ordinary.

After reading this paragraph, close your eyes and slap your thigh vigorously with your hand. Pay attention to the cascade of feelings, both in your thigh and in your hand—pulsing, vibrating, tingling, sharp sensations. Stay with them while they fade. Now go to something subtler. Become aware of the place where your buttocks make contact with whatever you are sitting on. Allow your Awareness to be like a laser beam, first feeling one buttock. Rest there long enough to experience the myriad sensations that arise from simply sitting. Can you feel pressure or tingling, warmth or discomfort? Allow the experience to develop like a Polaroid picture. Now move your Awareness to the other buttock. How is it different? How is it the same? Go to something even subtler, like your little finger, keeping your eyes closed. If it is hard to find in the field of sensations, ask yourself how you even know there is a finger there. What is the feedback from Life that says, "Ahh, finger?" If it is still hard to experience, move it around, feeling its existence, and then stop moving and pay attention.

Working with touch does not mean feeling *everything* in our lives. That is physically impossible. What we are doing here is using touch to retrain our Awareness in order to pay attention to Life. Amazing things can be discovered—things that we usually miss when attention is caught in the forward tumbling of thought.

In order to become curious about touch, be willing to explore your world with your eyes closed. If you have a friend who can do this with you, put on a blindfold and either have them lead you around or else bring you a variety of objects with different surfaces—ones that are smooth and rough, moist and dry, hard and soft. As you come in contact with an object, move beyond mass, weight, height and contours. Move beyond forming ideas about it and stay in the realm of experience, exploring the object exactly as it feels.

When we rely predominantly on sight to experience our world, our fingers become nothing more than tools that do sight's bidding, and we miss *so* much.

Without sight to rely on, the fingers can discover amazing things. Everything is unique and highly different and also has a Presence. *Everything is radiating itself.* With eyes closed, we can perceive that when we touch something, *it touches back.*

We can also open to the realm of touch by connecting with another person. Amazing things happen when one human being touches another. We need touch, but most importantly we need conscious touch, a moment when somebody is connecting with us skin to skin and is also aware that this is happening. When we touch another, pathways of sensations travel at lightning speed throughout both our body and the one we are touching. Whole worlds are born with a simple touch. The body becomes alive with energy and information, digesting that simple touch and allowing it to transform the whole organism's experience of the world.

Be willing to touch someone today with conscious Awareness, whether it is the simple holding of a hand while you're watching a movie, a hug, a handshake or the overall bodily experience of a massage. Have moments when you allow yourself to be awed by the experience of contact.

Listening

When we were very young, we lived inside of a symphony. The trilling flute of a bird song vibrated within us and was as fascinating as the percussion of a slamming door. We didn't just hear with our ears. We heard with our whole being. We lived in a world of music, every sound a note in the tapestry of Life. Everything had its own song—our house, the trees in our yard, the fly on the window sill.

As we began to contain ourselves and become guarded towards Life, we closed off, placing filters over our experience of hearing. On some level this closing off is necessary in our extremely noisy society. We hear more new sounds in a year of our lives than our grandparents heard in their entire existence. But this filtering has become an ingrained habit rather than a conscious choice and leaves us little ability to be open to sound in ways that can heal and touch us—nourishing sounds like birds singing, the gentle patter of falling rain and the whisper of the wind in the trees.

We can understand sound when we comprehend that it is energy in motion. The Universe *is* vibration. Absolutely everything, from every single cell to your whole body and even the Earth itself has a frequency at which it vibrates. Whether it is the sound of a bee or the clarion call of a trumpet, we can hear these vibrations because the atoms and molecules that comprise them are moving to and fro. Once you start listening to Life, you see that the Earth is a world of rhythms, ratios, relationships and harmonies that create everything from the number of petals on a flower to the mathematical precision of the Earth's dance around the sun. We have called upon these same mathematical laws of nature to create the music we play in great concert halls, over the radio waves and in homes all over the world.

Our ears hear only a minuscule portion of this vast, vibrating world we live in. The sounds that we do hear are an exquisite translation of air molecules into perception. It begins with the vibration of an object, such as the movement of a person's vocal cords. Air molecules that are moved in this process come crashing like waves upon our eardrums. These wonderful membranes vibrate like ancient tribal drums. This awakens a series of tiny bones that press against the fluid of the inner ear. In this inner sanctum, there are tiny hairs that awaken the auditory nerve cells which then send this information to the brain. What a wondrous process this is of transforming airwaves into liquid waves into electrical impulses and finally into perception.

Sound can be a magical invitation back into Life. When I was first awakening, going into my body was too terrifying for me, but listening was a place where I could anchor. To turn away from the ever-struggling mind and to keenly listen would bring a thrill throughout my body. "This is it!" Awareness would say. "I'm eavesdropping on my own life." Another thrill would run through my being as I realized that every sound I was hearing was totally brand new, never having been heard before and never to be heard again.

Really listening to my life evokes within me the peace of childhood. One memory is of being put to bed before the rest of the neighborhood had quieted down for the night. I felt such contentment in simply listening to Life unfolding, both in my own home and in the neighborhood. In those moments I was fully *being* with Life.

The song of birds is another sound that brings me back to the present. Once when I was speaking to an auditorium full of people, my mind caught in judgment about what I was saying, my ears picked up a distant bird song and suddenly I was back in the living moment. I have also found myself walking through parking garages, deep in the maze of a city, and a far-off trill would awaken me again. Birds constantly remind me to reconnect all of my being with the preciousness and uniqueness of the living moment.

The joy of consciously opening to the ever-changing river of sound is almost incomprehensible. From every point in space, the river of sound arises out of Mystery and melts back again in an amazing and continuous symphony. We can use sound to connect with Life throughout our day. When we tune in— deeply listening—we immediately enter the living moment of our lives.

The joy of sound is that it is always with us, always unfolding underneath the restless, wandering mind. When you find yourself caught again in struggle, just a moment or two of listening can re-center your Awareness.

Have fun with sound. When you are in a public place, close your eyes and hear the symphony that is language. Try to move beyond the content of what is being said and hear it as the rising and falling of music. You can also put in earplugs and tune into the internal sounds of your own body, the singing of the nerves, the whooshing of your blood through arteries and veins, the comforting rhythm of your heart. Know that you are listening to the Intelligence that created Life expressing itself as you.

Tasting

Eating is something all of us do many times every day, but rarely do we really taste. Most of us inhale our food, getting ready to shovel in the next mouthful before we have even finished chewing the last. Or we are preoccupied in conversation, TV or reading while eating. We are lost to the sensual wonder of food, cut off from the living experience of this gift. As a result, we are a society that lives on antacids, laxatives and pain relievers.

One of the most essential parts of the digestive process is to recognize, *to really see*, what we are going to eat. This allows us not only to eat wisely but also to create a very healing relationship with this food that is going to become a part of ourselves.

This is why saying Grace has been around for centuries. True Grace is a grateful recognition of the gift that Life is giving you. With Kirlian photography (the ability to photograph energy patterns), we have been able to compare the energy patterns of food that has been blessed and food that hasn't. The simple action of seeing and giving thanks literally transforms the energy of the food. Rather than eating unconsciously, we can use chewing and tasting as a place for grounding and remembering the miraculous process we are a part of and as a place for cultivating deep gratitude for the gift of Life.

I invite you now to find a piece of food, preferably something small like a grape, raisin, strawberry or nut.

Take a moment and see it as intently as you would a loved one's face. Discover it on a continuum from seed to seedling to ripening and harvesting, on to the store and finally to this moment in your hand. Be fascinated by its colors and contours. Give it your full attention, being deeply grateful for the vast network of creativity that brought forth this piece of Mystery.

Recognize that in a moment it is going to become a part of you. To really see this being and to be grateful for its willingness to give itself to you literally transforms it on a cellular level and changes the relationship it will have with your body.

Now close your eyes and place it in your mouth. Before chewing, just experience it. Feel its texture with your tongue and see what it tastes like in this form. Play with it like you did when you were a child.

When you are ready, bite into it and become intimately aware of what tastes you are experiencing. Is it sour, sweet, bitter, or pungent? Is it salty, bland or possibly a combination of these tastes? And where on your tongue do you experience it? Are you aware of it anywhere else in your mouth?

When you have thoroughly chewed it, swallow and acknowledge that it is now becoming a part of you. Honor the awesome Intelligence that knows exactly how to break it down and reweave it into blood, bone and muscle. Now notice if you are more satisfied by having taken in food that you actually saw and really tasted.

The wonderful thing about eating is that we do it numerous times throughout the day. In each experience of partaking of the wonder and mystery of food, we can awaken our senses and thus clear a pathway back into Life.

My mind has been so used to going unconscious around food that at one time my resistance to being present felt almost insurmountable. I then began to war with this resistance, demanding that I be present when I was eating. Of course, that only further removed me from the process. It was when I stopped fighting the resistance that I could allow myself to at least be present for one bite. If my mind wanted to space out for the rest of the meal, that had to be okay, but at least I would give myself the gift of one bite with Awareness. Sometimes that one bite invited me into a meal of Awareness and sometimes not. But these few bites with Awareness have transformed my relationship with food and my relationship with my life.

Smelling

Smelling is the stepchild of the senses. This hasn't always been so. When our ancestors lived on all fours, it was one of their predominant feedback systems. When they learned how to stand, sight then took over.

We don't create artwork or symphonies for the activation of smell, but smells surround and caresses us every moment of our lives. They evoke warm feelings within us such as the smell of sheets hung to dry in the warm summer sun or bread baking in the oven. And they can contract us into disgust and withdrawal as the smell of decaying garbage overtakes us or the noxious odor of strong chemicals engulfs us. Smells can also move us to distant memories and powerful emotions almost faster than any other sense.

We breath thousands of times during the day, each breath bringing us molecules that were once a part of everything in our environment. When they float back into the nasal cavity, they are absorbed by the mucosa which contains over five million cells that float in the breeze of our breath. These cells trigger the olfactory nerve, sending a message to a part of the brain called the olfactory lobe. In many animals this lobe is very large, but in human beings— because smell is not usually a necessity for survival—it is relatively small. From the olfactory lobe, these nerve impulses travel to the cerebrum where they are translated into information about the odor.

Smell can be the sense that is the hardest to use for grounding because much of the time it seems like there is nothing to smell. Animals know Life differently. They know that everything radiates a smell, not only objects and beings, but emotions like fear and anger.

To reconnect with the joy of smelling, we have to begin with the most basic of smells. Be willing to be a smell detective. Fully take in the rich aroma of coffee, the joyful scent of newly mown grass or the sweet fragrance of chocolate. Smell your skin and that of your lover. If you have a friend to play with, take turns blindfolding one another and bringing different objects to experience just by the sense of smell.

The senses are a pathway that we can return to over and over when we again discover ourselves lost in the maze of the mind. It is important to recognize that the senses are a pathway, not a destination. They are useful in that they help us to edit and divide Life into digestible parts, but they can take us only so far in the opening into who we really are because they don't accurately perceive all that is really going on.

The world we perceive is but a creation that our mind builds out of these little bits and pieces and the information we receive is a minuscule amount of what is really going on. This book you're holding is nothing but a vast dance of energy, and yet your senses say it is solid. We see only a small band of the light that is present and hear only a fraction of the symphony of sound vibrations. This makes our one view out of the vast array of possible views rather limited and simplistic, considering how complex Life really is.

Even though our view is very limited, to use our senses to come, for moments, out of the maze of thought, connecting into the magical mystery of the living moment, is to stand at a doorway. This is a doorway to the mystical reality that we live in all of the time, yet are separated from by the boundaries of our everyday thinking.

BREATH

Without mastering breathing, nothing can be mastered.

G. I. Gurdjeff

Besides making friends with our bodies and reconnecting with our senses, another very skillful way to ground in the living moment is to reconnect with the sensations of breath. This wonderful rhythm is always happening in the living moment. Fifteen to twenty times every single minute we have been alive, the breath has been flowing in and out of our body. How many of those breaths have we been aware of? The depth to which we are cut off from connection with our breath is the depth to which we are cut off from Life. To know this ancient river that is always moving through us and to reconnect with it many times throughout our day gives us a sanctuary, a place to rest from the ever-struggling mind.

To breathe is to live. We can survive a month or more without food and a number of days without water, but only a few minutes without breath. It is the great animator of Life. From our very first in breath until the last and final exhale, Life is a continuous river of breath on which the experiences of our lives are hung.

This river was breathing us when we learned to walk and on our first day of school. It was also present when we fought with our parents, fell in love or had our heart broken. When we are driving, the people in the cars passing by are being breathed by this process, just as each person who is committing a violent act or feeding the homeless is also connected with this river. The same flow of breath that is moving through you as you sit here reading this book has recently been a part of maple trees, eagles and butterflies, and eons ago moved through dinosaurs, mastodons and saber-toothed tigers.

It is fascinating to watch a young child breathe. As their belly rises and falls, there is no holding, no glitches in this wondrously rhythmic river. We once breathed like that, but as events in our lives confused, frightened and over-whelmed us, we began to hold our breath. Learning to be wary of Life and of our feelings, we pulled our breath up out of our belly and into the upper regions of our body. As the breath became more shallow, our center of consciousness rested more in intellect and will, cutting us off from a sense of stability and the great unity that we are part of.

To reconnect with an open breath is an amazing thing. When we take a full in-breath, it fills us with both visible and invisible energies. There is no accident it is called inspiration. To exhale completely is to ride the waves of letting go, trusting ourselves to the living process of Life. Breathing fully is the master healer of most of what ails the body. It allows us to access, not only a vibrant vitality, but also a connection with our primal unity with all of Life. To breathe fully is to be fully alive.

Also, with every breath we are connected to the whole of creation. Every time we breathe in, we take in trillions of atoms—atoms that were once a part of Shakespeare's pen, dinosaurs, stars, rainbows, Jesus, mountains and oceans. When we breathe out, we send on their way particles that were once an integral part of our own being, letting them go to a life of infinite adventure.

Take a few moments to close your eyes and follow your breath. Begin to perceive it as an ancient river coming to you from all over the planet, having moved through starfish, noble firs and mountain goats high in the mountains. See yourself sending the river onto children playing on the beaches of the Atlantic Ocean and seals congregating on its shore. Comprehend that there was a point when this river entered and began to animate you and there is also a point when it will leave. Be as present as you possibly can for just the next breath and be grateful to Life in its willingness to gift you with it.

The Four Gifts of Breath

There are four ways that breath can create a sense of ease and centeredness throughout our being. The first is purely on the physical. Our cells need two molecules of oxygen to every one molecule of glucose for fuel. The factory of a cell is much like a fire. If you want it to burn more brightly, you open the vents to more oxygen. As our supply of this life-giving fuel becomes more scarce through shallow breathing, the efficiency of our cells lessens dramatically, lowering vitality and creating many more waste products.

A well-fed fire leaves very little ash. A smoldering fire, without enough oxygen to fuel it, leaves much debris. We live in a sea of inefficiently fueled cells and thus inefficient energy. We are a society of shallow breathers and yet we wonder why we need caffeine to get us going. To breathe fully is to revitalize, cleanse and nourish the body, creating a much purer blood stream that bathes every cell of our being.

The breath is also the great internal exerciser. Each full breath gently massages and kneads our organs, stimulating a river of circulation in blood, lymph and intercellular fluids, facilitating nutrition and elimination. Its very simplicity has caused it to be bypassed in our western medicine. We spend thousands of dollars and countless hours on doctors and complicated systems of healing. All the while the gift of deep breathing is waiting to be discovered. To breathe deeply every day is to access a level of health we may not have known for a long time.

The second powerful way that breath affects us happens in the nervous system. This awesome communication network needs pure fuel in order to function at its peak (remember how fuzzy your thinking is after being cooped up in a stuffy room for awhile). The part of this network that is in charge of all that is automatically happening in the body is the autonomic nervous system. We do not need to think in order for our heart to beat or for our glands to perform their wizardry.

This system has two halves, the first being the sympathetic. This is the "Oh my God, a tiger!" place, where the heart starts beating quickly, the adrenal glands kick in and blood is shunted to the muscles for flight. When the threat is gone, the other half of this exquisite system, the parasympathetic, takes over, calming and reversing the fight or flight response.

The difficulty we are faced with is that we live in a society that is addicted to the sympathetic nervous system. We love scary or violent movies, we live our lives at break neck speeds, and we ingest coffee and sugar to whip up our body. To keep the sympathetic nervous system on, even at a subtle level, is deeply wearing on our bodies and is a deathblow to our hearts. The Chinese character for *busy* is made up of two characters: *heart* and *dead*.

The balanced rhythm of doing and being, of fast and slow, of rest and work is broken by our love affair with speed. To breathe deeply is one of the most skillful ways to turn on the parasympathetic nervous system with all of the ease and peace that it brings.

The third gift of deep, intentional breathing relates to a truth that shows up in many of the world's religions and healing systems. It is the understanding that breath is made up of more than physical components. Many words are used: *prana* (India), *chi* (China), *ki* (Japan) and *num* (the Bush people of Kalahari) to name a few.

It is understood that this force is in all forms of matter, although it is not matter, and it is taken in with every breath. Research done with respected T'ai Chi, meditation and Chi Kung masters has shown that this energy can not only greatly empower a person, but can heal. To breathe normally is to receive some of this energy, but to breathe consciously, deeply and rhythmically is to replenish and store this vital substance.

The final way that free-flowing breath can transform is in reconnecting us to the center of power that resides in our bellies. When we were very young, our center of gravity was in the pelvic region. This allowed us to move freely and with balance, dancing our way through our lives. We hadn't yet pulled our-selves up into the upper regions of the body, where we learned to rely solely upon will and intellect to maneuver through our lives.

Even though the mind has allowed us to do amazing things, to be caught in our head ensnares us in a web of concepts that cut us off from a source of intelligence, wisdom and empowerment that is always with us. Many different systems of healing, along with a variety of religions from various countries, all agree that it is life-affirming to cultivate the power center that resides in the belly. People in the Far East have called this center *Hara* or *Tan T'ien* and have known about it for thousands of years. This place of power resides a few inches below the belly button. To breathe into this region is to again awaken and reweave our connection with an Intelligence that is much greater than our struggling mind.

I was once told a story about a Zen Archery Master who had a bow that was so heavy very few people could lift it, let alone pull it back. To demonstrate the power of acting from the Hara, he brought it to his shoulder as if he was lifting a feather, and when he pulled back on the string, he asked his students to feel the tension in his arms. Much to their amazement, there was very little. He then explained that he had used the power from his belly. to draw the bow. Much more can be accomplished in our lives when we access this vast source of power than when we try to maneuver through our lives with just the mind.

Deep Breathing

Giving ourselves super fuel, calming and centering the nervous system, accessing a source of healing and energy, and breathing ourselves back into center are all accomplished through deep belly breathing. The diaphragm is the key to a deep breath. Because we usually only breathe in the upper half of the body, we rarely engage this muscle which was intended to be the main engine of breath.

The diaphragm muscle is a domelike sheet that dissects the entire body in the midsection. It is the roof of the abdominal cavity with all of its organs of digestion and it is the basement of the thoracic cavity with its heart and lungs. For most of us this muscle has fallen asleep, hardly moving with each breath. It needs to be re-awakened. When we experience a full breath, the diaphragm descends into the abdominal cavity, pushing the contents down and out in order to make room for the expansion of the lungs.

To know a fully alive and vital breath, we need to reawaken this sleeping giant. It is an art that is best cultivated on a daily basis. The rewards far outweigh the time and patience required to invite the muscles and nervous system back into the natural breath we knew as infants. At the beginning it will seem somewhat alien and possibly a little forced, but it is like the process of cleaning and oiling a severely rusted hinge. Fairly soon the resistance from corrosion is removed, and the hinge flows easily back and forth. In the same way, you will eventually find that taking a shallow breath requires more energy than resting in a full and open breath.

Let us explore the art of a full breath. Begin by either loosening your belt or changing into clothing with no restrictions around your waist, and then find a comfortable place to sit.

Assume a relaxed but alert posture. Close your eyes and spend a few minutes breathing through your nostrils, becoming fascinated by breath as it enters and leaves your body.

Now, as you come to the end of an exhalation, slightly pull in your belly, expelling the residue of air that is still in your lungs. Then let the belly drop and open as you begin to pull in air. Imagine you are filling a pear-shaped balloon with the bottom resting in your belly and the opening at your mouth. First fill up the bottom of the balloon, allowing the belly to expand, and gradually work your way up the body to your chest.

When you come to the fullness of the in breath, slightly pull in on the belly to push the air out and to keep the upper chest from collapsing. Again, when you come to what you think is the end of the out breath, create a vacuum by breathing out even more. You will be amazed how much air is left in the lungs. Then let go and feel the in breath rushing in.

If it is difficult to experience this, try lying down with a heavy book on your belly and practice breathing so the book rises and falls with each breath. Allow this to come from the breath rather than forcing the book up and down with your abdominal muscles. Another skillful way you can discover a full breath is to watch yourself in a mirror from a sideways view, noticing the gradual expansion of your body from the belly up. If you get a little light headed while breathing deeply, it is simply because you are not used to such rich nourishment. Back off into shallow breathing for a few breaths, and then resume the deep breathing again.

As you become more comfortable with deep belly breathing, there are two variations you can do that will enhance its benefits. The first is to add a pause for a few beats at the end of both the *in* and *out* breaths. This moment where you consciously pause alerts the whole system that you are shifting gears into the parasympathetic nervous system. After you become comfortable with a rhythmic breath that has pauses, you can play with how long these pauses are. In order to receive the maximum cleansing and nourishing effects of oxygenation and the revitalizing effects of prana, breathe in for the count of four, hold for four, breathe out for eight and hold for four. There are many variations of how long you breathe and hold. Do not make your pauses too long and make the out breath longer than the in breath. If you get light headed, know that you have progressed too quickly.

The second variation is alternate nostril breathing. We live in a world of opposites—left and right, up and down, in and out. To breathe in one nostril and out the other is not only one of the most effective ways of turning on the parasympathetic nervous system, it also is a great balancing breath. It coordinates communication between the left and right side of the brain, spreading this balancing throughout the whole body. I have found this breath to be one of the most calming and centering tools I use throughout my day. I've done it while waiting for doctors or while watching a movie. I've also done it in the middle of a chaotic day when I find myself becoming harried. When I do alternate nostril breathing, I can access equanimity and ease.

To experience this breath, place a finger over one nostril and breathe in the other. At the completion of the in breath, transfer your finger over to the other side and breathe out the formerly closed nostril. At the end of the out breath, breathe in the nostril you just breathed out of and, when done, transfer the finger and breathe out the first nostril.

When you're comfortable with this flow, add the deep belly breathing to this breath. When your body has adjusted to the joy of deep and full oxygenation, add the pauses to this breath.

At the beginning, it is very important to add only a few alternate nostril breaths into your daily practice. It is a powerful balancing tool that needs to be used wisely. Remind yourself to allow in deep healing breaths throughout the day. It can be skillful to set a timer or to connect the Awareness of breath to something you do repetitively. Pause and take a breath every time the phone rings, every time you come to a stoplight or flush a toilet. Notice whether you have been holding your breath or not.

Noticing my breath became the place where I could see how often I react and disconnect from Life. I first became aware of how much I hold my breath while watching cartoons with my children. Now, to watch TV is not life-threatening. But, in the middle of watching the Road Runner approaching a cliff with Wily Coyote hot on his trail, I saw that I had pulled up and contracted my whole body, especially the right side, and was hardly breathing at all. I began to retrain this ancient response by softening my body and taking a deep breath whenever I noticed how contracted I had become.

At first I could only do this when I was sitting still, as when driving or watching TV. As my awareness became more receptive to the experience of my breath, I could then begin to do it in the middle of conversations and then even while speaking in front of hundreds of people. The breath is the most exquisite biofeedback mechanism you have. Whenever you are caught in the mind, with its continuous addiction to reaction, the breath will tend to be more shallow and contracted. To become aware of your breath is to stand on the threshold of a world of connection and adventure.

THE MAGIC OF OUR DAILY LIVES

It isn't necessary to seek out adventure. Opening to what is around you will produce the most extraordinary experiences.

Edward Lewis

To cultivate the Awareness of our body, our senses and our breath, and to use them as doorways back into our lives opens us up to the experience of sacred moments when our minds, bodies and hearts are all in the same place at the same time. To be present for Life is a love affair. *It is the art of giving ourselves to Life and allowing it to love us in return.* As we open into Love, we transform the world by the depth of our Presence.

Yes, this takes discipline. At the beginning, you may only be able to stay here for a few seconds before the mind takes you away again. As Diane Ackerman says in *The Natural History of the Senses*:

There is that unique moment when one confronts something new and astonishment begins. Whatever it is, it looms brightly— its edges sharp, its details ravishing— in a hard clear light. Just beholding it is a form of revelation, a new sensory litany.

But the second time one sees it, the mind says, 'Oh, that again— another wing walker, another moon landing." And soon, when it's become commonplace, the brain begins slurring the details, recognizing it too quickly, by just a few of its features; it doesn't have to bother scrutinizing it. Then it is lost to astonishment, no longer an extraordinary instance but a generalized piece of the landscape. Mastery is what we strive for, but once we have it, we lose the precarious super-awareness of the amateur.

"It's old hat," we say, as if such an old weather-beaten article of clothing couldn't yield valuable insights about its wearer and the era in which it was created and crushed. "Old news," we say, even if the phrase is an oxymoron. News is new and should sound an alarm in our minds. When it becomes old, what happens to its truth? "He's history," we say, meaning that someone is no longer new for us, no longer fresh and stimulating, but banished to the world of fossil and ruin.

So much of our lives pass in a comfortable blur. Living through the senses requires extra energy, — a sense of marvel — and most of us are lazy. Life is something that just happens to us between birth and death.

The more we use our senses and our breath to groove a pathway back into Life, the more the ordinary becomes extraordinary. In seeing this, our daily activities can move out of the commonplace and take on an aliveness and a mystery that deeply nourishes us.

Let's use the example of taking a shower. Rather than staying unconscious during the entire time—planning your day, rehashing some problem or just spacing out—you can become deliciously aware of this living moment of your life. You have probably taken thousands of showers in your lifetime, and for 99.999% of them you haven't really been there! Next time, use your senses to be as fully present for your shower as you can.

Feel the coolness of the air on your skin, the texture of the faucet as you turn it on, the moisture that touches you even before you enter the stream of water and the powerful changes in your body as the water initially hits you. Continue by feeling the difference in the places where the water is streaming down your body and the places where it is not. Are there different temperatures in different places of your body? Smell the soap as you lather up, feeling the slippery texture of your skin.

Become aware that this is the same fresh water that was created at the Earth's beginning. Feel the joy of it blessing you now. What does the water sound like? Can you hear other sounds in the house, outside of the house? Can you feel the dramatic difference in sound as the water is turned off?

Be awed by all of the vast experimentation that has gone before you, allowing you to lift your arm to pull back the curtain and grab your towel. As you dry yourself, treasure this body, this exquisite gift you have been given from the great mystery. This is your life.

The most ordinary of moments can awaken us. I rarely just *wait* anymore. If I find myself with time on my hands before an appointment or while standing in line, very quickly Awareness kicks in and I bring my attention into the living moment. I sometimes use listening, deeply hearing the symphony of sounds that are arising all around me. Sometimes awareness of my breath brings me back. In lines, I often drop into the experience of standing and being held by the Earth. The joy of being fully present is almost too great for words. I know in some deep way, that because I am present, my attention has touched every person around me in that moment.

In the beginning, you will only be able to be present for maybe just a moment or two. In order to know more and more moments of full Presence, it is skillful to choose one thing every day that you practice doing with Awareness. It can be your morning cup of tea. Take time to sit quietly and hear the symphony of water heating up. Then feel the weight of the teapot and the warmth radiating from the cup as it is filled with water. What is the aroma of your drink? Can you be present as the cup is brought to your lips and feel the smoothness of its rim? Explore the warmth as it enters your mouth and then down into your body. These are moments, simple moments, of giving ourselves the gift of paying attention.

If tea cups don't call to you, it could be petting your cat or brushing your teeth. We are so used to the pell-mell pace of the mind with its Technicolor visions that the first forays into the experience of Life itself may seem very boring. But each moment of true connection, even if it is only one swallow of your morning beverage, takes you another step closer to Awakening.

These moments ay not seem like much at first, but they make a difference. It is much like watching a bucket being filled by isolated drops of water. It seems like it will never become full. Then one day you look and, much to your amazement, it is overflowing. With moments of paying attention, there will come a time, without even noticing the deep changes that are happening, when you discover that your entire perspective of Life has changed.

THE GIFTS OF PAYING ATTENTION

You're real self is a field of Awareness.
Deepak Chopra

In order to reconnect with Life, we need to comprehend that nestled in the core of our thinking is the belief that being inside the controlling mind means safety. As children, we had our connection with Life disrupted over and over again. It could have been a teacher saying something judgmental about a picture we just drew or possibly a neighbor's dog raging around the corner, barking at the top of its lungs. It might have been a sibling telling us how dumb we were or a parent who repeatedly discounted the validity of our feelings. Our attention became diverted from Life into trying to control what was to come. We sealed the door to the living moment with tape, super glue, rope and chain, swearing in the depths of our being to never open that door again because we believed it was the doorway to terror, rage and grief.

In counseling, a woman once asked, "What do you mean about being here?" She had her chin resting on her hands. I responded that it is the ability to ground in the feeling of your two hands touching and from that place again trusting the unfolding of your life. She immediately threw up her hands in fear and said, "No, I don't want to hear that!" The membrane around the experience of being fully *here* is the membrane of terror that was sealed around the living moment. It says that if you come *here*, you will die. But we are not children anymore, and to come *here now* means to thrive.

We also have to be very careful not to hear this invitation back into Life from the place of duality. This perspective says that being *here* is better than being lost in thought, and so our ancient urge to always want our lives to be different begins to judge and struggle with how much we are not *here*. In doing so we will just stay lost in the maze. We need to understand that being totally identified with thought has been an essential phase in our evolution, but we are now standing on a threshold. Just as creatures once lived exclusively in the sea and only slowly moved onto land, most of us have lived exclusively in thought. We are just beginning to learn how to use thought to reconnect with Life as it unfolds from Mystery.

In order to do this, we need to acknowledge without judgment that we have been lost in thought for a very long time and will continue to do so for large chunks of our day. The last time most of us were fully here was either in childhood, or possibly in the first phase of falling in love. It also can happen during a great trauma like an automobile accident or while inside the experience of a sense-opening drug such as LSD or mescaline. But since these are not usually a part of our everyday existence, we can use our senses to reconnect *for moments* throughout our day. The expectation is not to have our attention fully open to Life at all times. This is simply not possible while still in a body. But those sacred moments of being *here* enrich and open our lives, connecting us to deep wells of creativity, wisdom and the healing of compassion that are all available in the living moment.

As we add moments throughout our day when we show up for Life, many wonderful things begin to happen. We begin to be moved by the absolute wonder of the experience that is unfolding before our very eyes. How does the process take a little bit of earth, a dash of water, a blessing of air and a shower of sunlight and weave a garden full of flowers? How did you arrive out of one cell and grow into the trillions of cells that all work together with hardly a thought? Wonder begins to intrigue the mind, and we finally notice how much we miss when we are not truly here. How often do we really see our loved one's face? We usually live in ideas about them. How often do we honor the fact that when we eat, we are eating the Universe? To feel this wonder and to then meet the grief of how disconnected from Life we usually are is a powerful step in our Awakening.

To show up for Life also re-weaves the thread of trust that has been so nearly severed in us all. We begin to notice that spring has come out of winter for eons without us doing a whole heck of a lot about it! We finally see that Life is continuously unfolding out of Mystery—elephants coming forth out of a womb and peas unfolding out of the heart of a blossom. We finally breathe not a single, isolated breath, but find ourselves being breathed by the unbroken river of breath that flows through all beings. Our wonder moves into deep acknowledgment and awe of the Intelligence that permeates and penetrates every particle of the Universe. The possibility that this same Intelligence is weaving our daily lives begins to dawn upon our Awareness. In other words, the whole process becomes trustable, and grounding becomes something that we naturally do throughout our days.

And finally, to come back into Life is to experience everything as if it were for the first time. Every sound you hear has never been heard in that exact way before. Every single breath you have had since your birth has been subtly different from all the other breaths.

This healing comes in the willingness to return to the living moment over and over again, whenever we find ourselves drifting off into the mind. To return with mercy is a labor of love. Slowly, without even noticing it, we begin to groove a pathway back into the present moment, and we again know the rapture of being alive.

Grounding not only gives us the gift of directly receiving Life, it also allows us to become clear about the enormous difference between *being here* and being in a conversation *about being here*. The next step is to actually be able to see the conversation that filters our experience of living. To see thought is to free up Awareness from the constantly struggling mind, for the moment you see thought, you are not lost in it. So let us now look at how we can relate to the conversation that flows through us all day long rather than always being lost in it.

May we come to discover the safety of the living moment.
May we cultivate moments throughout our day
when we are fully present for Life.
And may we all know the rapture of being fully alive.

Core Intention: I'm here

Chapter 3
Our Addiction to Struggle

PRACTICE

Sometimes small mind looks me straight in the eye,

    so seriously that I burst out laughing, count my blessings,

    and find myself listening to the flowers conversing in the yard.

Sometimes small mind speaks and I listen in dead earnest

    to that same dried-out tired song.

And I drift, just drifting, drifting in….slow…….motion.

Sometimes small mind speaks to me and I sit with it,

    hold its hand, weighing each word,

    and help it on its way with stories from the Middle Way.

Sometimes small mind speaks to me and we do a wild,

    dervish-like polka, each struggling to lead the way,

    going faster and faster till we burst apart, exhausted.

    Stunned, we go our separate ways, exhilarated and a little confused.

Sometimes small mind speaks to me,

    and I just don't hear a thing.

Jim Ayala

THE STRUGGLING MIND

What man most passionately wants is his living wholeness, his living unison, not his own isolated salvation. I am a part of the sun as my eye is a part of me. That I am part of the Earth, my feet know perfectly, and my blood is part of the sea. There is nothing of me that is alone and absolute except my mind, and we shall find that the mind has no existence by itself. It is only the glitter of the sun on the surface of the waters.

D.H. Lawrence

When the morning alarm shatters the deep peace of sleep, the first thought that may grab your Awareness is the universal mantra, "Oh, shit!" Still nestled in the womb of slumber, your arm gropes for the snooze alarm, and sweet oblivion takes over once more. After what seems like a very short time, the pesky alarm again interrupts your peace, and the mind begins to say, "You should get up!" "No," it answers itself, "just one more snooze alarm." But even though the button is pushed, the escape of sleep does not return. After a seemingly endless war between "I should" and "I won't," you finally crawl out of bed, only to be met by the cold morning air. With grumbling mind and resistant body, you make your way to the bathroom for your morning ablutions. A moment of comfort from the hot steaming shower cuts through the struggling mind, and Awareness kicks in. "Oh, this is it! This is my life. I'm here. I'm alive." The wanting and resisting mind quiets down as you bring your full attention to the living experience of the moment.

But the struggling mind has only begun its day. Fear then makes its presence known. "This is the day of the big presentation, and I'm not prepared enough," it says. Your awareness begins to wrap around a maze of struggle, and the living experience of your life is left far behind. You throw your clothes on and rush to the kitchen for breakfast. Shoveling down a bowl of cereal, your focus is on your notes, hoping that a review of what you wrote last night will give you fresh inspiration. Instead, the mind begins to doubt your ability to even give the presentation, let alone to do it well. When your partner asks you a question, irritation flares through your body and mind. In a huff you collect your papers, throw on your coat, and rush out the door.

On the road, the other drivers feel no more supportive of your big day than your partner does. They are either too slow or too fast, too erratic or too conservative. Your mind boils over as you find yourself lost in a whirling maze of struggle.

For most of us, most of the time we live inside a struggling mind that feels it has to *work at* Life. On some days its struggles are subtler than the example of our friend above, but they are still there. This conversation that moves through us all day long is busy liking or disliking our lives. Leaning forward into the future or leaning away, it either wants what is not here or resists what is, endlessly lost in thought wherever it goes. No wonder we are exhausted at the end of the day.

Lost in this web of wanting and fearing, we live in afterthoughts about our lives—ideas, desires, beliefs, judgements and fears that are laid on top of our living experience. With our Awareness ensnared in a maze of struggle, we not only miss our lives, but we also fail to notice the support, the wisdom and the benevolence that are always available.

This conversation that so often grabs our attention is a story *about* Life. It has been woven out of bits and pieces of our experiences and is full of ideas about what Life is, who we are and what should be. To get the sense of how lost in a story we are, after you read the next two paragraphs, put down the book and try the following:

Take a moment and look around the space where you are sitting. Pretend you were raised in an entirely different culture and have shown up in this one for a few minutes. Use some of the grounding techniques from the last chapter to let in the living experience of your life. Be completely available to the moment.

Now raise your closed fists in front of your face. You can still see Life, but there is a barrier that blocks your sight. Your fists represent the beginning of the conversation about Life that you now live in most of the time.

One by one, uncurl and spread your fingers. Each one represents a part of this story—judgements about yourself and others, desires and aversions, shoulds and shouldn'ts, triumphs and failures. All of these pieces make up your conversation about Life. At times you can look through the fingers and connect with the living moment of Life, but most of the time you are focused on your hands.

Now bring your hands closer together and towards your face. Notice that eventually all you can see are hands. This is where you usually live, absorbed by the story in your mind. Very rarely are you present. You live in the fuzzy world of ideas about Life—plans and expectations, wants and fears, judgments and despairs. You whiz through the present moment as you careen from the past into the future and back again. And you wonder why you never feel the deep peace you long for!

Now slowly let your hands drop and really notice again what is around you. This is your life.

Lost in our story, we have all tried to create the perfect life, hoping that this would feed our deep hunger for peace. Instead, it has taken us even deeper into the maze of struggle. We also hope that if we just understand where the fingers come from (counseling) or are able to get beyond them into higher realms of consciousness (positive thinking or meditation), then everything will be peaceful again. Our attempts to change or get rid of our story may have brought us moments of peace, but most of the time we are still victims of the struggling mind. The freedom we yearn for doesn't come from fixing, changing and rearranging our story. Our true healing comes from discovering that we are not the story itself. *We are that which can see our story.*

I invite you to again bring your hands close to your face. This time, instead of constantly trying to get around, under or beyond these hands that are blocking your view of Life, move them a few inches away from your face so that you can see them clearly. For a few moments, explore your hands with your focused attention.

This kind of attention—this exploration of the story—is what heals the perceived rift between yourself and Life. You don't need to create the healing you yearn for. You only need to see what *stands in the way.* In this seeing—in this ability to be with the story without falling into it—the fingers automatically relax and your hands move back to your side. An expansive view of Life and the ability to be present the moment Life emerges out of Mystery are available to you again, and you rediscover the rapture of being alive.

MEETING THE FEAR OF WHAT IS THERE

Investigate what is. You can experience great insight by just watching struggle. Indeed, a moment of seeing struggle as just another state of mind, just an impersonal process passing through the vastness of your true being can allow you release from the painful shallowness of the mind. The mind insists it is so solid, and yet these thoughts are just bubbles, fragile impermanences passing through.

Stephen Levine

One of the main reasons we have been unaware of the benefits of relating *to* the story in our minds rather than being lost *in* it is that we're embarrassed by and afraid of what is there. We have been taught from early on that a *good* human being has particular kinds of thoughts and behaviors and a *bad* human being has another kind. So we hide from and try to exorcise those parts of our mind that we consider unacceptable. But we all have them all.

Right now, as you sit here reading this book, people all over the world are living the extremes of human states of mind. There are people in terror, rage, grief, lust, and greed. Every single one of us has experienced each one of these feelings at moments in our lives. And even though the feelings that we experience throughout our day are not usually so extreme, they effect us just the same. Little griefs build up into despair; little fears compound into mistrust of Life; moments of irritation keep us separate from our brothers and sisters; and greed can often compel us to overconsume.

To see that our mind is capable of any state is to also see that what moves through us all day long is not much different than what moves through other human beings. Everyone's mind, to greater or lesser degrees, has been as petty, fearful, arrogant, revengeful, self pitying, lustful, controlling and self absorbed as ours. What would our lives be like if we collectively comprehended that this is just what an unconscious mind does?

Take judgment for example. I have sat in numerous silent meditation retreats and I am still constantly amazed at how much the mind judges. It dislikes people for blowing their noses, walking too slow, walking too fast, closing doors, asking too many questions, and on and on. Rather than simply seeing what the story is up to, we become so busy trying to adjust it—believing that if we think like this it must be defective—that we never quite wake up to the fact that who we are is something bigger than thought.

So we go about wearing our masks, trying to constantly be whatever we feel *together* is, thinking our minds should always be focused, in control, loving, kind, reverent, thrifty and hope nobody will discover the truth. This *somebody* who is endlessly having a conversation in our head is on the job practically 24 hours a day. It's constantly pruning and editing, shoving down and rearranging, ignoring or trying to exorcise the parts we deem unacceptable. It causes us to live in the narrowest place human beings have known.

The first time I met Stephen Levine was at a workshop he gave in Seattle. When he said, "I would like to create a hat that, when you put it on your head, would instantaneously broadcast over a loudspeaker all of your thoughts," a collective groan of horror swept across the room. When this wave of fear had moved through, Stephen shifted our perspective from one of fear to curiosity.

It became evident that the depth to which we are embarrassed and afraid of the thoughts that stream through our mind all day long is the depth to which we compartmentalize ourselves and thus cut ourselves off from Life. The amazing thing is that to simply deny or ignore them doesn't make them go away. In fact, it gives them free reign to cause all sorts of chaos, confusion and despair in our lives, for an unattended mind has a tendency to get itself into trouble. Stephen described it very well when he said, "The internal dialogue is always commenting and judging and planning. It contains a lot of thoughts of self, a lot of self-consciousness. It blocks the light of our natural wisdom; it limits our seeing who we are; it makes a lot of noise and attracts our attention to a fraction of the reality in which we exist."

We are not only embarrassed and ashamed at what we may discover as we put on the hat, but we are also terrified of what we may find there. We sealed most of what was unmeetable in our childhood far away from our conscious Awareness. And there it lies, deep inside of us, molding and shaping our lives more than we can possibly imagine.

Our fear is that if we become present for these mind/body states, that they will swallow us forever. The opposite is true. Rainer Maria Rilke wrote:

> "We have no reason to mistrust our world, for it is not against us. Has it terrors, they are our terrors; has it abysses, those abysses belong to us. We must try to love them. And if only we arrange our lives according to that principle which counsels us that we must always hold to the difficult (go towards what we don't like), then that which now still seems to us the most alien will become what we most trust and find most faithful. How should we be able to forget those ancient myths that are at the beginning of all peoples, the myths about dragons that at the last moment turn into princesses; perhaps all the dragons of our lives are princesses who are only waiting to see us beautiful and brave. Perhaps everything terrible is, in its deepest being, something helpless that wants help from us."

Our aloneness is lonely, and our terror is afraid. Our rage is upset, and our depression is sad. All of the parts of ourselves that we have formerly hated and feared are desperately in need of us, in need of our undivided and merciful attention. Our fear is that if we go towards these mind/body states rather than constantly managing, fixing, running or hiding from them, we will be engulfed. But there are ways of becoming present with these feelings that bring us freedom.

I sometimes liken these mind/body states to the image of a village that has lived under the fierce and frightening power of a mighty dragon. After having tried endless times to destroy the dragon, most of the people stay hunkered down in their homes, half alive, afraid to live their lives. There is a little boy in the village who sees clearly that either trying to destroy the dragon or hide from it wasn't bringing people the freedom that they yearned for. He decides that he is going to get to know the dragon.

Sneaking out one night (for everyone in the village has told him not to go), he makes his way to the dragon's cave and finds a rock to sit upon (out of fire breathing range). When the dragon appears, rather than running away from him, the little boy says, "I want to get to know you." The dragon, very unused to this response, puffs up his chest and makes a lot of noise as he breathes out fire in the boy's direction. The boy flinches, but he does not move. He again says, "I want to get to know you."

The dragon finally recognized what the boy was saying and it began sharing all of the loneliness that came from being hated and feared. The little boy discovered that the dragon just wanted someone to listen to it. As it was heard, it became kinder and gentler and eventually became the guardian of the village.

Our dragons within us desperately want to be seen—not hated, feared or ignored. They want to be recognized and heard. I now deeply know and trust that going towards and engaging with mind/body states that I formerly resisted does bring the healing that I yearn for. But my automatic reaction when something arises that I have not yet included in the community of my being is to turn my back and run. And the faster I run, the faster it runs after me! I find, however, that my times of running are shorter now, and my willingness to sit with it—out of fire breathing range—is getting stronger.

We also have difficulty putting on Stephen's hat because we have been lost inside of our own conversation for so long that we have forgotten the *safety* of the living moment. There is something wonderful here waiting for us that can only be discovered when our Awareness is fully engaged in the present.

In trying to describe what is waiting for us here, the closest word I know is Love. For me, the word Love points to the activity that holds the planets spinning as they do, that draws together the cells that make our bodies, that brings forth spring out of winter and that heals the cut on our skin. It is everywhere and with us always. And it can only be known in present time. Everything else is a conversation about it and will never bring us the connection, communion and healing we are ready for.

To get an experience of what we have been exploring, imagine you are sitting in a movie theater with a group of friends, all of whom understand that you are something much bigger than thought. Watching the contents of your mind projected upon the screen, each of you knows that thinking is a wonderful tool but a horrible master.

Feel the wondrous freedom as your friends exclaim over and over again, "I know that place. I have felt that same self pity, desire for revenge, hatred, confusion, doubt, despair, self loathing, pettiness, greed, loneliness."

This moment of collective acknowledgment of the similarity in the contents of our minds is a moment of freedom. It allows us to let down the masks we wear to fool people. Realize that on the screen you are watching not only your own mind, but you are seeing the collective dream we are all lost in. Allow your heart to open to yourself for the courage to have taken on this dream that cuts you off so completely from Life.

Now expand your Awareness beyond the theater and feel all of the people on the planet who right now are completely lost in the movies of their mind. Then realize that no matter how much we are all caught in our stories, struggling with Life, we are still being breathed by, held by and loved by Love. Know that these few moments of remembering take us all one step closer to our freedom.

BECOMING FREE

Life is what happens while you're busy making other plans!

John Lennon

Having been lost in the maze of the story for so long, it is not only very difficult for us to notice that we are dragged around by thought all day long, but it is also very challenging in the beginning to see what the story is doing. It is much like trying to describe the type of house you're living in if you have never been able to go outside and see it in its totality.

In order to see clearly how addicted we are to our conversation about Life, I invite you to try the following:

Bring your finger into the space in front of your eyes. Begin to move it all around— up and down, side to side—and follow it with your eyes wherever it goes.

This finger represents the story that passes through you all day long, and wherever it goes, you go. If the story feels sad, you say you are sad. If it says that Life is terrifying, you live in fear. Without even a thought about thinking, you are dragged around by your conversation all day long. It has been said that we have 60,000 thoughts a day and that 90% are repeats from the day before! And by far the greatest percentage of them are involved with our own individual story, keeping us caught in a maze of struggle.

Lost inside our story, we are always trying to create the life we want and all the while the Life we yearn for is right *here*, unfolding in the present moment. But we don't know how to connect with the moment, and we've been gone for such a long time that we are afraid of it. So on and on we go, trying to get it all together in order to snare the peace we are yearning for.

Tumbling from one idea to another all day long, we exhaust ourselves with our constant searching. Very rarely, if ever, does it penetrate our consciousness that we are not thought. It is a tool just as our thumb is a tool. As a man once said in one of my retreats, "The liver makes bile, the kidneys make urine and the mind makes thoughts." You would think it ridiculous if someone thought we were bile. It is just as ridiculous to say that we are our thoughts. We are Awareness. We are that which can see thought rather than thought itself.

Again move your finger around in the space before you, tracking it wherever it goes. Now, keeping the finger moving, look straight ahead and focus on what is directly before you. This is what it is like when our attention is not following thought. Thoughts think themselves, and our freedom comes when we realize we do not have to follow them wherever they go. Because we are focusing on something other than thought, we can also notice that we are the ability to see the finger moving rather than the finger itself. Thoughts come and thoughts go, and, as we learn to see the story rather than identifying with it, we can access levels of freedom that were incomprehensible when we were enmeshed with thought.

As we watch thought rather than being lost in it, the first thing we see is how busy it is. It carries on a running commentary about our lives—planning, regretting, wishing, hoping, clinging, rejecting, rationalizing. We can get very tired just watching how busy it is, and we can see that our attention has been pulled up and out of our whole being and has become focused in our heads.

As we step back into a more spacious place and watch the conversation that moves through us all day long, it becomes easy to see that thought is mainly focused on struggle. It struggles with our bodies, our mates, our children, our co-workers, our boss, our emotions and even with itself. It is absolutely certain that if it gets rid of what it doesn't like and acquires what it does, then we will finally know peace. If the desired object is attained, we feel a moment of peace, but then the fear of losing what we have gained kicks in.

If the story's main addiction is to struggle, then its main flavor is fear. It is terrified of being embarrassed, hurt or abandoned. It is afraid of what might be, afraid of what might not be and afraid of the consequences of it all. We are afraid for ourselves, for our family and for our Earth. The story, like the news media, thrives on high drama, turning everything into an emergency.

It has been said the only thing we have to fear is fear itself. This is because most of what we fear are phantoms in the mind. Now, however, we are ready for the next step. We do not need to be afraid of fear. Years ago, while I was spending a weekend with Patricia Sun, a powerful teacher of Awakening, she reminded me that the fear we all have is genuine, but it is not real when seen through the light of Awareness. In truth it is a paper dragon, a conversation in our heads. Our job is to let go of the fear of fear so that we can listen to it rather than having it lead the way.

The seemingly endless conversation in our heads also believes at its core that who we are is defective. One of its favorite pastimes is to continually reform itself. It prunes and edits, shoves down and tries to exorcise what it finds unacceptable. For many years I had a sign on my bathroom mirror that was so faded from the steam of the shower that no one could read it. But I knew what it said: *The thinking mind is based upon needful not-enoughness.* "We need to be different because we are not enough," subtly chants the mind.

This is not only true inside of your mind, but it is the truth for every single human being there is. No matter how powerful or accomplished one becomes, this belief still lies deep in the heart of the story until we see it and know that we are not this story. All we have to do is hear interviews with people who are considered to be successful and, if they are honest, their self-doubt and fear always surface. As long as we keep on buying into this belief, the story will continue to be fueled.

One of the story's main games is control. Cut off from the Sea of Intelligence, this web of concepts feels that it is in charge of Life. It tries to orchestrate it all, feeling that if our lives haven't yet become *perfect,* it's only because we haven't done it right. If we do attain some level of control, it is usually accompanied by a subtle feeling that we should be doing it better. If we exercise three times a week, we should be doing it five. If we commit to being kind in our lives, we are appalled at the slightest inkling of irritation.

We seem to be constantly jockeying and maneuvering for control because we have lost sight of the fact that the awesome Intelligence that has brought forth galaxies and wildflowers is present in our daily lives. Our story has created a split in our minds between us and this Intelligence. We may accept that our heart beats from a power greater than us, but the story says that we are responsible for the rest.

64

Control is ultimately an illusion. Remember a time when you felt you had it all together or really understood your life? It usually came with the sense that you had finally gotten it nailed down. But it changed, didn't it? It is much like trying to hold down a dozen rubber duckies in a tub full of water. Just when you think you have them all corralled, you take a deep sigh of relief, and they all pop up out of your grasp. The mind doesn't want to accept that Life is a constantly changing show. Every thought will turn into another. Every object we desire will eventually become tattered and old. Every person we love will either watch us die or we will watch them die.

To come out of the illusion of solidity and permanence into the constantly changing flow of the Sea of Life is not as scary as one might think. People who have been given a terminal diagnosis initially react with great horror and grief. Many then go on to rediscover Life. Everything becomes fresh and clear, new and very precious. I have heard people say that a life-threatening diagnosis from their doctor was the greatest gift they were ever given. It propelled them out of their story and its illusion of permanence and connected them with the breathtaking wonder of being present for Life the moment it appears out of Mystery.

When we are in the flow of Life rather than being lost in thought, our attention is then available for the living moment, and the power of focused attention is enormous. Have you ever noticed what it is like to stare at the back of somebody's head while on a bus? Eventually, that person will turn around. Whatever Awareness focuses on becomes more alive! If a simple gaze can penetrate the normal state of unconsciousness that most people live in, think of the possibilities that come from human minds that are focused and available to Life. The power is awesome.

Not only does undivided attention enhance and enliven whatever it focuses on, it can also help us to access deep wisdom that is unavailable when we are lost in the struggling mind.

A good example of how attention can bring us out of struggle, allowing us to become connected, compassionate and skillful in our lives, comes from an experience I had with my son Micah.

One Saturday morning, running up the stairs, he enfolded me in a dancing hug. "It's mine," he said. "I bought it, and it's really mine." After years of saving and at least two months of searching, he had found the car of his dreams and it had received a clean bill of health from a mechanic. He had given the previous owner two thirds of the money and was going to complete the deal the next day when the banks opened. "Close your eyes," he said. "I want to take you out to see it, but I don't want you to look until I give the signal."

Down two flights of stairs, out to the driveway and onto the lawn we jour-neyed, him leading and me following. When I got to just the right place, he turned me around and said, "Okay, now you can look." Tears of joy sprang to my eyes. It was exactly what he had dreamed of and had come close to many times in the last few months, only to see the deal slip away. "I'm off," he said. "There are so many people I want to show it to!" As I watched him drive away, one of those precious moments in the long journey of parenting flooded my being—deep contentment in my child's happiness.

The next day he was up early, much earlier than usual for an 18 year-old. There were deals to complete, licenses to purchase and stereos to be looked at. When I arrived home later that afternoon, there was a message on the answer-ing machine. "Mom, please be there. There is something wrong with the car." I checked the time. The call came in 40 minutes ago. Paging him immediately, I waited for his call. When I picked up the phone, all he said was, "You need to come right now. The left front wheel fell off the car and caused a lot of damage." In shocked silence I picked him up from where he had placed the call and took him back to the car. It was like a sleek, beautiful panther who had its left front leg chewed off, and it lay wounded and tilted by the side of the road. I pulled in behind it, and as I put on the hazard lights, Micah got out and sat on the curb, his head in his hands. Only one half hour ago he had signed the bill of sale and in a 30 minute span he had his dream in his hands, only to watch it dissolve right in front of him.

As we waited for the tow truck, my mind became caught in the maze of struggle. It was whipping around at lightning speeds, opening into a deep sadness, only to become consumed by rage at Life for seeming to be such an unfair process, and then falling into helplessness. Because of the cold, Micah eventually came back into the car, and we sat there silently, each one of us dealing with our grief. He was in such a deep place that words were noise and touch an invasion.

After what seemed like a very long time (actually only around five minutes) faintly, through the cacophony of my mind, I heard the beat of the hazard lights. "Come back." Awareness said. "Rest for a moment in this steady beat." At first my mind resisted it. I was strongly pulled by the tidal waves of thought and emotion that were moving through me. "Life is not safe. It's out to hurt you and the ones you love. I don't know what to do. What I am doing is wrong." As the voices screamed in my head, Awareness whispered gently, "Come back. You're getting lost in your story. It is not necessary to identify with these ancient and familiar patterns of your mind." Over and over again I returned to the hazard lights.

Slowly my Awareness became more available to the living moment. I began to see rather than react to the story in my mind. I recognized that all of the millions of moments of my life had brought me to this moment, sitting by the side of the road with two hearts breaking and the steady beat of the hazard lights. I then became very curious about what parts of my story were making themselves known to me. As the waves moved through, rather than becoming lost in them, I named them: "Ahh, rage. Yes, I see you. Self-judgment. Of course. Sadness." As I went through layer upon layer of my story, I discovered despair at the core. This was not only the deep despair within me that I had hidden from my whole life, and it was not only Micah's despair at learning that Life is an uncontrollable process, but it was OUR despair, the despair that all of us feel because of our separation from Life.

I knew then that the most skillful thing I could do in this situation was to meet this despair—not to be swallowed by it, but stand *with* it. I did this not only for Micah and myself, but for all human beings. My heart opened to this deep despair, and I was able to be present to it and allow it a voice in the community of my being.

Because I was able to see rather than react to what was moving through me, from that moment on, the place out of which my words and actions came was much different than before. Not getting lost in my inner struggle, I was again connected to the wisdom, compassion and curiosity that allowed for actions that were skillful and healing. I became present to the process in a way that was unavailable to me when I was lost in thought. The very atmosphere in the car changed, and over the next few hours and even on into the next few weeks this experience brought both of us much more than it had taken away.

THE POWER OF ATTENTION

Whatever there is that arises in the mind or in the heart, just watch it. Let go of it. Don't even wish to be rid of thought. Then the mind will reach a natural state. No discriminating between good and bad, fast and slow, hot and cold. No me and no you. No self at all. Just what there is.

Achaan Chah

To make the leap into a mind that can live beyond its own story is to include rather than exclude, observe rather than fight, and hold vision rather than becoming lost in doubt and fear. In order to know this, one of the most important steps we can take is to transform the way we use thought. We cannot use our old style of thinking to heal the maze of pain and struggle that we find ourselves in. The old style says that we have to discover what is wrong and fix it, change it or get rid of it. This only fosters more struggle. If we try to get out of this maze by claiming that we are wrong for being here or that we just need to exorcise the bad parts and all will be well, we will only stay lost in the endless world of struggle.

As soon as we label something bad, wrong or defective (including thought), we give it energy. Using our old ways of trying to change whatever we don't like, we activate a law of physics: what is pushed against pushes back. A good example is weight loss. The statistics from the Surgeon General of the U.S. show that 98% of the weight that is lost by Americans is gained back within a year and a half. And yet, one of the most successful topics for books on the *New York Times* Best-seller List has been dieting. This tells us something about how much we believe in a style that says just overpower what is wrong, do it right, and then everything will be okay. We go to this mode over and over again. Oftentimes it does work in the initial phases—many people have lost countless pounds—but the long-term evidence shows that most weight loss doesn't last.

We have done this same thing with thought. We believe that if we just think right, then everything will be okay. We don't see that thought is like the tides or the seasons. If there is a low tide, then there will automatically be a high tide, and when the tide goes out again, we are left struggling on the beach, wondering what we did wrong. *The healing we are yearning for does not come from constantly changing the content of the mind, nor does it arrive by trying to understand where particular patterns came from.* These are both important tools for maneuvering through our minds. But the depth of the healing we are ready for arises out of our ability to simply *see* and acknowledge the story in our mind and to recognize that its core addiction is to struggle.

A good metaphor for the shift in healing we are ready to make is a messy house. The core intent of our healing up until now has been to clean it up, creating a more livable mind. This is an important part of our journey. But what we most yearn for is to go outside and play, to become bigger than the 'house' of thought and to again reconnect with Life.

My life is a good example of these two different styles of healing—trying to fix and change what is or becoming willing to see it and thus discover that who we are is something bigger than the stories in our mind. Because of the level of unsafety in my childhood home, I had slowly retreated into a maze of contraction, terror and self judgment where nobody could contact me. This heralded a gradual but steady descent into alcoholism, mental illness, drug addiction and behaviors that have taken years of forgiveness to heal. All the help offered was based on the classic belief that since I was hurting, something was wrong and I needed to be *fixed*. It was doomed from the beginning

68

because people related to my *brokenness*, not to my *wholeness*. Not one of the people I went to for help recognized me as something other than a problem that needed to be solved. I didn't need to be fixed; I needed to be seen and accepted.

The turning point in my life came the third time I tried to kill myself. Two attempts before had not worked and I was lost in self-hatred that said, "You never do anything right; you are even a failure at suicide." The last time, I slit my wrists over and over again becoming more furious at my body with every stroke. because it wouldn't bleed enough to die. On that night I asked my first honest question, "If I can't stand the pain in my life, and if I can't leave this body, what is this all about?" In hindsight, I can now see that this simple question was the beginning of my journey out of the maze.

People and books started showing up that opened me to the world of meditation. My first forays into this world were done through the more traditional forms of chanting, visualizing and focusing on accessing expanded states of consciousness. At moments, especially after a particularly centered meditation, I could touch a place of peace. The glow would last for awhile, but then the mind, with its roller coaster of thoughts, feelings and experiences, would erupt into this sanctuary and again I would be tossed into the cauldron of confusion, self hatred and despair. The intention of these forms of meditation, just as with the counseling, was to get rid of or move beyond states of mind that were considered undesirable. Both brought healing into my life, but they also kept me caught in the endless struggle of trying to do it right or better.

I can still remember a time when the staff of the school of natural healing that I worked for had a party. We began it with a group meditation in the back yard. When it ended, the leader said to her friend, "Wow, did you go there?" (alluding to a level of consciousness). When he answered, "Yes," she responded, "Wasn't that wonderful?" Well, I hadn't gone anywhere! I left, retreating to the shower and remember beating my hand against the wall while raging, "When am I going to do it right?" For years I struggled, becoming a part time meditator, while constantly chastising myself for my lack of discipline and for my chaotic and unordered mind. I felt like a closet failure for not being able to *control thought* or create the *right* levels of consciousness.

Then one evening, as I was sitting in front of the fire after putting my young children to bed, I was hashing and rehashing one of my favorite struggles when all of a sudden a very clear voice inside said, "You know, this is only thought." In that moment it was like having been in a cold room my whole life that all of a sudden became warm. "All that is happening is that I am *here*, sitting in front of a fire, and my mind is spinning a tale of chaos and confusion," said Awareness. At that moment, I discovered a freedom that I had never known before. Of course, by the next morning that knowing seemed very far away, but a part of me knew that the next phase of Awakening had shown up.

A different kind of meditation then came into my life, one that taught the art of simply paying attention. This wasn't about constantly trying to make myself and my life different. It was about becoming very curious about *what is*. These skills and techniques opened me up to the possibility that who I am is something bigger than this stream of thinking that I had always been trying to exit or change.

At first, whenever I was with people who taught and counseled in this way, I felt the same feeling I had felt by the fire that night—deep peace. But I couldn't hold onto it or make sense of it when I left their presence. I was continually trying to understand the ability to become bigger than thought from inside the maze of struggle. But I kept trying.

Then, in 1984, I was given the grace to meet Stephen Levine. He spoke wonderful insights and enclosed them in a merciful and compassionate heart that allowed me to soften around the experience of struggle. Slowly and surely I was able to see my story rather than being lost in it, and I began to experience moments of belonging to Life, pure moments of truly being alive.

In the beginning it was hard. My ability to ground in the moment and to become curious about what part of the story was appearing was not very strong. At times it felt like every state of mind and emotion that I had tried to escape was realizing that there was finally somebody home—a part of me that could meet these states with a merciful attention rather than always trying to change them—and they all lined up, pushing and shoving into my conscious Awareness in order to be seen.

Over time I began to see that these were not random experiences flailing themselves at my Awareness. I understood that the story which removed me from Life was built slowly and painstakingly out of myriad experiences and that there was an order to it, just like in a novel. There was a preface, introduction, unfolding chapters replete with footnotes and bibliographies. And I saw that this story could be dissipated like the ephemeral cloud it was, just by the act of seeing it. One of the core sentences that remained in my heart from my very first teacher, "In the seeing is the movement" began to make sense. Being able to see the voices that had run me my whole life was moving me into a space beyond them. Fixing, changing and understanding can bring a more ordered mind, but we are still caught in the mind. I was ready for freedom.

I became deeply committed to meeting the story and then returning to the living moment. It was not easy, nor was it simple. In the beginning, waking up to the story meant becoming available to it, and at moments when my Awareness was not strong enough, I would fall deeply into the maze. But every time I fell, I eventually returned again to Life, sometimes a little bruised, but more aware of how my story was put together and more connected to the rapture of being alive.

THE POSSIBILITY OF AWAKENING

The purpose of a spiritual life is not to create some special state of mind for they are always temporary. It is to work directly with the most primary elements of our body and mind, to see the ways we get trapped by our fears, desires and anger and to learn directly our capacity for freedom.

Jack Kornfield

Imagine two fish jumping out of the water. Before they dive back in, one says to the other, "Now I know what you mean about water!" We are doing the same thing with thought. In moments where our attention is connected to the living moment, we recognize the big difference between being lost in a conversation about Life and being with the real thing. To see the story in our mind rather than being lost in it, our attention is again available to Life. We then discover that there is something here that can only be experienced in the living moment. Behind the veil of conceptualization and all of our attempts to control Life is the essence of Life beyond thinking.

We are being individually and collectively shifted out of the separate, struggling mind, back into intimate connection with this essence that permeates and penetrates absolutely everything. We are now at a crisis point where this shift is necessary. It is a crisis that has arrived, not because we have screwed up, but because this is the way Life unfolds. Over the eons, whenever Life was ready to shift to a new level of evolution, it always moved through a time of crisis. And that is where we find ourselves now. We are being cracked wide open and invited back into Life.

We have gone as far as we can clothed in the experience of separation, lost in the style of thinking that divides rather than unifies. Our communication systems are sophisticated enough now for us to see that we have been denying the harmful effects of this separation on ourselves, our loved ones, our society and the planet as a whole. Through this comes the possibility of understanding that we will destroy ourselves if we continue to stay lost in the maze of the separate mind.

To become conscious of what thought is doing allows us the freedom to use it in ways that connect, unify, engage and embrace Life. This begins with acknowledging that each of us lives inside of war most of the time and, because of that, the world lives in war. In this recognition, we can then gather the commitment, curiosity and compassion it takes to relate *to* the struggles of our minds rather than being lost *in* them. Every moment in which we relate to the content of our mind rather than being lost in it, we take ourselves, along with everyone else, another step into healing. So let us now explore how to strengthen our attention so that we can relate to thought rather than from it and thus heal ourselves and the world.

May we come to know that who we are is something much bigger than the stories in our minds.

May we learn the ability to see the story with great curiosity and compassion.

And in that seeing may we again reconnect with the living moment of Life.

Core Intention: Ahh, struggle

Chapter 4
Moving Beyond Struggle

HAVING TEA WITH FRIENDS

The Moon found the trap door to my heart,
jumped in and made itself at home.
We invited the Tulip sisters over for tea
and enjoyed the afternoon, watching the Sun making the rounds.
Who would have ever guessed that having tea with friends
could be so much fun?
One day, bats of all sizes started flying out of my eyes!
Hundreds of them, even thousands, a continual stream
that would approach the lip of my eyelids
and become tears melting like wax, day and night.
They keep coming and coming!
It was a flying bat flood that wouldn't stop.
Like a good parish priest on any Sunday afternoon
I would greet the winged, teary ones and say:
Good Morning!" and "How nice to see you."
and "Nice you could come," and "Have a great afternoon!"
When it was finally over and done with,
the bats left behind a vast, silent cavern, previously unexplored.
You couldn't hear a pin drop, there was nowhere for it to fall!
You couldn't use a lamp, it wasn't dark, nor was it light!
You couldn't go anywhere. There was nowhere to go and no one to go there!
The Moon found the trap door to my heart and jumped in,
    and made itself at home.
We invited the bats over for tea and my God, what a chatty lot!
And peckish too! They ate all the cookies before the first cup! Bloody hell!

Jim Ayala

IN THE SEEING IS THE MOVEMENT

Meditation is anchoring your boat so you don't go out with the tides.

Joan Borysenko

In my-mid twenties, I was hospitalized in Europe off and on for the better part of a year. My life had come crashing down around me. A week before I entered the hospital, I was told that if I didn't stop all of the destructive behaviors I was engaging in, I had only five months to live. My response was that I knew I would die. Everything I had tried to make me *better* had failed, driving me deeper into a maze of struggle. Drugs, alcohol and overeating were the only things that numbed me enough that I didn't have to feel an almost constant, debilitating shame, and I wasn't willing to give them up. The day I arrived home from Europe, I tried to take my life, only to have my stomach pumped out in time. Two other attempts at suicide also failed, driving me deeper into the world of self-hate and despair.

Then one gentle spring weekend, my mother gave me the gift of a workshop with Joel Kramer. He was a Hatha Yoga teacher who taught much more than yoga. He taught the art of seeing *what is*. As he talked about the power of Awareness, I felt a ray of sunshine flooding the dark and dreary maze I had lived in for so long. For a brief moment I recognized that I was Awareness itself. *I was the ability to see the story that moved through my mind all day long, rather than the story itself.* I could also see that the path I had been taking—constantly trying to make myself different or better than I felt I was—would not take me beyond struggle. For moments, I connected with a clarity and peace greater than anything I had ever consciously known.

The next time Joel came to town, I took in a tape deck and recorded the whole weekend. I then went home and transcribed every word. I still couldn't hold onto whatever it was that triggered the clarity and peace. The words and concepts would seep through my consciousness as quickly as water through sand.

After having spent many weekends with him, I had distilled what I was hearing down to a few words. I went up to him and said, "What I am hearing is: In the seeing is the movement. It's not in the fixing, changing and rear-ranging of all of the states of mind and body we so try to control. *The healing is in the seeing—in the ability to relate to them rather than from them.*" He smiled as he said, "Yes." I went on to say, "It seems that the whole sentence should be, "In the seeing is the movement, until the observer and the observed become one. What does that mean?" With a twinkle in his eyes he said, "Go find out!"

Lost inside of a *story about Life*, cut off from the living experience, a good deal of our energy is spent in manipulating the story. We try to get rid of the parts we don't like, and we try to find and nail down the parts that we do. But at our essence is something that lies beyond the story, beyond the constantly wanting and fearing mind. *Who we really are is already here, right now.* We don't need to try to get to it. We need to SEE the story that covers it over the way a fog bank hides the land.

Every moment of recognizing what is happening in the mind, without falling into identification with it, is a moment of not being caught in the story—a moment of freedom. These moments then become the movement that takes us beyond the constant struggle that we live in most of the time. The part of ourselves that can see the story in our head is Awareness.

Take a moment and think of a wonderful memory, possibly holiday times as a child with all of the anticipation and joy. Now shift your attention into planning your day tomorrow. Notice how it takes a moment to settle in. Get into the details. Now shift again into a fantasy. What would it be like to win the lottery? Put some juice into it. Shifting your attention again, notice the emotions that come from this fantasy. Finally, shift back into the room where you are sitting and hear the sounds of life around you as they arise and pass away.

Notice that with all of these shifts, there is something that is steady and constant, *something that can perceive what is happening.* It can tell the difference between a thought, an emotion, a sensation, a fantasy or a memory. This is Awareness, the ability to see *what is.* Most of the time our attention is focused on our experiences, enmeshed in the world of thoughts, feelings and sensations as they appear and disappear in our lives. Freedom comes when we can watch our experience rather than being lost in it.

The summer of 1996, I broke my leg while hiking with my son. At the same time, my mother was approaching her death in a city six hours away from me. I had spent the last few months traveling back and forth, becoming intimately involved with my mother's process. Slow progress with my leg made it appear difficult, or even impossible, for me to be with her, and I began to struggle with what was happening. Also, with little exercise, I felt like a toilet that hadn't been flushed.

One morning, I awoke into the maze of struggle, completely lost in a fit of resistance. As I sat down to meditate, my mind said, "Oh good, at least there will be a little peace now." It was focused on "let's get out of this state and into a better one." And of course, it didn't work. Trying to get into peace only created more grasping, resistance and fear. I was so caught in struggle that I had totally forgotten about paying attention.

Finally Awareness kicked in. "*What is*?" it asked. In other words, "What is happening here?" In a flash, my attention moved out of identification with my spinning and resisting thoughts and I became deeply curious. In response to the question, "What is the experience of my life right now," I could see that my mind was caught in wanting things to be different than they are.

In asking the question, "What is?" I began to relate *to* the thoughts in my head rather than being lost in them. It was like I had been in a whirling washing machine and all of a sudden I was standing outside of it, watching the clothes being tossed around. As I stayed with the question, *What is?*, I began to feel more spacious around what was happening.

As my field of Awareness opened, I connected with the overall experience of just not feeling well. I was able to intimately feel, without fear and judgement, the subtle flu-like feelings all over my body. As my attention became more focused, I made contact with the tightness in my solar plexus, the fist of resistance. As I settled there I could then see, without falling into them, the voices that fueled this contraction in my belly.

I listened to the song of grief that came from not being able to be there for my mother, the deep chant of fear that she would die before I saw her again, and the litany of rage that spoke of how seemingly unfair Life can be at times. Rather than identifying with these voices, I made space for them, remembering that they were all a part of the passing show of my story.

Slowly my belly began to soften and my heart opened. I realized that the roots of these feelings went much deeper than the experience of not being able to be with my mother. The grief and rage were core support beams in the maze of my story. By relating to them rather than being lost in them, I began to rest in the place beyond the story. With great joy, I could now use attention to watch the struggle in my mind and not identify with it. Everything began to come back into balance. My mind became quieter; my body felt better; and my heart trusted that I would again be with my mother exactly when I was supposed to be.

Of course, when an urgent thought would again catch my attention, off I would go, and that thought would flow into another and then another, and pretty soon I would wind my way back into struggle again. But then the discomfort of the struggle would awaken me again. Re-asking the question, "What is?" would take me back into keen curiosity about what my story was doing and into a sense of merciful spaciousness.

For the rest of the meditation I went back and forth, identifying with the struggle, waking up to *what is* and stabilizing in deep curiosity, only to become caught in the mind again. But every time I got caught in the whirlwind of the story, I was able to drop back into my body and simply watch the thoughts and feelings that were now flowing through me. And as I did so, everything became lighter and clearer.

Why are moments of seeing *what is,* rather than identifying with it, so powerful? Because it is Awareness in action. We are not the story in our minds. We are Awareness itself. This is the spacious field of our own true nature. When you focus this Awareness, it becomes attention—the ability to be present and deeply curious about exactly what is happening right now.

In the past we have used struggle to try to get out of struggle, only to find ourselves still enmeshed. Attention is the doorway out of this maze of the mind. It is the only activity that can take us beyond our story because it is the only place that is bigger than the struggles in our mind (including the struggle to become free). It doesn't fight with *what is* nor does it wish it to be any different. It is simply willing to see it.

Through attention we discover more and more moments of being immediately with Life. We also become able to see, with great compassion and deep curiosity, the story that takes us away. The more we see the story, the more we are *here.* And the more we are *here,* the more we can see the story. Slowly and surely we become bigger than the maze of the struggling mind and know the breathtaking joy of belonging to Life.

BRINGING AWARENESS TO THE STORY

Those by chance who have likened our lives to a dream were more right, by chance, than they realized.

C. E. Montague

We have been exploring, step by step, the ability to be awake. We are now ready to shine the light of our attention on our story. As long as we are identified with the conversation in our minds, we will be unable to see that what we formerly thought of as ourselves is simply a story. It is a story that is woven out of our experiences and is full of ideas about ourselves and about Life, keeping us away from truly experiencing Life itself. To be able to see the story gives us great freedom.

Many years ago I had an experience that clearly highlights the healing that comes from being able to see the conversation in our heads. I was a single parent for most of the time my children were growing up. We lived very simply and at times even less than that. I had received a $10,000 settlement, more money than I had ever seen up to that point in my life. The temptation was to spend it on so many things I felt we needed. But I also knew I had no back up set aside for emergencies. Nor did I have a nest egg for my later years. Long term goals won out, and I decided i should invest it.

Having never had money, I didn't have a clue about what to do, so I called a friend, and she connected me with her financial advisor. After thoroughly explaining our financial situation, he said he had just the thing for me. After a few days, a stack of official papers arrived with a note saying that the investment would take care of itself for five years, and then I would need to invest $2,000 every year thereafter. Being a fairly trusting individual and also being highly uneducated around money, I filed it away. Four and a half years later I called him, only to find out that he had moved to Mexico. The first feelings of trepidation began to appear. Tracking down the parent company, I discovered that what I had thought I had invested in and what really happened were two different things.

On my way to a meeting with a new financial advisor, I was still operating on the belief that I could retrieve a good deal of my initial investment, so my mind was fairly quiet. It was one of those breathtakingly beautiful winter days in the Northwest where the first hints of spring were in the air. Crocuses were appearing, heralding the soon to arrive celebration of all of the other spring blossoms. On the drive downtown, I was either fully *here* or was able to easily return, being present with the garage attendant and with the people in the elevator. As I got off on the 40th floor, I was greeted by the view of Puget Sound. The Olympic Mountains were pristine white with snow, framed by the exquisite blue of both sky and water, and I was very glad to be alive.

When I left his office an hour later, instead of being present, I was caught in the web of my story. He not only told me that I would be lucky to get back a fraction of my investment, but he also said that the original advisor had pocketed a $10,000 commission. Lost in my story of helplessness, I felt violated, abused, used, stupid, inept and enraged. Needless to say, I didn't notice the view on the way out of his office. Nor could I connect with anyone on the elevators and escalators as I descended to the garage.

I had a number of choices of what to do with this state of mind that so thoroughly had me caught in its grip. I could try to rise above it, thinking positive thoughts. I could ignore it by either denying or numbing (I did think briefly about stopping and getting something to eat—even though I was not physically hungry). I could stay lost in it, caught in the whirlpool of my mind. Or I could become curious about it.

Having cultivated deep curiosity about the unfolding of my life, it didn't take very long before curiosity cut through the upheaval. The first thing that captured my attention when I asked the question "What *is?*" was a sharp pain in my wrist. My whole body had become very tight, reflecting the struggle in my mind and I was gripping the steering wheel tightly. There was clearly much more going on than just a sore wrist, so again I asked, "What *is?*"

At first nothing was very clear because the story in my mind was so loud and overwhelming, but repeatedly I brought myself back into the actual sensations of the present moment. I could feel the rage, the sense of injustice, the fear for my financial future. A piece of me wanted to revel in the experience of self pity and righteous anger. But I had been aware too long to easily forget the price my body and heart pay for this level of chaos and confusion. With great compassion, I acknowledged that I was lost in a very contracted part of my story. Without judgment, I met each voice as it ricocheted throughout my body and screamed through my mind.

With this spacious and focused attention, my body relaxed, my heart opened and my mind calmed down. I moved from the victim stance into one of empowerment. I recognized that money will always come and go and I chose not to let its abundance or its scarcity define my life. As I arrived home, I found again that I was in that centered place where clarity and wisdom abide and where I felt deeply grateful to be alive.

Asking *What is?* brings our attention from the struggling mind into engagement with the living moment. This not only connects us to Life, but it allows us to see the story that takes us away. Freedom comes when we can bring the full light of our attention to this story. This art of seeing thought, rather than always trying to fix it, change it or rearrange it, is the doorway into the field of Awareness that thought is flowing through.

CULTIVATING AWARENESS

Don't think.
Don't get lost in your thoughts.
Your thoughts are a veil on the face of the Moon.
That Moon is your heart,
and those thoughts cover your heart.
So let them go.
Just let them fall into the water.

Rumi

We have been caught inside our stories for so long that it does take effort to learn how to see the story and to discover that underneath it rests the living moment—the place where Love is. While we all experience great joy in connecting with the living moment of our lives, it soon becomes evident that, even with the best of intentions to be present, the tide of thought can easily again capture our attention.

The most skillful way I know to become bigger than the endless conversation in our heads is to set aside time everyday to strengthen the 'muscle' of our attention and then to learn how to use it to watch the story—the story that you think is you. I call this Awareness Meditation, the foundation which comes out of Insight Meditation (best known by the work of Jack Kornfield, Jon Kabat-Zinn and Stephen Levine). It is a much different way to meditate than we have done before.

Meditation was usually seen as the act of stopping thought or of creating better states of mind. This kind of meditation is about focusing on *what is right now* rather than about trying to create something different. It is the art of reconnecting with Life exactly as it is appearing in this moment, including both the vibrancy of the living moment and the veil of thinking we place over it all. In this exploration, we can then discover that who we really are is that which can see thought rather than thought itself.

For most of us the muscle of our attention is flaccid, having been pulled around by the maze of thought for so many years. We can usually only pay attention for a moment or two before thought captures us again. Wes Nisker, who had an ongoing column in the periodical, "Inquiring Mind," once wrote a humorous piece on the wandering mind called "Empty Thoughts on a Full Stomach." The following are excepts from this hilarious piece that says a lot about how busy our minds are:

...In breath...out breath...I'm resolved to stay mindful this hour...in

breath...just move the knee over a little...there...out breath...maybe I should count...in breath one...out breath....in breath two...out breath...if I get to twenty-five, I'll start over...in breath, whoa, did I miss one? ...can't remember. OK...in breath one...did I just judge myself?...out breath...judging the judging...oh no...judging the judging of the judging...what a mess these synapses are...luckily it's not ME...it's just synapses firing...sin apes, or sin snaps...that's cute...must write it down later...

OK, in breath one...out breath...in breath two...now we're getting down to it... "Let me take you down, cause I'm going soon, Strawberry Fields"...what a great song that is...I wonder what ever happened to sweet Sue...the park days...am I less optimistic than I used to be?...optimistic...optical mistake or optimal mystic...that's clever...

OK, time to meditate...in breath one...out breath...in breath two...or is that three?... I've been in the zone for at least five minutes...my mind has been destroyed by rock and roll...rocks in my head...and too much thinking...if that's what you call this stream of lower consciousness...I'm just a smelly chemical stewpot...Descartes should have said, "I stink, therefore I am,"... Got to remember that one...

OK, in breath one...out breath...in breath two...now we're getting the rhythm...in breath three...if I sit real good this hour then I'll go for a walk...out breath...or go sit in the dining room and watch yogis...I wonder if that cute girl is with the guy she came to registration with...what great posture...and great eyes...oh, oh, here come the dirty movies...forget it, it's not useful, not making me feel better, lust...lust...lust...lusting...lusted...hey, it went away...mindfulness strikes again!...OK back to the breath...get serious...in breath one...I could die in the next minute...out breath...in breath two...out breath...in breath three...out breath...alright, I feel the space in my mind starting to expand...in breath four...out breath...in breath five...nice, nice, I like it...out breath...in breath six...a little peace...out breath...I should sit more often...in breath seven... "nothing is real, nothing to get hung about. Strawberry Fields Forever."...

Even though this is humorous, it is not too far away from what we experience all day long—following thought wherever it goes. In order to not always be lost in thought, we need to strengthen the muscle of our attention. This is done by choosing a primary focus, a place where our attention can not only rest, but also return to over and over again when we find it captured in the web of our story. This focusing can be done while in meditation, while driving down the road, while eating our food or while washing our hands. Any moment in our lives can be used as a focusing moment.

It is best if the focus, rather than being a word, a mantra or a concept, is something that we are actually experiencing. It is a wondrous moment when we discover that underneath the ceaseless becoming of the mind are the sensations of aliveness. No matter what thought is doing, our hearts are beating, a symphony of sounds is unfolding all around us and within us, and our breath is continually rising and falling. All of these can be used as a focus and as we allow the wandering mind to rest in these sensations, this brings it to a place of calm and clarity.

Anything in the field of sensations can be used as a focus—sound, our sore knee, the breath. If we choose listening, we can become intensely fascinated by the constantly changing dance of sounds all around us and in us, each one entirely brand new. If we choose focusing on the pain in our knee, it becomes fascinating to see how movable and changeable pain is. If we choose breath, we can discover the joy of riding these rhythmic waves. The focus becomes a sanctuary in which we can rest for moments out of the ceaseless *becoming* of our mind. This kind of focusing, where we aren't trying to go anywhere, do anything or become anybody, reconnects us with the living moment of our lives.

BREATH AS THE PRIMARY FOCUS

And now I see with eye serene
The very pulse of the machine;
A being breathing thoughtful breath;
A traveler betwixt life and death.

William Wordsworth

Whatever you choose as a focus becomes an anchor, a place to return to over and over again. While anything can be a focus, breath has advantages that have been recognized and cultivated for eons. The most basic gift it holds is that it is with us in every single moment of our lives. Each experience we've had since the moment we were born has been accompanied by breath.

Feel it now as you read this book, rhythmically rising and falling. It was there when you first learned how to ride a bike, fell in love, showed up for your first job, learned how to swim, or sucked your thumb. And every single one of these breaths mirrored what was happening in your mind. When you were contented and safe, the breath was open and free. When you were caught and struggling, it became tight and contracted. When you were exhilarated, it became rapid and strong, and while you were deep asleep, it was slow and gentle. It is a rhythmic, ever changing and wondrously fascinating river to pay attention to.

Breath is our connection with Life. It is no accident that the literal meaning of inspiration is *in breath*. Breath is the space in which spirit and matter meet, where the invisible becomes visible. As we learn how to pay attention to our breath, it draws us into the still, clear pool of insight, clarity, support and Love that is awaiting us at the center of our being. Resting in the breath is like diving under the surface of a stormy sea where it is quiet and calm. Breath is also the place where we can see that something bigger than us is in charge of this dance. We are breathing, and at the same time we are being breathed. (Just try to stop breathing!)

Before I began to awaken, I created an illusion of safety by shallow breathing in order to hold back the terrors that I believed Life held. I often had a tight fist in my solar plexus as I contracted my diaphragm, cutting off the possibility of a full breath. When I discovered the safety of the living moment, my breath clamored to be free.

It became clear that whenever I was lost in my old story, my breath would be tight. So my breath became an exquisite biofeedback mechanism. Many states of mind screamed that they were real and absolutely necessary, but all I had to do was notice whether this state opened or closed my breath, opened me to Life or kept me caught in the maze of struggle. If my breath was tight, I knew I was lost in my mind. I began to breathe deeply in cars, in theaters or standing in line at the post office. These moments beyond the restless sea of my mind became much-appreciated sanctuaries and began to enliven and heal my body, as well.

Slowly, breath began to reweave the tattered thread of trust. Rediscovering the river of breath taught me that I was not alone in this process. It revealed to me the rhythm with which Universal Intelligence orchestrates Life. This rhythm is inherent in the dance of the planets around the sun, the ebb and flow of the tides and the drumbeat of our hearts. It shows up in the music of the seasons, the cycles of birth and death, and our breath. The great Sea of Life is swelling and receding, rising and falling all around us, in us and as us. Our bodies are but a small inlet of a great sea of rhythmic Intelligence, and we can deeply connect and attune with this sea through our breath.

To learn to pay attention to breath exactly as it is appearing is to open a book of wisdom. And as we make a commitment to return to it over and over again, it will take us into the deeper regions of truth that lie at rest in the core of our being.

Let us now explore the art of meditation in which we bring our attention to breath exactly as it is appearing. Either have a friend read this next passage to you or, if that is not possible, put it on tape and listen. If neither of these work, slowly read this and then become as curious as possible when you close your eyes.

Bring your attention to your body, feeling yourself sitting in the middle of the living moment of your life. As your attention settles in, notice there is something quite dramatic happening - the rising and falling of your breath. This is the great river of Life passing through you, arriving from the sweet breath of babies, the gifts of a cedar tree and even from the age of dinosaurs. Breathe in Life in your next breath, and then let go. It is true you are breathing, but it is also true that something far greater than you is breathing you. Let go of doing it yourself, and allow yourself to be breathed by Life.

As you rest in this great rhythm of Life, the mind will again capture your attention. To stay connected, become very curious about how this breath feels as it flows in and out of your body. Do your shoulders move? Rest your attention there a few moments, and see what is happening. How about your arms? When you are ready, move to your back, and see if you feel the breath there. As you explore each of these sensations, stay a while before you move on. Does your belly rise and fall, or is it quiet? Do your clothes move with you, or is there a place where they subtly rub against your skin? Can you feel the air caressing the inside of your nostrils? If so, how far back into the nostrils do you feel the air? Are there sensations on the top of your lip as you breathe out?

Now choose the place in your body where you are most aware of your breath, and allow your attention to rest there, riding the rhythmic flow of Life. Recognize that your breath is a circle - in breath opening the body until the circle begins to turn into an out breath, the letting go that is an out breath, the pause in between and then the swelling of the in breath again. Ride the circle, staying focused as much as possible on the living experience of the breath. If the mind gets bored, bring it back to curiosity. Explore the difference between the in breath and the out breath, or become fascinated by the length of the pause in between.

You will be repeatedly taken away from this sanctuary by thoughts. The power is not in staying on the breath. The power is in returning over and over again. For the next few minutes be willing to gently return to the actual physical experience of breath whenever you find yourself lost in thought. To end, give thanks for the gift of these breaths and the ones to come. When you are ready, open your eyes.

We live in a society that loves stimulation—action packed movies, MTV and channel surfing. After a few minutes on something so seemingly bland as a breath, the mind will become bored and start looking for excitement. It goes out into the future or creates a wonderful fantasy. It may rehash yesterday's events, judging everyone's performance (including our own), or it will drift off into daydreams until, with a start, we remember that we are meditating.

The key to long term meditating, and thus lasting healing, is to know that meditation is not about *staying* focused on the breath. It took me years to understand this. If we say that we must stay focused on the breath and a good meditation is measured by how much we are there, then we will still be caught in struggle. *The healing comes in returning over and over again whenever we've drifted off into the dream.* And we *will* drift off into the dream. We've only been tracking thought for decades! But every moment we return, we are not only strengthening the muscle of our attention, we are also clearing a pathway back into Life. At the beginning it will be as faint as a deer trail, but every time we return, the path widens and becomes clearer.

At times the story can be so loud and persistent that it is difficult to keep track of the breath. Words, silently said to ourselves, can be a skillful way to remind ourselves that we are paying attention to our breath. It can be as simple as counting the in breaths up to 10. If we *space out*, we simply start at one again. We can also say "in breath turn, out breath turn." Another favorite of mine is "here" on the in breath and "now" on the out breath.

Thich Nhat Hahn created a wonderful meditation for children at his retreat center in France. He suggested that they find 10 small stones and hold them in one hand. As they meditated, he invited them to say silently to themselves these following pairs of words. The first word of each pair is said on the in breath (the first two words in the last line) and the second word (second two in the last line) on the out breath:

> *In, out;*
> *deep, slow;*
> *calm, ease;*
> *smile, release;*
> *present moment, wonderful moment.*

At the end of each round of words, he told them to shift one of the ten stones to the other hand. When all of the stones had been shifted, they were then invited to either do another 10 rounds, or else simply explore the breath exactly as it is. When the adults in the community learned of this meditation, they began doing it and teaching others how to do it. It has now traveled many times around the world, touching numerous lives.

Know that our minds will be gone a good deal of the time. In our old beliefs around meditation, we believed that we were supposed to do something with thought—transform it, get rid of it, or get above it. Trying to do this, however, usually creates more thought, causing us frustration which results in our becoming part time meditators or closet failures.

We may go wandering around in the thinking mind five minutes or more before Awareness kicks in and says "Ahh, I am lost in thought." When we notice we are gone, we simply return to the breath, even if we only stay there for half of one breath.

Each moment of returning is more powerful than you can imagine. A participant at one of my retreats was sitting beside a pond, caught in the struggling mind. When Awareness kicked in and she again returned to the living moment, her mind tried to catch her in struggle again by commenting that just a few moments of returning wasn't enough. Wisdom opened her up again by reminding her that the pond in front of her had been created from drops of water. Our healing happens in the same way. From a moment here and a moment there where we reconnect with Life, a pool of peace and connection is cultivated. In time this peace—rather than the struggling mind—slowly becomes the ground of our being.

The deeper into meditation we go, the more we see that it is not only in returning that we become clear, but it is also in *how* we return. For a long time in my meditation practice, when I noticed that I was lost in thought, I would force myself back, chastising myself for having been gone. Now I can gently and with great tenderness bring my attention back to the breath.

Even though breath has been proven to be a skillful focus, it may not be the one for you. Because I had been deeply scared out of my body when I was young, in the beginning it was terrifying for me to even contemplate paying attention to my body or breath. So I used sight to ground myself here, describing the colors and shapes of the room I was in. Then, when I closed my eyes, my primary focus was the symphony of sounds. Over time, I began to inch my way into my body and eventually into my breath.

THE POWER OF NAMING

The range of what we think and do is limited by what we fail to notice.
And because we fail to notice that we fail to notice,
there is little we can do to change, until we notice how failing to notice shapes our
thoughts and deeds.

R.D. *Laing*

The ability to discover and return to our breath takes us into the next step of Awakening—the ability to *see* our story. The more we return to a focus, the easier it is to see how busy our minds are. Our experience becomes dramatically different when we can have moments of relating to what this busyness is doing rather than being lost in it. Go back to the experience of moving your finger around in front of you and, rather than tracking it, keep your eyes looking straight ahead. This is the place where your attention is stable and centered. Just as you can see the finger moving without having to follow it, you can see thought without having to follow it.

The way we see thought, without getting caught-up in it, is to name what the mind is doing when we notice that we are not with our breath. Whenever we name to ourselves what thought is doing, we have stepped out of it, at least for a moment. In the beginning, it is difficult to see thought because most of the time we are lost in it. Because of this, naming progresses through stages from a very general noting to eventually a very sharp and clear ability to see the entirety of the story we took on. The most general level of naming is to silently say to ourselves, when we notice that we are no longer on the breath, "thinking, thinking" or "story, story." It helps to say it twice because it notifies the mind that you are relating to the story rather than identifying with it.

Being able to name what thought is doing is very healing. Self judgment is an example from my life. The counseling and meditation that I did for years seemed to minimize the voices of self-judgment enough that I could function in society, but they still lurked in the depths of my being and could come and devour me in a moment. Of course, when I began meditating, they kept up a running commentary about how miserably I was doing. One of the most glorious moments of my life came when, rather than believing what these voices were saying, Awareness kicked in and said, "Ahh, self-judgment." In that moment, for the first time I *saw* judgment, rather than being lost in it.

After you read this paragraph, put down the book and close your eyes. Allow in a few deep breaths. Bring your attention to your breath, and become keenly attentive

The key to naming is not only to be gentle and non-judgmental, but also to be persistent. The mind will throw up all sorts of ideas about why this is a waste of time; why it isn't working; and why we'll never do it right. Simply note "thinking, thinking" and return to the breath.

NOTICING WHAT THOUGHT IS DOING

The mind is happening all by itself. Struggle arises uninvited. It is your resistance to it that makes you think it is so real. And you have often cultivated very little trust in the natural process of the mind and body because you have fought with it so often, thinking you have to be someone else. No blame, just something to notice. Big surprise there is struggle in the mind. Who doesn't have it? But the way in which we meet it can create an even deeper faith within us that all we are experiencing is simply passing show. Nothing you need to fight. Just something to soften, to acknowledge, to open around, to let go, to let be as it is and greeted with curiosity and heart.

Stephen Levine

Once we have cultivated the ability to return to a focus, noting when thought takes us away and then naming it, the next step is to see what thought is doing. The easiest way to do this is to name the direction thought is going—whether it is leaning into the future or into the past.

After you read this section, put down the book and close your eyes. Take a few deep breaths. Bring your attention to a focus. When you become aware that your mind has drifted off into thought, notice whether it has wandered into the past or the future. If it is in the past, squeeze your left hand and say "past." If it is in the future, squeeze your right hand and say "future." If it takes more than a split second or if you discover yourself spacing out, squeeze both hands and say "thinking, thinking."

In that moment of noticing what thought is doing, you are not identified with it and have opened a bit more into the spaciousness of your true being. Continue noting whether thought goes into the past or into the future for at least five minutes. When you are done, open your eyes.

Naming *past* and *future* is one of the primary ways I bring myself back into the moment. In my early years of meditation I usually experienced a healthy dose of wandering mind. I learned to cut through the fogginess in my mind by noticing if I was thinking about the rest of the day or trying to rework yesterday. In that moment of noticing whether the mind was in the past or in the future, the present became more clearly defined. The mind lets go and I discover myself *here* in the living moment.

Another way we can see the direction thought is moving is to use the words *planning* and *remembering*, for the mind loves to do both of these. Two other pairs of words can help us to watch the mechanics of thought—*liking or disliking* and *wanting or resisting*. Or you can come up with your own words. Seeing and naming the mechanics of thought allows our perspective to broaden, giving us more freedom from the story in our minds.

The next step is to see the actual content of this story. It takes awhile to create the stability of attention in which we can actually see what thought is doing without becoming lost in it. Over time, as our attention stabilizes, we will be able to notice and name many different states of mind that formerly caught us in their web—anger, fuzziness, self pity, agitation, happiness (yes, it can take us away too!), wanting, fearing, numbness, boredom. Every time we note a thought without judging or getting lost in it, this weakens its power over us and strengthens our ability to become bigger than our story.

As we see the different parts of the conversation in our head, it becomes easier to make contact with the deep and ancient feelings that have run us our whole lives underneath the level of our everyday awareness. In making contact with them lies the possibility of freeing ourselves from their grip. For most of my life I was terrified. This feeling was so big I wasn't even aware that I was afraid. All I knew was that I didn't like to be with people. As I became able to see it and feel it in my body, I came to know it so well that it no longer controls me. I have now learned how to work with it rather than having it define how I live my life.

As we explore the story in our meditations, this centered clarity begins to show up in our daily lives. I can still vividly remember one of the first times I was able to relate to anger rather than being lost in it. After having seen and gotten to know anger as it appeared during my meditations, I found myself one day in the middle of a rather heated argument with an acquaintance. Awareness kicked in and said, "Ahh, anger." Rather than being swept up in the argument, a part of me became fascinated by how anger talked and felt. As I made space for it, I became less invested in being *right* and more interested in the actual experience. My words and actions began to come from a different place, and we ended up laughing about how deeply we had been caught and how passionately we had defended our positions.

The ability to see thought and name what it is doing will be, at moments, very crisp and clear, only to move back into the haze as we again become lost in our story. We are not in charge of making or breaking these moments of clarity. All we can do is be willing to return over and over again and name that which takes us away.

Don't expect these tools to progress in a linear and tidy fashion in your practice. It just doesn't happen that way. We have built gradually from focusing in the moment, into simply returning over and over again to Life itself, and on to the step of naming *thinking* when it takes us away. We then opened to noticing the mechanics of thought and finally to noticing the actual content. But on any given day, we could be back at square one again, having difficulty finding a breath or, without a clue as to how or why, finding ourselves sitting for long moments in a stable and attentive Awareness. The key is to simply show up for *what is*, inviting the comparing and judging mind to take a break. To get to this level of Awakening takes time and commitment, but it is definitely worth it.

THE GIFT OF STILLNESS

Rest in natural great peace.
This exhausted mind,
beaten helpless by neurotic thought,
like the endless pounding of the waves.
Rest in natural great peace.

Unknown

There is something that happens when the body is still that seems to be unavailable when we are moving. The analogy that Jack Kornfield, a well-known meditation teacher and author of *A Path With Heart*, gives is that when a glass of cloudy water is still, the silt falls to the bottom and everything becomes clear. A daily sitting practice is the place in which we can see the silt fall away.

The power of setting aside time each day to be present for our breath and then noticing what takes us away is enormous. There is something waiting for us here in the living moment, something that we have yearned for our whole lives. It can only be discovered as we stabilize and center our minds.

Take a moment and ask yourself if you are willing to gift yourself with daily meditation. This is a much different approach than saying it is something that we *must* do. To make it a *should* only creates resistance. I saw this clearly around flossing my teeth. Despite dire warnings from my dentist, I was a part time flosser for years and came to hate those little boxes of floss that I had left everywhere in order to force myself into flossing. A major shift came when I realized it was a kind thing to do for my body! It got scratched off of the *I have to do* list, becoming something that I *wanted* to do for myself. I am now a daily flosser.

The same is true for meditation. It is one of the most precious gifts we'll ever give ourselves. Be assured that you will wobble with it just as when you learned how to ride a bike. The important thing is to keep on returning. Know that every act of being present for Life is powerfully transforming.

Once we are willing to gift ourselves in this way, rather than following the many rules that have been created over the years around mediation (such as: we need to sit in front of an altar; it is best to sit cross legged on the floor; our hands must be placed in a particular way; early morning is best; we must sit for 20 minutes twice a day), the most important thing to do is to discover what works for you. You may not live in the kind of environment where you can only sit at night or you may have an injury that precludes you sitting without support. Find the location, position and time that is right for you.

For most people, to sit in the morning before the mind begins to move very fast is most conducive to clarity, but this may not be true for you. Listen to yourself and keep it simple. Allow the place where you meditate, how you sit and the length of time that is right for you to come out of your own life and needs. Also allow them to change and transform over time.

It is skillful to choose a quiet place where distractions are at a minimum. Turn off the phone and, if you live with other people, notify them of your intention to have this time entirely to yourself. At the beginning, set aside 10 minutes. If you find 10 minutes too much, try five. To start, consistency is much more important than the amount of time. If we over-exercise our physical muscles after having taken a break from working out, we can easily injure ourselves. The same is true for our muscle of attention. Demanding too much may just invite frustration.

The mind is like a speeding train with a lifetime of momentum that propels it into constantly becoming. To break this narrow addiction to thought, at the beginning of a sit it can be skillful to connect with a more spacious perspective. What works for me is to feel myself being held by the chair, that is being held by the floor, that is being held by the foundation, that is being held by the Earth. As I allow myself then to be held by the Earth, I open up into the knowing that the Earth is allowing itself to be held by space. In that I discover that I am dancing through space in the exact moment that I am sitting here. In that precious remembering, I pop out of the narrow absorption with only my own story and realize myself as a part of a grand and mysterious process.

I then open to the astounding realization that it took the creativity of the Universe billions of years to make this moment, and I become very curious about *what is*. I then begin to draw the lens of my attention into a more finely tuned focus. First I pay attention to the space that I am sitting in, grounding in one of my senses in order to enhance that experience. My favorite is hearing. I find it fascinating to focus my attention predominantly on listening, eavesdropping on my own life! Hearing the symphony of sounds appearing and disappearing and noticing that they are always different connects me to the moment that Life appears out of Mystery.

Once I've opened to spaciousness and reconnected with the living moment, I ask *What is?* to my body, noticing what my present experience is. It may be tiredness, exhilaration, contentment or discomfort. There may be a particular sensation that needs my attention—a pain in my neck, a hungry stomach, a sore back. Realizing that the field of sensations that is my body is a constantly changing dance, my commitment is to not push anything away and to remain open to whatever I am experiencing. With this curiosity, I finally bring my Awareness into the breath, grounding in the actual experience of breathing. I then return to the breath whenever I find my attention pulled back into thought, naming what thoughts had grabbed my attention.

You can also work with the lens of your attention during meditation. If you find yourself struggling, maybe even having difficulty finding a breath, you can expand your attention into listening; or open into seeing yourself from the moon; or go into exploring the sensations of your body. All of these create more space in your consciousness. When the tightness in your mind begins to let go to spaciousness, you can then refocus the lens of your attention on the breath.

A close cousin to working with the lens of attention is the ability to change one's focus. There will be times in your meditation when sounds, sensations, feelings or emotions become so strong that naming them does not free up your attention. You can then shift your focus to the distraction. If it is a

92

sound, name it as "hearing, hearing" and then listen to it, really listen. Pretend that this is the last time you will ever hear this sound in your life.

If the distraction is a sensation in your body, name it by saying "sensing, sensing." Describe it to yourself, allowing your mind to be like a finger, intimately exploring what is happening. In that one area there are many sensations arising and passing away—tingles, searing, warmth, coolness, throbbing, aching, pulsing, shooting pains. Observe if it is dull or sharp, moves or has boundaries, appears and disappears or is constant, or if it is connected with any other sensations.

If it is an emotion, say "feeling, feeling" and then bring your attention to where it lives in your body, describing what you find there. When you are done exploring it or you discover that you have spaced out again, return to your primary focus. Eventually, your attention will be stable and strong enough to be present for all of your thoughts, feelings and sensations.

When something is repeatedly grabbing your attention, become fascinated. See how it behaves. Does it come and go? Does it stay? Is it sharp or fuzzy, loud or quiet, agitated or subtle, light or heavy? Does it have a vibration? Watch it change and move in the living experience. If you lose connection, go back to the breath. This can be done with a pain in your knee, boredom, sleepiness, anger, a full tummy or even joy.

You can end a meditation in a number of ways. Some people set a timer to go off at the end of a predetermined amount of time. If your life allows it, you can also sit until it feels right to end. If a timer is too invasive and if your schedule does not allow for an open-ended sit, you can record nothing on a tape for the length of time you want to sit and then add the sound of a bell at the end. Then, whenever you sit, you play the tape and the bell will notify you when the allotted time is up.

The beauty of this kind of meditation is that nothing is truly a distraction. Everything can be included. All of your life experiences can be quite fascinating when not resisted. This sound or that thought or the feeling racing through your body *is* your life. The place you are heading to is an open and spacious Awareness that can include it all.

As your ability to be present becomes stronger, you may only spend a few minutes at the beginning of your meditation grounding in a primary focus and then you simply watch, with an alert and receptive attention, the unfolding of Life within and around you. A moment of sound, a sensation in your foot, a thought from the past, all arising and passing away; nothing to hold onto, nothing to push away; all received by an attentive and spacious acceptance.

Practicing Returning & Connecting

Knowing that nothing needs to be set in stone and that our job is to listen to what works for us, the following is an example of a possible sit. The only necessary thing to do is to choose a focus, returning to it over and over again, noticing what takes us away. The rest of these suggestions are all tools that can aid in this returning and noticing.

1. Use your breath to cultivate a quieter mind/body experience:
    - Drop into the rhythm of deep belly breathing.
    - Add pauses at the end of each in and out breath, gradually lengthening the pause at the end of the in breath.
    - When your body is accustomed to more oxygen, add alternate nostril breathing.

2. Open the lens of your Awareness and connect with Life. Some mind opening ideas are:
    - Become aware that you are being held by space.
    - See yourself from the moon, and recognize that all of the moments of your life have led you to this place and this meditation.
    - Feel all of the stars above you, below you, to the left and to the right of you.
    - Connect with all of the activity happening on the face of the planet: the roar of waterfalls, people arguing, the unfolding of flowers, rush hour traffic, buildings being built, babies suckling, children dying. Now feel the preciousness of this quiet oasis.
    - Acknowledge all of the beings through the eons of time that have gone before you to make this moment possible. Know that this willingness to sit with *what is* will affect all of the children coming after you.

3. From that spacious place acknowledge the space you are sitting in, becoming curious about *what is*. Use one of your senses to intimately connect with Life. Remember that your life is made up of individual moments and that this is the only one that matters.

4. Connect with the living experience of your body through the question *What is?* Become very curious about what sits here, for your body is a constantly changing river of sensations. Name to yourself what the predominant experience is. Then discover the rhythm of your breath, choosing the place where it is most evident that breath is happening. If need be, use words to remind yourself that you are paying attention to the breath. Without any judgement for how much you are gone,

return over and over again to the breath.

5. When you notice you've become focused on thought again, work with the tools of naming in order to become familiar with what takes you away. Choose the more general words when the mind is easily distracted (ahh, thinking, thinking). When your Awareness is more stable, move into the deeper levels of naming, either noticing the direction it is moving (past and future or liking and disliking) or the actual content of thought itself. Some of the qualities you will see are fear, judgment, boredom, anger, desire, sadness, confusion, doubt, resistance. Become curious about the physical manifestation of these mind states.

6. Throughout your meditation, cultivate moments where you expand your Awareness and ask the question, "What is?" Of all of the possible human experiences, *what is* yours right now? When your mind begins to wander again, bring your attention back to your breath.

At the beginning, you will find yourself captured by thought for most of your meditation. The amount of time you spend in thinking doesn't matter. The power is in the returning. Doing this work is like sitting in front of a gigantic boulder, so big that it is all that you can see. It feels like someone has given you a little tiny hammer and pick and he said, break open this rock. Thought may laugh hysterically, saying that this is impossible. But, as one of my teachers told me, we chip away here and chip away there at the seeming solidity of thought. Then one day we hit a fissure in the rock, and it cracks open in front of us, allowing us to see what the rock had always blocked—the actual experience of Life.

Don't let the mind rush you in this process of Awakening. You may spend a week or a year just adding moments of Awareness into your daily life before you are ready for a sitting practice. And even with meditation in your daily life, you may not notice for a long while how much this art of simply returning is transforming you until you find yourself in the middle of a crisis with a sense of calm and clarity you've never had before. Stephen Levine titled his book about this kind of meditation, *A Gradual Awakening*. Each moment of returning to your focus is another drop of water in the bucket of your Awakening. One day, without being aware that the bucket is filling, you will discover that you are really present for the miracle that is your life.

INCLUDING THE DIFFICULT

...could you keep your heart in wonder at the daily miracles of your life, your pain would not seem less wondrous than your joy.

Kahlil Gibran

Sitting in meditation strengthens the muscle of our attention so that we can be awake for our own lives. To see the benefit of adding a daily sitting practice to our lives and to discover the joy of belonging to the living process, we need to explore the role of pain in Awakening. It hurts to stub our toe, to give birth, to watch a loved one die. Our standard relationship with the difficult and challenging times in our lives has been to get away as fast as we can. We take pills, overeat or become terribly busy. If these don't work, we try to manage, fix and understand. Very rarely do we meet the difficulties with a keen curiosity and a heartfelt compassion.

The place where we can learn how to do this is in our meditations. Rather than being something to ignore or annihilate, the uncomfortable parts of our meditations can help us to transform our whole relationship to the difficulties of our lives. During a sit, the difficult whispers to us, "Don't run away. Be with me, and I will show you the doorway to freedom." The greatest teacher we have to invite us out of struggle is the pain in our lives. If we are lucky— and I do mean lucky—the things we don't like about our lives will not leave and will become even louder and more insistent over time. They will cause us to try everything we can think of in order to get rid of them until the only option we are left with is to pay attention. That which we don't like highlights for us the maze of struggle that we live in and repeatedly gives us clues about the way out.

There is no accident that in most fairy tales the treasure is hidden in the cave where the dragon lives, in the castle where the evil prince holds court or in the lake where the serpent abides. The old style of solving difficulties says, "Don't go near these unwanted guests." The new style realizes that what we truly are *includes* the dark and the light, the comfortable and the uncomfort-able. And it uses the dark to help awaken us. These unpleasant visitors carry the keys to the door out of the maze of struggle.

This is not to say that we should never manage, control, fix and understand. These techniques are necessary steps on the path of our Awakening and will continue to be so at moments on the journey. But these skills will only take us so far. We are now ready to add the ability to be with *what is*, especially that which disturbs us. It is in learning how to respond rather than react that we become free.

A story that I have shared with many people speaks of the healing that comes from transforming our normal knee jerk reaction to one of response.

Imagine coming home one day to find a monster sitting in your living room. "What are you doing here?" you ask with great indignation. Getting no response, irritation takes over, and you order him out of the house. He doesn't move. Racing into the kitchen, you ask the other family members about this intruder, and nobody has a clue. Returning to the living room, you announce that you are going to call the police, and he still does not respond.

Calling 911 you say, "There is an emergency. A monster has moved into my house, and I want you to take him away." Kindly but firmly they tell you that this is not their job. You call social services, moving companies and even the zoo, hoping to get rid of this unwanted guest. Nothing works. In desperation, you even toy for a while with the idea of calling in a hit man (your Uncle Joey could probably arrange it), but that is too abhorrent for your tastes.

Being a good student of consciousness-raising practices, you decide that since you create your reality, he is only here because you have not yet figured something out. So off to counseling you go. You describe this stranger in your living room and the counselor takes you back into childhood, discovering a trauma there. You let go of a big chunk of self-judgment and, with a sense of relief, you go home, fully expecting that the monster will be gone. It isn't.

So now you decide that it was bad karma from a past life. Off you go to be regressed and discover a life when you were the underdog and he represents all of the people who persecuted you. Things begin to make sense. This understanding brings deeper layers of mercy, and again, with great hope, you enter the living room, only to discover that the monster is still there! The sense that he would be gone if only you could figure it all out and understand how to "do" this right begins to eat at your heart. The edges of despair flood your being, but with great strength you resolve that you will just try harder and then it will have to work.

Everything you have done so far has made it easier for you to live with him, but you still want him gone. Thinking that you are responsible for everything, you close your eyes and say powerful affirmations, repeating to yourself over and over again "I am healed, and this irritant is gone from my life." You feel more empowered as you say these words and you know that he is evaporating right now as you speak. In a very confident move, you take a peek through your closed eyes, only to discover that he is still there!

So you call on your friends to come and do a healing circle, cleansing your house with sage and cedar and visualizing white light surrounding and transforming this unwanted guest. The atmosphere in the house is lighter and clearer, but he isn't gone. As your friends leave they assure you that all you have to do is continue these practices and eventually he will leave. "After all," they remind you, "you are in charge of your life."

Then, after a particularly rigorous week of counseling, affirming and visualizing, it begins to sink into your consciousness that maybe he isn't going to leave. "If that is the case," you say, "I will at least make him more presentable." You call in a barber and a fashion designer to spiffy him up. And it does become a little bit easier to live with him. He is not quite as scary and abhorrent.

But one morning, sitting on the couch and doing all of the varied practices that promised to get rid of this uncomfortable visitor, the feelings of deep grief and rage at yourself begin to overwhelm you. "If I create my reality," you say, "then I am a failure. Nobody else has a monster in their living room. (They all do, but they never speak about it.) And if I can't get rid of mine, there must be something terribly wrong with me." You collapse on the floor in a flood of tears, self-judgment and hopelessness.

In the middle of this storm you hear, very faintly, a melodious voice. "Ask me why I am here." In shock you look up at the monster. In this whole time he had never before spoken! "What did you say?" you ask in amazement. "Ask me why I am here," he repeats. "Well, I don't want to talk to you. You are the enemy. I didn't invite you in to my home. You came unbidden and are deeply unwelcome," you respond. In a huff you turn your back to him. "What have you got to lose?" he asks. "Nothing else has worked. I haven't gone away."

In your desperation you realize that this is true. Picking your self up out of the heap of self-failure, you slowly approach him. (This whole time you've never come any closer than 10 feet.) Your heart is racing wildly. "This is the enemy. What am I doing? I must be crazy. If I get close he will beat me, rape me and maybe even murder me." But your desperation urges you on. As you sit down on the chair across from him, the question, "What is?" burbles up from the depth of your being. "This is my life," Awareness says. A surge of joy races through your body, and you become curious about the monster rather than living in reaction.

As you hone your curiosity, the first thing you notice is that the monster has kind eyes! "Why, you have beautiful eyes," you say. "And they are even twinkling with joy and laughter. Why have I never noticed before?" "Because you made me the enemy," he says in his melodious and healing voice. "I am not your enemy. I have come from the depths of your being into your life in order to awaken you. I am not here to disturb you, even though I do evoke that in your mind. I am not here to harm you, even though I do bring up your fear. I am your destiny, highlighting the maze of struggle that keeps you separate from all that you yearn for.

If you listen to that which is upsetting in your life, it will teach you that there is no "there" that you need to "get to," no mythical place where everything will finally be fixed, understood, managed and controlled. The healing is in learning how to show up for the dance exactly as it is appearing. Beneath all of this becoming, trying and doing that you live in most of the time, what you yearn for is right here, in present time. The way to get here is not to try to get here. It is to simply see the illusion of struggle that stands between you and the freedom that you are."

In some corner of your being you know that what he says is true. Rather than wanting to run away, you begin to listen to this monster that had formerly bothered you, and your heart begins to melt. "You truly are my friend," you say. His laughing eyes answer "yes." "And you have been waiting a long time for me to pay attention and listen to what you have to say." With a big sigh, he affirms this truth.

Even with this connection, at moments your fear and confusion take over. But you notice the kindness in his eyes and again you find yourself present for this former enemy. Something he has been saying over and over again finally becomes clear to you: "Life is for you. Who you really are includes both the dark and the light, and it uses the dark as a tool of Awakening. When you understand this, it becomes evident that your life—all of it—is trustable. It then is easier to show up for your own adventure—for the moment that Life appears out of Mystery."

The words he spoke were true and they quieted the racing of your mind and opened the fist around your heart. As you drink from the nectar of truth, fear begins to take over again. "This is so beautiful and so right that I am afraid I will forget," you say. "I am afraid I will make you the enemy again." "You will," he says. "But that is okay."

"Remembering and forgetting are a part of the process that you are in. Right now, the most skillful thing you can do is to be willing to pay attention to me. That intention—the willingness to listen rather than ignore, and communicate rather than manage—will take you out of the maze of struggle, birthing you into freedom."

The monsters in our lives—that which contracts, disturbs, disgusts, terrifies and confuses us—are here to bring us into our center. It takes great courage to even begin to let go of our resistance to *what is*, moving towards our experience instead of away. But it is only in the meeting that we can discover that our monsters come from the depth of our being to heal us, not to destroy us. As a friend of mine says, "What is in the way, is the way."

STEPPING INTO FREEDOM

Any heavy state is only the surface level of a beautiful wellspring of energy within us, an unrestricted flow of creativity. When we do not get involved in its story, a marvelous transformation occurs, and they become a source of Awareness.

Jack Kornfield

To begin to relate to thought rather than being lost in it by living in the question *"What is?"* allows us to see the conversation in our heads. In the beginning we will only see bits and pieces of this familiar story, pieces that seem unconnected. But slowly, over time, we become able to see the whole layout from beginning to end. Seeing it in its entirety allows us to discover a place beyond the story, the place where we are Awareness itself. In discovering this, we become present for Life in a keenly attentive and deeply compassionate way.

An image that can illustrate this is one of a magical land that is filled with beauty and wonder. But there is something very puzzling about this world. All of the people live underground. They have burrowed deeply into unconsciousness and only rarely surface to experience life above ground, the place of being awake to Life.

At first it can be scary. As we have lived for years underground, we have lost trust in this land. There are all sorts of things and experiences that cause us to again dive underground, burrowing back into our story of wanting, fearing and numbing out. But as we learn how to see the underground stories that keep us separate from Life, we begin to live 'above ground' again. Then there come moments of true exhilaration when we make immediate, moment-to-moment contact with Life.

Over time, as we explore being open to Life, we discover that Life is *for us* and that the doorway to the healing we yearn for is to show up for the process. It becomes easier to see that there are no accidents in what is happening in our lives. On the surface it may look like meetings, parties, commuting, relationships, shopping, etc., but we realize that behind the surface something very grand is happening.

As we reconnect with curiosity, wonder and courage, we discover a deep commitment to see what makes us go underground again. As we explore all of the facets of our story, there is a moment when we discover ourselves in a hot air balloon with a view that can see it all. In that place, the unfolding of our lives makes sense; the flavor of the story that we took on makes sense;

and what is happening on our planet—all of it—makes sense.

This image reminds us that slowly and surely we are being invited back into the living adventure that is Life. This is the place where grounding, noticing and naming are taking us—the place where we will know moments when we are simply Awareness itself. Sensations arise and pass away, sounds appear and disappear; thoughts come and go as it all moves through the spaciousness of who we really are. All of it becomes simply a passing show, nothing to hold onto or push away, nothing to identify as us. We rest in the very center of it all, and at the same time, are connected with everything.

The more we become Awareness itself, the more curiosity becomes the hallmark of our lives. Rather than struggling, we are moved into engaging. Rather the doubting or fearing, we know a deep and abiding trust. Rather than judging and hating, we become the healing balm of compassion. Rather than managing, we learn to deeply listen to Life and act from a place of connection rather than disconnection. And rather than being separate, isolated and alone, we discover ourselves belonging to our own lives.

This is the work of a lifetime. It is birthed in the willingness to return over and over again to the living moment and to watch with great tenderness what takes us away. At this point of evolution we have to be content with just moments, knowing that as more and more people connect with Life, we will collectively wake up. And we need to remember that evolution always flows at a seemingly microscopic pace. In this Awareness, we will learn to deeply honor even a moment or two out of our day when we are fully here. The power of each precious moment of connection with Life is beyond our comprehension. Collectively they will birth the Earth into the next level of its unfolding.

May we each cultivate the art of curiosity, living in the question, 'What is?"

May we see, with great tenderness, the struggling mind that keeps us separate from Life.

And may our daily practice bring freedom in the midst of it all.

Core Intention: What is?

Chapter 5
The Power of Inclusion

LIVING IN QUESTIONS

I used to be an answer machine.
Toss in the problem.....
ching ching,
out came an answer.
The mind got A's
while the heart languished.
So I came here and you asked me to
live in questions like:
Is it kind?
Can I meet myself here?
What is the flavor of my wall?
And the mind went....
ching, ching, ching, ching, ching.
Yes? No? Vanilla?????
TILT!
You smiled.
And finally....
my heart answered,
without a word.

Dee Endelman

THE RIVER OF LIFE

Healing is bringing mercy and Awareness into that which we have held in judgment and in fear.

Stephen Levine

Imagine that Life is a river. Most of us are trying to control this river, hoping that we can make it do what we think it should do. So we head our boat upstream, furiously paddling against the current, trying to make Life into what we think it should be. All the while we are struggling with Life, not only does the majesty and the mystery of the river completely escape our attention, but we are also unable to dance with the powerful flow of water.

Going upstream, we live in *what should be* and *what is not*. In this mindset, we don't notice that the pull of the river is more powerful than our attempts to control it and that all the while we are furiously paddling, it is taking us down the river of our lives backwards! Unable to see where we are going, the rapids and waterfalls catch us off guard, and we spend a lot of time cold, wet and shivering in the face of these powerful forces. What we truly long for is to allow the boat to turn around and follow the current of Life.

As we turn our boat around, we learn the art of showing up for the river of Life. Rather than just relying on our own limited intelligence, we now have the force of the river at our disposal, taking us turn by turn to our destiny of becoming aware.

The two main skills that allow us to maneuver down the river of Awakening are attention and inclusion. These are the two components of Awareness— deep curiosity that brings us into immediate engagement with Life and a spacious heart that knows how to make space for *what is* rather than resisting it. They are the tools that birth us out of the maze of the struggling mind, and they are also the truth of our being.

We explored the skill of curiosity in the last chapter, highlighting it with the words *what is*. Now we are ready to explore the second skill, inclusion, the place where lasting healing occurs.

The power of inclusion has been alien to most of us. We are geared to controlling, denying, fighting, resisting, managing or understanding *what is*. As we begin to come out of the fog of separation, it becomes evident that we have continually struggled with what is too much and too little, too big and too small, too painful and too boring, too loud and too quiet, too fast and too slow. We have believed we're both too much and too little at the same time! Most of the time we've thrown most of our lives out of our hearts.

Inclusion is the opposite of the struggling mind. It is the ability to move beyond struggle and meet *what is* exactly *as it is*. It is the art of meeting everything in our lives, especially all of the formerly disowned and disliked parts of our lives, with deep mercy. This *allowing* is magic for as long as we are resisting what we are trying to change, we stay stuck to it like glue.

The phrase *this too* mobilizes the activity of inclusion. As we say "this too," we let go of struggling with Life and become present for it instead. This allows us to skillfully maneuver through the rapids, waterfalls and whirlpools of our journey rather than spending energy fighting with them. From a place of inclusion, we can make skillful and creative choices about how fast or slow we need to go, about how much we need to rest and about which rapids we will ride and which we will transport around.

This too is not about floating directionless in the river. It is a place of engagement with the powerful forces that have created the river and us. It is about being responsive *to* the river rather than feeling that we are responsible *for* it.

While working with this river analogy in my Awakening groups, some people decided that they would like to go river rafting for a weekend. After having checked out a number of companies that could supply us with boats and guides, I narrowed it down to two possible choices and set out for a day on the river to check one of them out. It was to be a day of discovering deeper levels of the power inherent in compassionate curiosity, the combination of *what is* and *this too*.

I awoke with feelings of trepidation. This was compounded by the fact that I was not feeling very well and was not all that certain that I wanted to take my body on a wild ride that day. For the first few minutes of my meditation, I was lost in reaction. When Awareness kicked in, I immediately asked the question, *What is?*

My Awareness went to an aching muscle in my body that contracts only in the face of terror. This confused me because I wasn't particularly afraid of river rafting. It was something new that I had never experienced before, but I like adventure. As I dropped into what this muscle was feeling, staying with the actual physical experience, it became clear to me that what I was afraid of was being a nuisance, a core part of my childhood story. The story said, "What if I get sick on the river and am a bother to every one else?"

Having seen *what is*, I began to make space for it. I literally talked to this muscle and to the old story that had caused it to contract. I asked it what it needed from me that day, and what I heard back was *inclusion*. "Don't abandon me. Please make space for me and listen to me."

With this connection, I felt it wasn't necessary to cancel the trip. In fact, it made sense to me that this was a day to make space for these feelings, even allowing them to be there for the entire time, if necessary. In other words, I said, "I can include *this too* as a part of my journey and bring to it the healing attention it so deeply needed." My mind had expected an entirely different day. Before the fear made itself known, I had imagined a day of wonderful experiences. When the fear began to take over, I then imagined a day of horrors. Now I was willing to show up for exactly what was appearing. In making space and connecting with the uncomfortable, I began to feel better.

The willingness to include rather than resist what was appearing transformed my experience. Even though a feeling of discomfort was still in my body, by including it, I stayed in a larger space. My heart was full of joy and my mind was available for the adventure. Even when the guide said, "When the waves crash over you..." and "If you fall out of the boat...," I did not contract.

About half an hour into the river, a different muscle in my body began to spasm. I contracted. This particular cramp had caused all sorts of havoc in my life. The only way I had ever been able to get it to let go was through hot baths, deep massage and lying down. None of these were available and I was trapped in a boat, sitting in a position that further tightened this muscle. The panic of *no way out* began to build and the fear of *being a bother* tightened its fist around my heart.

In the middle of my reaction, I began to hear the whisper of *What is?* from the core of my being. When Awareness kicked in, I took my attention into the muscle and began to soften around it. My heart immediately said, *this too*. I literally talked to this cramp, asking what it needed, becoming as attentive and spacious as possible. Again it said, "Can you meet me without hatred and fear?" My heart flooded with the words, "I'm here," and "this is workable." My reactive mind quieted down and was replaced with conscious connection.

The cramp let go about 15 minutes later, never to return that day! I had met a big rapid in my inner life, a place that I had been very afraid of for my whole life. Now, rather than meeting it with resistance, I stayed conscious and connected and discovered the joy of riding through this rapid in a spacious and attentive way.

Inclusion is magic. It can make bearable and even heal the hardest heart, the deepest grief and the sharpest pain. *This too* makes our journey immeasurably easier as the energy that was formerly caught in the struggling mind is transformed in the spaciousness of the heart. It also invites us into the knowing that in order to discover the deep peace that is always within us, we need to learn how to not fight what lays over the top of it.

As we combine *what is*—bringing our Awareness back into present time—with *this too*, we are brought back into the healing of the heart and then on to engagement with Life the moment it appears out of Mystery. We then can flow through the river of our lives with curiosity, compassion and trust.

After you read this paragraph, put down the book and allow in a few deep breaths, softening your belly and focusing your mind. To hone your Awareness, ask the question, "What sits here?" What is the living experience of your life in this moment?

Start in a more global way, discovering what, of all of the possible human experiences, is happening right now (sitting, lying down, standing). Now become more focused. What is your body feeling? Allow your Awareness to be like a flashlight, highlighting the experience (tired, exhilarated, content, upset, uncomfortable).

Now go to one particular feeling, something that is speaking louder than all of the others (a headache, a sore back, an overall feeling of fatigue) and begin to explore it, allowing your Awareness to be like a finger, discovering exactly what is there. Say to yourself, "This too. For just this moment I choose to include this as a part of my journey. I let go of resisting, controlling and of even wanting this to be any different than what it is. For this moment, I allow it to exist as a part of my being."

Stay there for at least a few minutes, returning when your mind drifts away. Don't expect any great healing. It takes time to reweave the severed threads of connection and communication, but with every moment of seeing what is and then including it, we take another step into our healing.

THE ART OF LISTENING

It is not about what is happening in our lives. It is all about our relationship to what is happening that is the difference between struggle and freedom.

Jack Kornfield

Now that we can see that it is in responding to and including *what is* rather than trying to change it that we become truly free, let us explore how to create a relationship with what we formerly hated and feared.

The key to this kind of relationship is in listening. The key is in how we listen. Just think about how powerful it is when someone meets our anger with an understanding attention rather than reacting to it. The same is true for the contracted and disowned parts of our being. Just as we all respond to wise, kind, interested listening, so do these states. It doesn't matter whether it is a physical sensation, an emotional feeling, a very intense thought pattern or a combination of all of these, they all respond to deep listening. They open and reveal themselves to an Awareness that is truly willing to hear what is trying to be communicated. This isn't about analyzing, lecturing, assumptions or pat answers—it's about pure, undivided listening.

To begin to listen to all of the parts of ourselves that we formerly hated and feared is like having had a major falling out with a dear friend with whom you haven't spoken in a long time. As it becomes clear that both of you want to mend the relationship, you realize that the love and care is still there, but it is caught under layers of distrust, anger and grief. Each of you needs to be heard by the other without judgment.

The story inside of ourselves with its concepts, sensations and feelings, needs to be heard in the same way. It is full of beliefs about who we are, created when we were young enough to be unable to see through them. These beliefs became characters in our story—terrifying ghouls, scared children, struggling elves, rage-filled dragons, helpless princesses, arrogant knights and self-absorbed prima donnas—and every single one of them is an essential part of the community that we are.

Imagine the colorful array of characters found in fairy tales. They all live inside of us! They all play essential roles in the grand theater of our Awakening. But most of us try to ignore, deny, put down or hide the unpleasant characters that are in our story. This only gives them more life, allowing them to run us underneath the level of our everyday awareness. They are like little children left in a room by themselves. The longer no adult is present, the deeper they go into chaos and confusion. And over time, they have a tendency to get louder, crying out for the healing of our attention.

Just like the monster in the living room, they not only need to be seen, they also need to be heard. Making a connection with what we formerly resisted, ignored, hated and feared is a major step towards our healing. As we open into communication with them, doors that we didn't even know were there reveal themselves.

What we are exploring here is compassionate listening. Imagine a child running to a parent after a playmate has called him or her stupid. There are several possible responses. The parent can ignore the child, respond with annoyance at the interruption, or agree with the assessment, telling the child that he or she really is stupid. In these reactions the belief is given life. Another possible response is that the parent listens, allowing the child to express all of the fear and the anguish that were brought up through this encounter. Through being validated and heard, the belief that he or she is stupid has far less of a chance of gaining a foothold in the child's story.

The same is true for our deeply rooted beliefs. They too respond to this same kind of compassionate listening. And the most important person we need this response from is ourselves. A woman in one of my Awakening groups had an epiphany last week. She was able to express to the group her deep fear that nobody liked her. As with most stories in our heads, the exact opposite was true. She was a deeply appreciated and respected part of the group. In being this honest about her fear, allowing this belief frozen from childhood out into the light of day, it was much easier for her to see how young it was. She left group full of respect and compassion for herself.

A few days later, she had an experience of scheduling two different things at the same time. Rather than simply rescheduling, she began to fall into the old story again. "I never do anything right. They will hate me because I am so inept." In a flash, she awoke and was able to listen to this voice with great curiosity and compassion—not hating it, not fearing it, simply allowing it to speak without becoming identified with it. She not only met the unmeetable with her heart, but she moved another step beyond having this fear be in charge of her life. The freedom that she felt from those few moments of listening to herself was enormous.

To meet these different characters in our story—to include them, allowing them to express the beliefs that were frozen inside so many years ago—is an act of enormous healing. These parts of us have waited our whole lives for us to gain enough Awareness that we could finally meet them without identifying with them.

In the beginning phases of responding rather than reacting to the parts of our story, inclusion can be like magic, quickly dispelling the conversations in our head. But as we move further into Awakening, it becomes evident that there are characters in our story that won't be so easily dispelled. Irritation will often dissolve the moment it is seen, but the ancient rage we have all carried since childhood is an entirely different matter. We not only have deep reservoirs of rage, but also of terror and grief. It takes time to build the bridges that we burned through denial, self-judgment and fear. It is the work of a lifetime, but the pay off is enormous. Every time a pattern is met in the attentive heart, the energy that was formerly locked into it is freed up and becomes available for the rapture of being alive.

THE POWER OF QUESTIONS

"Live in the questions now. Perhaps you will then gradually, without noticing it, live along some distant day into the answer."

Rainier Maria Rilke

The key to a healing relationship with the formerly hated and feared parts of ourselves lies in asking questions. As in the analogy of healing a relationship with a friend, as we listen to this person, it is important to ask questions: What were you feeling when we parted ways? What was triggered inside of you when this happened? What were you trying to communicate? These questions give your friend a space into which she can speak her experiences. The same is true for every part of our inner story.

To ask questions of what is showing up in our lives puts us into direct relationship with it. We usually run and hide or try to change what we don't like. Neither one of these allows for direct contact where we can heal and be healed. These patterns not only need our undivided attention, they long to speak their truth to us.

To ask questions gives us moments when we are not caught in struggle. They also allow us to respond rather than react and it is in response that healing happens. It doesn't matter if this only lasts for a second. Just like throwing a small pebble into the middle of a huge lake, the ripples eventually make it all the way to the shore. One question sets things in motion, moving us farther down the path of Awakening.

The true power of questions doesn't work in a linear way—ask a question and get an answer. Answers will come in their own time and their own way. If we focus on the answer, we break the power of the question. *The power is in asking questions.* Looking for answers just flips us back into the controlling, analyzing, planning and comparing mind. Questions make space for the sea of Intelligence that is waiting for an opening.

We will explore questions more deeply later on in the book. Until then some of the most powerful questions you can work with are:

- *What is asking to be met?*
- *Who are you?*
- *What are you trying to communicate?*
- *What is it you need from me today?*
- *What is the treasure that you hold?*
- *How have you served me?*

♦ *How are you healing me?*

♦ *What shift in consciousness are you birthing me into?*

The flavor of these questions is compassionate curiosity, the combination of *what is* and *this too*. It is the art of approaching these mind-body states in an accepting and curious way. Again, ask, but don't look for an answer. Answers will come in their own time and their own way. To keep our questions open-ended is to understand that *challenges come with the solution woven into them*. The solution comes as we pay attention, listen and live in questions.

The time when I really learned the power of asking questions was when my Mother was dying. As I explained earlier, I had broken my leg. The first day I was up on crutches, I went to be with her. I had my daughter come and pack for me the night before and my son pack the car the next morning. Arriving in Victoria, I was exhausted. I had forgotten what a challenge it is to maneuver around on crutches, especially with a newly broken leg. The next morning, after a night of intense throbbing pain, I woke up into the fear that I didn't have the strength to be with my Mom. In my meditation, as I stabilized on the breath, Awareness said, "What is asking to be met?"

I dropped into my body and touched with attention the actual place that was holding my fear. It is a few inches above my navel and felt as if someone had pulled the energy plug and everything had drained out. This feeling was a predominant part of a debilitating illness a few years ago, and it could still terrify me. Rather than running away, I went to it. "I recognize you. What is it that you need from me today?" This question moved me into non-resistance. It also signaled to these feelings that I was willing to listen and learn rather than resist and deny.

Instead of spending energy fighting this feeling, I softened and opened, feeling a shift in my body, a closing of the energy drain. By not running away from what was happening, I was able to stay in contact with myself. Many times throughout the day I asked my body, "What is appropriate now?" Rather than getting caught into the whirlwind of "support person" for my Mother, I could pace myself, allowing my body to say when it was time to support and when it was time to rest. Before in my life I would override my weariness and continue with whatever I was doing because I believed I "should" perform up to a mythical standard of perfection. Now I was listening and staying in balance.

At the beginning it may not be easy to actually connect with what is presenting itself. We then simply ask the question, "What wants my attention?" or "What is asking to be met?" Know that if our mind is agitated and upset, underneath that chaos an old pattern is usually asking to be seen.

110

INCLUDING THE BODY

The body is solidified mind.

Stephen Levine.

The stories that we get lost in—that deeply need our attention and our compassion—move through us as thoughts, emotions and sensations in our bodies. It is oftentimes much easier at the beginning of our Awakening to bring curiosity and mercy to the parts of the stories when they show up as sensations in our body. Caroline Myss says it so well when she states, "Biology is biography." In other words, the entirety of our story is held in the very tissues of our body.

Absolutely every state of mind—terror, joy, longing, rage— manifests in our bodies in a particular way. Think of a sexual fantasy and notice what happens in your body. Think of a person you are having difficulty with. Notice how the energy in your body shifts. Now think of someone you love. It changes again.

Different emotions seem to effect different parts of the body. Rage is often stored somewhere around the solar plexus. It is in this region that the liver (I am livid), the gall bladder (that really galls me), and the spleen (I was just venting my spleen) reside. And grief often shows up in the thoracic region, with tightness in our throats and constriction in our chests (I have a heavy heart; I have a lump in my throat). Some people can even read the story of your personality by looking at all of the lines on your face or noticing your posture. How we walk, move, sit and stand all say volumes about the stories that we live in.

Using the body to pay attention to our story is also facilitated by the fact that it has held our confusion and pain all of these years, but it can only do this for so long. The parts of our story that keep us lost in delusion—whether it be our fear, judgment, sadness, grasping or resistance—affect the energy flow in our bodies. We can usually function with constricted energy flow until our 30's or 40's, and then the tissue surrounding the cramp will become affected.

A good example is the stomach. If we think of times when we were very afraid and had narrowed our world down to the isolating and self-absorbed world of fear, we'll recall that there was usually a knot in our stomach. We could be at a party, completely oblivious to how anxious we are, when all of a sudden our stomach begins to signal to us. In paying attention, we can then become aware of the fear pattern we are being run by, and in that Awareness we have the choice to do something about it.

The gift of this tissue breakdown is that it grabs our attention. We can no longer live unconsciously in our old patterns for they are calling to us directly from the living tissue of our bodies, revealing the struggles that we haven't yet seen and freed. As we pay attention to the area of discomfort, first recognizing it, then feeling it and finally dropping into it, it will reveal to us the story, the delusion in our mind that goes along with this energy constriction.

In my own life, whenever my stomach tightens, I am usually experiencing dread, one of my core patterns. Underneath this tightness is often a sense of shame that I am not doing my life right, combined with a sense of terror about what price I am going to pay for these "mis-takes" (it's usually some theme of "they won't like me.") As I am able to meet the fist in my stomach and then explore the underlying feeling of dread, I am able to see the old conversation in my head that is always there when my stomach tightens up. Now when it arrives, because I am familiar with it, I don't have to identify with it. In that compassionate curiosity, my Awareness is then freed to be *with* Life rather than with my old conversation *about* Life.

The two components of compassionate curiosity—*what is* and *this too*—intimately engage us with the story in our body that is asking to be healed. *What is* brings attention out of the restless, searching, wandering mind and focuses it in the present. If my mind is still lost in a fog, when I ask this question, I remind myself that it took billions of years to make this moment, and I say again, "What is?" It signals my mind to pay attention—to stop leaning forward into Life or leaning back away from it.

Another way I access this focused place is to ask, "Knowing that all the millions of moments of my life have led me to this moment, what is this one like?" At the beginning it may be hazy and even difficult to feel anything. That is why it is helpful to start globally with an overall sense—describing the room you are in and the general feeling of being in a body—and then finally coming into direct contact with what is asking to be met. It may be vague and formless at first, but slowly allow *what is* to reveal itself to you and *listen.* Go back again and again to the question "What is right now?"

As we discover what is there, the body will graphically teach us. The opposite of *this too* is *not this.* When we respond to a discomfort in our body from *not this,* it causes the muscles around the discomfort to contract, becoming a breeding ground for more pain. When we can physically soften with *this too,* we generate the opposite. It takes away the fuel for continuous tightening and also allows us to make space for the healing energies to flood in. This is also true with our emotions and our thoughts. Fighting and constricting around unpleasant ideas and feelings creates more pain, while cultivating the spaciousness of *this too* opens the doors to healing.

My sister called one night, caught in a web of fear. As our Mother lay dying in another city, core patterns that each of us took on in our childhood were rising to the surface of our Awareness in order to be seen, accepted and moved beyond. One of her patterns is free-floating anxiety. She is four years younger than I and thus experienced our Mother's journey into paranoia at a very young and vulnerable age. On the phone she was lost in the fear of this anxiety, becoming almost paralyzed in the process. She was in complete reaction with no ability to respond.

I asked her to pay attention to what was happening in her body. As she described the tightness in her chest and the pounding of her heart, she was able to name this nemesis that had tortured her for so long, the feelings of panic that were now moving throughout her body. With great trepidation she moved towards them, feeling this fear that had been such a predominant thread in her life. As she was able to be with it rather than fight it, she began to sob from the depths of her being. The last thing I said to her was, "You grew up in a sea of paranoia, and there was no one there to acknowledge and hold your fear. This anxiety has waited your whole life for you to see it without falling into it, for you to meet it with tenderness and mercy."

When she called the next day, she said that after the phone call she lay on the floor, brailling her way into the anxiety as it lived in her body. For moments she became bigger than the anxiety itself and was able to relate to it rather than being lost in it. The racing of her heart slowed down, and the constriction of panic let go. Into that spacious attention, the truth of her perfection and wholeness became clear to her. It so profoundly shifted her perspective that she was able to move through a chronically resistive place with her husband later that evening, a place they had been trying to get through for a long time.

As you learn how to listen to your body, seeing the story of the struggling mind that is manifested in your tissues, allow what wants to reveal itself to you to show up in its own way and its own time. Your job is to generate over and over again a sense of curiosity and mercy. Trust where you are. Whatever is grabbing your attention, begin to explore and describe it to yourself. You can take this as deep as you like. You may describe it with only one word, "ahh, pain," or you can go onto examining it in minute detail—tight, full, warm, throbbing, pushing, pulsing, shooting.

Describing it is an important step, for it not only puts you into direct contact with *what is*, but also every time you name it, you are relating to it rather than being lost in the middle of it. Whatever you discover, say, "This too. For this moment I allow you to be a part of my experience." The ability to be present in a compassionate and curious way moves you beyond the story.

THE HEALING OF THE HEART

This being human is a guest house, every morning a new arrival...a joy, a depression, a meanness, some momentary awareness comes as an unexpected visitor.

Welcome and entertain them all, even if they're a crowd of sorrows who violently sweep your house empty of its furniture. Still, treat each guest honorably. He may be clearing you out for some new delight.

The dark thought, the shame, the malice, meet them at the door laughing and invite them in. Be grateful for whoever comes because each has been sent as a guide from beyond.

Rumi

We have grounded, and we have opened. We have cultivated paying attention and awakened to the art of inclusion, coupled with the power of asking questions. All of these steps are moving us into the place of allowing these formerly feared and hated parts of ourselves back into our hearts. That is where the healing lies. The heart is the place that is bigger than the opposites of the struggling mind.

My journey into Awakening has been a journey into tenderness and mercy. At one of the ten day retreats I go to every year, I made a list of all of the parts of myself that I had formerly hated and feared that were now woven back into my heart. I cried tears of gratitude and mercy for how deeply I had been locked out of my own heart and how this very prison of the judging mind had pushed and pulled me along the path of Awakening.

When we discover the power of allowing the disowned parts of ourselves back into our hearts, we may at first meet them in the hope that they will go away. They will become more manageable with every meeting, but they won't go away. The good news is that they will be transformed into our allies when they are finally embraced as welcomed guests.

It is the most unwelcome parts of ourselves that hold the power of Awakening into the healed heart. I discovered this at a retreat titled African Drumming, Dancing, Ritual and Art. "Aha," said my mind, "that sounds like a weekend of rhythm, music, opening and fun." Well...it was unlike any retreat I'd ever been to. Instead of being fun, it was an unbelievably painful but ultimately freeing experience that finally allowed me to embrace a core part of me that I had always run from before.

On the first evening, I began to get an inkling of what I was in for. There was no schedule, no idea when meals would be. A transformer had blown just before we arrived, so there was no hot water, heat or lights in the cabins and very little warmth in the big, drafty hall. A number of people left in the course of the retreat, and at times I wanted to, but I stayed, for I knew that discomfort always brings up the next layer of what is ready to be seen.

The second night, we began a ritual with very little preparation and with no guidance about how it was going to unfold or how long it would take. At 3:00 in the morning, after having gone through many phases—some scary, some boring and some enlightening—the leaders sat us in a circle of stones on the wooden floor with the admonishment that if anyone left, the ritual would be compromised for everyone. (Two people had tried to leave a few hours before, and we were thoroughly educated on how they could have opened up the circle to dark forces). The leaders then left without any indication of when they would return.

Up to this point, I had checked in with myself over and over again and had gotten the sense that it was important to stay with the retreat. But now, in the middle of the night, exhausted and cold, sitting on a hard, cold floor with no end in sight, I wanted to leave. Panic began to build in my body and mind as I was pushed to my limit and my body felt like it was going to explode.

Awareness was obscured by a mixture of terror, despair and self-hatred. "I can't handle this. When is it going to be over? I should have left. You are so inept and besides, you're such a wimp," my old voices screamed at me. Then Awareness kicked in. I asked *What is?* and my attention came out of reaction and back into the living experience. *What is* brought me back into the living moment. I recognized that of all of the possible human experiences, I was sitting on a cold, hard floor with 50 other people. Moving out of reaction, I remembered that my life is a journey of Awakening where everything is *grist for the mill* of becoming conscious. I then asked, "What is asking to be met?"

I began to see with deep curiosity and a heartfelt compassion the feelings that were ricocheting through my body. As I made contact with the feelings flowing through me, from the depths of my being came flooding memories of other times in my life, mainly in childhood, when I had the same experience of feeling caught in an overwhelming situation *with no way out* and no end in sight. But this time, for the first time in my life, someone was there meeting me in this indescribably painful place. And that someone was me.

I began to talk to this core feeling of *no way out*. It was too enveloped in fear to respond to questions. But I could say, "*This too.* I include you as a part of this experience." As my heart opened, I could say to the terror, "I see you. I want to get to know you. You were a core part of my childhood, and I'm not going to abandon you or get lost in you. I'm here for you."

Rather than becoming caught in reaction, my heart cradled these feelings with a deep sense of tenderness and mercy. This softening and opening of inclusion warmed my body. When sensations of cold or panic began to seep back in, I found myself repeatedly returning to the warm glow of compassionate curiosity. As the room became colder, my heart became warmer. What had been an indescribably painful situation was transformed into one of the major healing experiences of my life. I knew as I packed to leave later that morning that I had been deeply opened and now trusted myself to the core. I saw that even when I am pushed to the maximum, I was now capable of being there for myself when I most needed myself.

My ability to be that present for myself on that cold floor in the wee hours of the morning came from the accumulation of many moments, both in meditation and in my daily life, where I met many of the core parts of my story rather than putting them out of my Awareness and thus out of my heart.

Because this was the first time I had ever met the experience of *no way out*, I now needed to begin meeting this core feeling when it showed up in my everyday life. At first, I could only be present for a moment before I would flip out into reaction again. But having learned from many skillful teachers that going towards a state that controls you is the way of freedom, I returned again and again to my approach.

Over time I was able to sit with this fear both in meditation and during my daily life. I would watch what would bring it to the surface, what words it would use, and how it would manifest in my body. At the beginning I would notice after the fact that fear had been present. But gradually I began to enter it, going through layer after layer so that when it was present, attention rather than fear would be triggered. "Ahh fear," Awareness would say.

In order to bring the amazing power of inclusion into your life, be willing to spend the next 24 hours working with *this too*. Whatever comes up—whether it is indigestion, a cranky child, a sleepy body, an agitated mind—be willing to recognize it and then say, "*This too*; I can include this too as a part of my life." If there is something that the mind refuses to stop struggling with—a bad cold, a major meeting at work, a difficult relationship—ask it, "Can I let this be as it is for just this moment?" Another helpful response is "It's okay." As the mind begins to let go of trying to turn this into an emergency, you can go back to cultivating the inclusion of *this too*.

As we begin to stabilize our minds by strengthening our ability to pay attention and opening into compassionate listening, we discover that whenever we really see with an inclusive heart, it is a profoundly healing moment. This is not the *quick fix* we've been taught to believe is healing—just give me a pill, a positive thought or a dose of denial, and everything will be okay. It takes time to learn to truly meet what has been formerly cut out of our hearts. But this is the pathway to freedom. Every time we go towards something rather than away, we have another opportunity to lessen our identification with these contracted states, freeing the energy that is locked in them so that we can be more available for the living adventure that is Life.

FIRST-AID KIT

When the demons become unmasked, you may feel you are going mad or doing something wrong, but in fact you have finally begun to face the forces that keep you from living in a loving and fully conscious way.

Jack Kornfield

Creating a relationship with our disowned parts is an art. There are times when our attention is not yet as strong as the pattern that is asking to be met and we find ourselves *falling into* the feeling, experience or sensation rather than *relating to* it. At such times, when compassion and curiosity feel light years away, it is beneficial to have an first aid kit. This kit is filled with skills that allow us to bring a sense of spaciousness around these challenging places in order to gain perspective. Then, from a more spacious place, we can become curious again and, when we are ready, touch whatever we are experiencing with our heart.

There are a number of things that can be done when the clouds of unconscious reaction have enveloped us and there doesn't seem to be any way to awaken in the midst of them.

1. Asking for Help

One of the most important "First Aid Tools" is to ask for help. Remember, there is an Intelligence that permeates and penetrates absolutely everything. When we are caught and struggling, unable to see what is there and unable to access any space outside of the struggle, asking for help opens the door just wide enough so that the Intelligence that is always with us can get a word in edgewise. In fact, it could be said that all of the challenges of our lives are here specifically to bring us to this place where the only choice we have is to let go and ask for help.

The contemplative priest and author Thomas Merton said that true prayer begins when prayer doesn't work. For a good portion of our journey, we have used prayer to stay in control, asking for what we want and trying to get rid of what we don't. There is a point in the journey when we realize this only keeps us separate from the Living Presence—the Sacred Intelligence of Life. When asking for help, we don't have to feel we are in contact with this Intelligence, we don't have to see any great transformation after we ask, nor do we have to hear an answer. Just asking is enough. *Help will come in its own time and in its own way.*

What works for me is to simply say, "Show me the way through this." It is also sometimes helpful to have a physical symbol that reminds us there is something bigger than ourselves that is in charge. I often light a candle and keep it burning all day long in my kitchen, a place where it is unusual to find a flame. Numerous times throughout the day, when I come around the corner and see the burning candle, I remember that I am not alone. When I am away from home, I will carry special rocks in my pockets or wear sacred gifts around my neck.

2. Shifting Attention

When we are visited by a heavy state, and it feels unmeetable, the most basic thing we can do is shift our attention. If you have ever been a parent, you have probably relied upon this simple but powerful tool when your children are getting out of control—you place their attention elsewhere. It is wondrously amazing to watch a two year-old winding up to a full-blown temper tantrum, and when you invite them to watch a lady bug on the window, they immediately shift from anger to fascination!

A woman from one of the groups calls this *engaging with Life*. I find cleaning house can help take the focus off the struggle. A movie or a good book works too. Know that the deep inner work continues even though we are focused elsewhere, for when the struggling mind isn't busy trying to get a word in edgewise, integration can happen in a much more effortless way.

3. Lightening Up

It is good to remember not to take ourselves so seriously. The mind loves to turn the littlest thing into an emergency and the slightest mistake into a major screw up. "You grow up the day you have your first real laugh at yourself," said Ethyl Barrymore. When a group of people over the age of 100 were interviewed, a common thread in each of their lives was an ability to laugh at and with the ups and downs of their lives.

I love that moment in my consciousness when my mind is gearing up for a big "drama trauma" melt down and Awareness kicks in with "ahh, struggle" and then laughs. I also ask, "Is this really going to matter tomorrow or next year?" And usually the answer is, "No." Of course, there are things in our lives we need to take seriously, but most of the emergencies we face are mind-created horror stories, and a little lightening goes a long way toward breaking this addiction to struggle.

A friend of mine shared with me the phrase she uses which combines the sense of how challenging Life can be with the knowing that it is here for us, no matter what is happening. Loudly and with great vigor she says to the process, "Fuck you very much!" My heart immediately explodes in mirth and joy when I hear this. It includes both the resistance of the personality and the openness of the soul that knows it is all an adventure. So, lighten up. Tell good jokes to yourself while you're in the car. Look for the humor. It is all a matter of perspective.

4. Movement

There are many states that are asking to be met that won't let us shift our attention or lighten up. We can then use movement to cultivate the opposite of this particular state of mind. If I am caught and struggling, I love to move in a way that is the exact opposite of what I am feeling. If I'm lost in self-judgment, sometimes I'll cradle my heart. If I'm caught in a disempowered mode, I'll put my hands together in front of me and forcefully chop down to the ground as I yell, "Ha!" If I'm feeling foggy and unresponsive, I take a power walk with head held high, arms swinging and long, strong strides. Putting on music and allowing whatever is coming up to be expressed is also very freeing. You can dance it out, letting your body reveal both the strengths and the weaknesses of this pattern.

It can also be helpful to go outside in order to get energy flowing again. To feel the sensation of rain on our face, the warmth of the sun, or the wind caressing our hair helps immensely. Nature can remind us that we are the Earth awakening and are a part of a greater process. Also, beauty is literally food for the soul. Something happens to every cell of our being when we immerse ourselves in the beauty of nature. I also love going to a place where I can see for a distance. (In a pinch I'll even use my roof!) It is very healing to the nervous system when our sight can extend beyond what is right before us.

At times, when a particular state of mind has been around for a while and I find myself unable to stay attentive, I will ask myself what is the opposite of this mind/body state. I will then *act as if* I am experiencing it. Let's say it's fear that is present. I will then cultivate strength and courage in my walk, in my words and in my actions. This is not to rise above the feeling in order to get rid of it, which results in staying caught in the pendulum of reaction. This is using the energy of the opposite of what is asking to be met in order to cultivate the stability and the clarity necessary to be present with it.

Another way to work with difficult states of mind is to enhance the contraction. There is something magical in allowing a particular pattern to express itself to its fullest. In that very act of nonresistance and welcoming, it becomes much easier to break our identification with it and to turn a difficult experience into an opportunity for awakening. If I'm irritated, I'll feed the smoldering fire inside of me by allowing myself to get very angry. I'll stomp around and yell and sometimes even pound the bed. If I'm sad, I'll rent a sad movie or read sad poetry. Stephen Levine teaches a technique in which you press your fingers deeply into your breastbone between your nipples. This is the grief point. As you press, you begin to wail and moan. At first it can feel artificial, but this technique has the ability to bring up the storehouse of grief that is resting under our sadness.

5. Impermanence

It can also be deeply freeing to cultivate the recognition of impermanence. Nothing stays around for very long—absolutely nothing—not planets or people, countries or civilizations, joy or depression, pain or bliss—not even the difficult state of mind that is saying it will last forever. When heavy states move through our body/mind, they are usually accompanied by the belief that they are the totality of us and that they will be there forever. And yet, if you think about it, no state of mind has ever stayed "forever," not even the pleasant ones. Just like the weather, they all arise and pass away. Through cultivating the truth of impermanence, it becomes easier to allow these states to flow through us rather than to identify with them and get lost in their content.

6. The Power of No

One of the most powerful tools in the first aid kit is the ability to just say *No*. There are two levels of a skillful *No*. The first happens when we can't get any space around our story. During those moments when a heavy state feels like it is pressing in from all sides, we can say, "No. I'm not ready to deal with you." This is not denial. It is the ability to put the experience on hold, for sometimes we do not have the strength, the time or the ability to deal with what is arising right then. It is important to watch the intention of our *No*. If it is done from an angry or fearful place, it can actually feed that state of mind or body. But if it is done with a caring firmness that realizes it is important to meet what is asking to be met, but that this is not the appropriate time, it will give us much needed space rather than throwing us deeper into contraction.

The other level of *No* comes when we have seen enough of our story that when it captures our attention, we can firmly but with great heart say, "No. I don't need to identify with that." This is the place of empowerment in which we recognize that we fully have the choice about what we are going to pay attention to.

7. Honor Resistance

At times it may be impossible to do anything. This is when the state of mind we're caught in rebels at even the thought of doing anything at all and cannot remember that there is something beyond our story that is supporting us every step of the way. With the depth of the heavy states that I've known, numerous times in my Awakening process I've had moments when I became paralyzed and any attempt to make a shift was met with resistance. Luckily, my mentor was able to show me the power of not resisting resistance. In fact, she taught me how essential it is to honor it. Resistance is the guardian at the threshold of our growth. It says that to open any more is to enter the territory where we do not yet have the skills to traverse. Both resistance and fear can keep us safe.

8. Patience and Support

There will be times where absolutely nothing can penetrate the contraction of our story. No matter how far along in the journey of Awakening we are, it is possible to know this place where it seems that no light can penetrate. But when we are on the path of Awakening, states that used to last for days or months and sometimes even years move through much more quickly and bring in their wake great gifts that help us move out of our story and back into Life. In those years when Awareness could not yet connect with the core parts of my story I was helped by a quote from Rainier Maria Rilke:

> I want to beg you as much as I can to be patient toward all that's unsolved in your heart and try to love the questions themselves—like locked rooms and like books that are written in a very foreign tongue. Do not seek the answers, which cannot be given you because you would not be able to live them and the point is to live everything. Live the questions now. Perhaps you will then gradually, without noticing it, live along some distant day into the answer.

So be patient. The process of Awakening is an organic one. It has soft summer days and raging winter storms. But the constantly changing kaleidoscope of our experience unfolds in an orchestrated manner, as rhythmic as the changing of the tides and finely tuned as the dance of the seasons.

9. The Phases of Awakening

The final tool in our first aid kit is the awareness that Awakening is a living process. Just like a plant, it sets down roots and then grows the support system of stem, branches and leaves. Only then does it have the capacity to blossom.

We could say that Awakening happens in three phases. The first is the one of being asleep—the normal consciousness of most people. It is the phase of holding onto and resisting Life, caught in the endless cycle of struggle.

The second phase is when we realize that something else is happening here beyond our narrow everyday focus. It is the spacious truth of our being that is present in every single moment of our lives. We are beginning to understand that in seeing our struggles rather than always trying to fix them, we discover something beyond our ordinary mind. Our daily lives become a dance of reconnecting with Life and of getting to know the story that takes us away. We still spend most of our time in the maze, but the moments when we can see the story of struggle and then connect with the spaciousness of being that resides beyond it become more and more frequent.

This brings us to the third phase when, having seen enough of our story, we become awake and consciously aware of being a part of something greater. The center of our being resides in Awareness. We find ourselves in the maze at different times in our lives, but we easily come back to present time, available for Life the moment it appears out of Mystery.

At moments in this process, it can feel like our fears, desires and confusions are stronger than before. This happens because whatever we pay attention to becomes more alive. But paying attention to something we have previously denied or ignored does not make it bigger. Rather it is more like a flashlight flooding a basement that has been in the dark for years. When we turn on the light, it is easier to see the cobwebs and the junk so that now they can be cleaned up.

It is very helpful during the second and third phases of Awakening to have a person or a group to share with that understands the Awakening process. The pull of the story is so strong that we need to be continually reminded that who we are is something bigger than our story. Also, in having a place where we can share whatever is happening without it needing to be fixed or changed, the grip our story has on our attention can soften. It is reassuring to hear where other people are and discover that everybody else has the same struggles in their minds. This can help us to see that the darkness that we carry is not unique or horrible. Instead, we realize we are meeting the delusions that everyone has, meeting them for the healing of all beings.

This first aid kit is essential in the process of Awakening. As soon as we move into another level of Awareness, the next layer of what has not yet been included in our compassionate Awareness will surface to be seen. And even though the action of inclusion and curiosity becomes easier to access over time, our initial response will still usually be resistance. For many of the divorced parts of ourselves, we will need to take a few steps forward, only to retreat, drawing upon one or more of these tools that can help bring forth equilibrium again. Slowly and surely, we will gather enough curiosity and compassion to meet these states without falling into them.

KINDNESS–A FIRST AID KIT UNTO ITSELF

It's a bit embarrassing to have been concerned with the human problem all one's life and find at the end that one has no more to offer by way of advice than 'Try to be a little kinder.'

Aldous Huxley

Kindness is a powerful tool for maneuvering around our story. While we are caught in the deepest parts of the maze, it can be practically impossible to cultivate kindness for ourselves. When we find ourselves this contracted, we can take the focus off of ourselves and place it on another. To be kind to another human being is not only a wonderful thing to give to the world; it also is healing for us. It opens the doors of our own heart, allowing us to be present for ourselves again in a spacious and merciful way.

In order to live a life of kindness, we need to understand that we are all in this together. We are accustomed to seeing everything outside of us as *other*— separate and disconnected from us. We see things and people as objects in our mind, objects that can either enhance or detract from the experience of our own lives. Something very radical happened when Einstein and then Hubbell discovered the expanding Universe. It began to seep into our collective Awareness that absolutely everything came from the same place and that the whole dance of the Universe is an interconnected web of unfolding. There is no *other*.

One of the most skillful ways to cut through the illusion of separation and struggle we live in most of the time is to act in our lives as if everything were a part of ourselves—for it truly is. There is so much more that we have in common than we have in differences. Your skin color, your religious beliefs and sexual preference, and possibly even your whole view of Life may be different than mine, but we come out of the same ground of Being and share the same air, water and planet. At the root of our existence we also carry the same fears and desires, the same confusions and hopes, whether we live in a tribal village in Africa or a high rise in Manhattan.

Think of a newborn child. Include Hitler, Bin Laden, Florence Nightingale and Abraham Lincoln in this vision. We are all born in innocence, with the urge to love and be loved at the core of our being. As the cauldron of daily life molds and shapes us, differences become more apparent, but still nestled in the heart of every being is the desire to be happy.

The heart truly begins to respond when it realizes that pain and sorrow exist in absolutely everyone's life. There is a story about a woman who lost her young son, her only child. When she approached the Buddha, overcome with grief, she said, "Master, please bring my boy back to life." The Buddha replied, "I will, but first you must go into the village and get me a handful of mustard seed from a home where no one has lost a loved one to death." She went from house to house, searching for the seed. But when she asked if anyone in the home had died, the answer was always "yes." Finally, she realized that what had happened to her happens to everyone—that all who are born will also die and that all people experience loss.

She then brought the body of her dead son back to the Buddha where he was buried with ritual and she asked the Buddha for teachings that would bring her wisdom and refuge in this realm of birth and death. The heart truly opens when it realizes that it is not only death that happens to each of us, but also upset, loss, heartache, craving, grief, judgment, confusion and despair, and that each of us is doing the best we know how. Understanding this, we can respond to all that we see with kindness.

There are many wonderful books out now about the art of kindness. In fact, the whole concept has taken this country by storm. A newspaper article once called it "guerrilla goodness." To consciously commit to being kind, both in known and unknown ways, can literally transform the world.

One story tells of a young woman who was at the end of her rope. She had broken up from a long and very painful relationship and had moved to a new city—without friends, without vision and without hope. Every day she would come home from work and just stare at the walls, sometimes crying, but mostly just sitting and wondering if she would ever know joy again. One

124

night upon returning from work, much to her amazement, the red light of her answering machine was flashing. When she played the tape, it was a wonderful male voice apologizing for calling the wrong number. He said that her voice on the message had sounded so sad, and he just wanted to tell her that it was okay to be sad, that to be able to feel that sadness was important. His message went on for almost twenty minutes, talking about going through pain instead of running away from it and how even though it probably seemed impossible now, things would get better. She never learned who this person was, but she said that this message was a healing catalyst in her life.

The most powerful gift of kindness you can give is the presence of caring. Generating this feeling as we hand our money to the clerk or listen to another's problems with compassion is one of the most transformative powers in Life. True healing comes not from doing anything. It comes from *being with*, whether it is a health condition in our body, an upset friend or a voice on the other end of the phone.

We cannot even begin to imagine the ripple effects of small acts of compassion, support and kindness. In some very deep way, these acts are the physical representation of the Awareness that we're all in this together with common needs and fears and that each of us is doing the best we know how.

One of the most delicious things about kindness, and why it is a first aid kit unto itself, is that we cannot give it away without it deeply affecting us. To leave smiles and kind words in our wake is to fill our own being with the same joy. The poet William Wordsworth gave us the gift of saying, "We are made kind by being kind. That is the best portion of a good man's life—his little nameless, unremembered acts of kindness and of Love." Acts of being present for others in a spacious and inclusive way automatically move us out of our contracting, struggling mind back into connection with Life.

ENTERING THE ADVENTURE

Follow, follow, follow, follow,

follow the yellow brick road.

From the film "The Wizard of Oz"

As we begin to show up for the unfolding of our lives, using *what is* and *this too* to remind us to be present for what is happening causes trust of the process to arise. Everywhere we look we see Intelligence, whether it is in the DNA nestled at the heart of every single cell in the world or in the exquisite timing of the seasons. This Intelligence exists in the dance of our daily lives, as well, and yet we usually don't see it. There is an ordered unfolding in this dance—whether it is the chaos happening between countries or the confusion in our minds. We don't see it because we haven't been taught how to pay attention. It is as if the instruction booklet for the living of each of our lives is in front of us every moment, and we're not reading it.

Paying attention reminds us over and over again that we are a part of an interconnected process and that unseen forces are with us every moment of our lives. The pieces of our puzzle are being spoken to us through symbols and dreams, bits of conversations overheard on the bus and lines from spy novels. But when we are caught in struggle, it is hard to see this, let alone to trust it. Cultivating compassionate curiosity allows us to step back from the multi-piece mosaic and see that it all fits together to make one picture. In that seeing, it becomes easier to belong to the unfolding that is our lives.

A woman I know was boating up a river to a weekend retreat, deep in the heart of small, somewhat primitive country. The boat in front of her was filled with people from a church in the Midwest who were sponsoring this retreat. Part way into the journey, her boat broke down, and they watched the lead boat disappear around the bend. Left stranded and alone, they made their way to the dock of an old hut on the shore and waited for help. Eventually the other boat did return, and in checking out the problem, the leader said he would drop off his people at their lunch place and be back in fifteen minutes.

Watching the boat disappear again around the bend, fingerlings of fear began to nibble at the edges of her story. Here she was, stranded on a river in the backwater of a foreign country. She shook off the fear with the response, "I can handle this." A half-hour went by and then an hour. An hour and a half and finally two and nobody came. As time slid by her story got stronger, moving from frustration into anger. "I wouldn't have left people in this way. Why didn't anybody in the first boat say they wouldn't go on until we were with them again? How could they continue, knowing we are stranded?" Fear finally got a foothold in her mind.

Eventually, a small boat arrived with a man who spoke very little English and who was evidently supposed to fix the problem. Discovering that it was beyond his capability and with darkness beginning to arrive, he rounded up another boat, loaded the people in and off they went in search of the other group. Upon arriving at the retreat center, nobody, including the retreat leaders, said anything about what the people in the second boat might have been experiencing. It was as if it didn't happen. Without any support to be conscious, she got lost in the struggling mind's arsenal of weapons:

126

Rage—"Why isn't anyone acknowledging what happened?"

Helplessness—"I don't know what to do."

Self judgment—"Everybody else seems to be fine. Why am I making such a big deal out of nothing?"

In her childhood, an uncle who had molested his daughter had sexually molested her too. He was an important part of his church and was respected by his community. When she shared the violation with her mother, she was discounted and told to keep it to herself. The feelings of being violated, betrayed, abandoned and unheard became frozen parts of her story, and she lived them out unconsciously for most of her adult life. Then came this dramatic experience in a primitive place (the abuse was also very primitive), that was perfectly orchestrated by Life to trigger these core parts of her story.

She was not able to stay conscious of this on the trip. The feelings were still too strong for her Awareness. But after the trip, when she came to the Awakening group I lead, all of us, including this woman, realized the perfection of what had happened. It took an abandonment way out in the wilds of a primitive country for her to bring up and meet all of the feelings that were locked away in her story by the double betrayal in her childhood.

Everything that happened to her on the river, including the different parts that everybody played, was a necessary experience in the theater of her Awakening. Everything was there to trigger the common illusions of struggle and separation that had so completely overtaken her life. Being able to see this experience as an invitation to awaken out of her story rather than just a traumatic event that happened on vacation brought all of us in that room into greater curiosity about our own lives and a deeper trust of the process.

She had also said that the predominant feeling she experienced while searching for the other part of her group was a deep sadness. Upon digesting all that we had talked about together, when we met again the next week she was able to make space for this grief. She shared with us that in being given permission to meet all of the feelings that came up as a result of this experience, she could see that they all converged together into one sentence, "I don't matter." Nestled underneath this was an ocean of sadness.

It became evident to her that most of her life experiences were touched by the belief that she didn't matter. Before this shift, the grief was so embedded in the core of her story that it had been impossible to see. Making space for this feeling to be there, she was able to see it and say, "*This too.* I can include this too as a part of myself." In that connection, she then said to this feeling, "You matter to *me.*" She gave herself the attention that was denied all those years ago. In compassionately meeting this feeling, she took a huge step away from it running her life underneath her everyday consciousness.

The Presence of Life that permeates and penetrates absolutely everything wants us to awaken. In fact, it yearns for this even more than we do. And it uses absolutely every moment of our lives (even a boat breaking down in a far off country) to move us farther along in the journey to connection and communion. Life is *for* us. Another way you can say this is that your life is your path. There is no accident who is your boss, what happens on your vacation and what type of body you have. And there is no accident what this all triggers inside of you.

To open to our lives allows us to get glimpses of the astoundingly creative adventure that each of us is on and to learn the art of trusting the process. It is only from a spacious perspective that we can begin to perceive the awesome Intelligence that weaves the seemingly happenstance experiences of our lives. It will use all kinds of occurrences and situations in order to lead us to the bloom of Awakening. Our job is not to try to understand it all. It is to notice what is happening so that we can bring *whatever is* back into our hearts. As we notice with compassionate curiosity, understanding wells up within us as automatically as salmon swim upstream. We then know the joy of belonging to Life and belonging to our own lives.

To become available to the living moment of Life is a journey. We are destined to take on a struggling mind, get lost in it and then awaken through it. In the next four chapters, we will explore some of the core structures of the separate mind that keep us lost in its web—fear, self judgment, resistance to pain and addiction to control—and we will see how we can move through them.

May we become deeply curious about whatever is happening in our lives.

May this practice awaken deep compassion for all of the parts of ourselves.

And in this inclusion, may we again re-enter the living adventure that is our lives.

Core Intention: This too

Chapter 6
Meeting Our Fear

DESCENDING INTO SILENCE

Descending into silence

    is a very noisy affair.

        The mind chatters like a squirrel,

            intent on just one nugget of wisdom,

When what it truly craves is…..

    Knowing…

        Opening…

            Belonging…

                Connecting…

                    to the Universe.

—Barbara Weiland

THE WAY HOME

For it is the dawn that has come as it has come for a thousand centuries, never failing.
But when that dawn will come—of our emancipation from the fear of bondage and the bondage of fear—why that is a secret

Alan Paton

Everything we have explored so far is an invitation back into Life—into the moment in which Love lives. Lift your eyes from the book and look. *This is your life!* All of the creativity that has happened since the beginning of the Universe has made this moment possible. Every single experience of your life, both the easy and the difficult, have led you to this one where, for just a brief second, you are connecting with your life. This moment is part of a grand adventure that is using absolutely everything in order to bring you to Awakening. On one level it looks as if you are working and shopping, eating and sleeping, struggling and playing. But the truth is that only one thing is happening, and it is that Life, inside each one of us, is waking up to itself.

In our yearning to connect, we're beginning to understand that the way home is not to try to get to any particular place. It comes in cultivating a relationship with what takes us away. It comes in our willingness to see, with great mercy, the story we've lived in our whole lives. It is a story that fills up our heads, clouding over the truth of who we really are.

The main beliefs of this story that we will be exploring in this book are: our fear of fear, our judgments of ourselves and others, our resistance to pain, and our belief that controlling Life will bring us the peace that we long for. We will first explore our fear.

COMING TO KNOW FEAR

Most people guard against going into the fire,
And so end up in it.

Rumi

Fear is one of the core building blocks of the mind that believes it is separate from Life. We all have fear. Even when our lives are going well, it is still there, concealed in the core of our inner story, ready to flare up at a moment's notice. We fear the unpredictable changes of Life; we fear our so-called inadequacy; we fear the dark side within us; and we fear our constant companion, death. Fear not only causes us to lean away from Life, resisting what we don't like, but it also causes us to lean forward, trying to grab a hold of something that will quell our fear. Unable to stand in the present, we miss our lives. We are like the little boy who had to live in a plastic bubble because he had no immune system. We wander around in a bubble of fear, one that keeps us as separate from Life.

When we come across the depth of fear we carry we try to contain it. But it is only by cultivating a relationship with fear that we can use it to invite us into Life rather having it leave us struggling and disconnected.

Fear is a powerful and mysterious force. It permeates all of physical life. Think of the sea anemone, rapidly closing itself if it perceives that danger is near. Even bacteria viewed under a microscope, when touched by a probe, scurry away in a flurry of reaction. Survival fear compelled the various forms of life to discover creative ways to adapt to the forces that threatened their existence. The chameleon figured out how to change color so that its predators wouldn't see it. The gazelle learned to run very, very fast. Plants created toxins that were poisonous to those who wanted to eat them into extinction. And lions, tigers and bears had their strength.

When humanity showed up on the scene, fear was an important part of our survival. The world was an awesome and powerful place to be. One day there would be food aplenty and the next day none. There could be cold deep enough to freeze us to death, powerful animals that could tear us limb from limb, forces of nature that could destroy our world in a moment, and disease that seemed to come from the anger of the gods.

Instead of strength, camouflage or speed, we had a survival tool that other species did not have—our minds. With this tool, we set out to control our environment. In order to overcome the fear of extinction, we tamed fire so that food and warmth were more plentiful. We learned to stalk and kill game that was far more powerful than we were, and we studied plants, learning both their healing and their destructive properties. Our skills at propagating food are so developed that nobody on our planet needs to starve. And our ability to respond to medical trauma is so astounding that even a heart attack is not necessarily a deathblow. We have come a long way from the caves where we were constantly threatened by our environment.

We may have lessened the threats to our survival, but controlling our environment didn't make fear go away. In fact, in some ways, it made it worse. For as we learned to control, we moved away from intimate contact with Life. That left us on the outside, looking in. We felt the terror of being separate, doomed to experience loss and death. In order to cope with this, we directed our energy to denying, ignoring, resisting and controlling fear.

With all of our energy directed toward managing our outer environment, fear has had free reign in our inner world. Most of us most of the time live in some level of fear. We fear that Life won't give us what we want. We fear that it will give us what we don't want. We fear that we are not enough and we fear that we are too much. We fear our power and we fear that we're not powerful enough. In other words, we fear living and we fear dying.

We believe that if we just gather more things, make more money, and have enough *good* experiences, then fear will leave us. And for moments it does, but it always comes back. We finally accumulate enough money, only to find ourselves afraid it will vanish. We starve ourselves to a size 6 and then are afraid of gaining a pound. *We are afraid of fear* and because of that, fear runs us. You can see it in our relationship to Life (it is too much or not enough), in politics (*they* are the enemy), in our religions (if you don't do it "right" you will go to hell), and, of course, in our race relations (I hate/fear that you and yours look different from me and mine.)

Fear is hyper-vigilant, dividing Life into polarities and deciding which is safe and which is unsafe. From the framework of fear, survival means divide and conquer. It was a necessary phase in the Awakening of humanity, but we can now see clearly the price we pay for living in fear. It keeps us caught in the separate, struggling mind, cut off from belonging to Life and thus cut off from connecting with the living adventure of our own lives.

MEETING FEAR

If you bring forth what is within you,
what you bring forth will save you.
If you do not bring forth what is within you,
what you do not bring forth will destroy you.

The Gospel According to Thomas

There is a new level of consciousness calling to us, a level that uses fear for the powerful tool it is rather than having it run our lives. It speaks of inclusion rather than exclusion, of trust rather than fear and of responding to Life rather than trying to manage it. Twenty-five hundred years ago, the Buddha opened into this level of consciousness. He saw through the fears that had been running humankind for so long. In the Four Noble Truths, he spoke of the suffering inherent in living from the struggling (desire and aversion driven) mind. And he said that there was a way out of this maze of struggle.

Two thousand years ago, Jesus also saw beyond the body of fear we have taken on. He reminded us that we are to live from Love—love of God and love for one another. He knew the truth that we are birthed by Love, we are breathed by Love, and we are being healed by Love, and he said this truth would set us free.

For the past 2500 years, we have been digesting what these and other aware beings have offered to us, and we now find ourselves living in a time of great transformation. We stand on the threshold of realizing that we are bigger than the body of fear we took on so long ago. Realizing this, then fear becomes a doorway, leading beyond our illusion of isolation and separation into our inherent wholeness. What we are awakening into is not about getting rid of fear, because we've learned that whatever we resist becomes stronger. It is about getting to know fear so that we relate to it with equanimity and wisdom rather than trying to control it—either running from it or being run by it.

Becoming bigger than fear takes us beyond the illusion of isolation and separation. In mythic terms, fear is the guardian at the doorway. It guards the sense of belonging to and trusting Life that is our birthright, and we are required to embark on a heroic inner journey to claim this treasure. To meet the fear that separates us from Life is a Herculean task, one that will call us to access our most passionate commitment, our deepest intelligence and our highest creativity. To meet our fear is to be initiated into who we truly are.

In the marrow of our bones, every single one of us knows that this is true. All the stories in which the hero meets the serpents in the deep, challenges wicked witches and stands against invading dark forces are speaking about the parts of ourselves that have to be met and healed. The witches, goblins and ser-pents lie in the very depth of our inner world, standing guard over the sword of our attention that will enable us to claim our true power.

People who have traveled the depth and the breadth of the inner journey, meeting their fears in the process, capture our attention and admiration. We were so enamored by Buddha, Jesus and Muhammad that we created religions around them. Great painters who depict the signposts along the inner way become timeless in our imagination. Poets who speak to our heart are still in print after hundreds and even thousands of years.

And yet most of us have not yet committed to this inner journey. We are so terrified of what lies inside that we have seduced ourselves into thinking that this is something only certain special people can do. However, if we listen carefully to those who have made this journey, we will hear, woven through everything they said, an invitation to go within and the assurance that it is safe to meet and go through our fears.

A dear friend of mine lost her 9 year-old son to a tragic accident after which her 11 year-old daughter spiraled down into a maze of pain. For years it permeated and penetrated her life. When she began to turn the corner, she wrote a most revealing piece on the journey of Awakening called *Through*:

> *There is this thing that I've been going around for years, this thing that I must go "through." I have gone to the left of it and the right of it. I've climbed over it and tunneled under it. But unless you go through it, it won't take you to where you want to be. You'll end up someplace else, which is where I find myself once again. This ritual passage through is something that I have feared and sought to avoid for years. And it <u>can</u> be avoided...for lifetimes even. But eventually we all must make the journey "through." I realize this now. I feel it even physically. It's time.*
>
> *There will continue to be excuses that I could use to abort this decision. There will always be excuses, especially for an imaginative and rebellious mind. But I am committed now. I know the rewards will be great. I have always known this, just as I have always known that I would make it to this light I seek that lies at the mythical but very real "other side."*
>
> *It is hard not to judge myself harshly for trying so long and so laboriously to overcome this obstacle by doing everything **except** going through it. But then again, that spirit that drove me to the hot sands of Crete, the misty streets of Munich, and the icy waters of Alaska is the same spirit that brings me to where I am today...which is face to face with this thing I have run from for so long. And although I have not yet gone through it, there is a small particle of peace that comes from simply looking it in the eye. It is ever so slightly smaller than I thought. It is definable...not infinite.*
>
> *I cannot deny the feeling of defeat I have for not having found a clever way around this. There is a part of me that feels if I were just a little smarter, I could have made it. And I still feel like there are crafty people out there who have made it successfully "around" even though I know that's probably not true. Nonetheless, I still feel inferior to these fictitious demigods who have beaten the system. I wanted with all my heart to be one of them. But I guess I will just have to settle for simply getting there, even if I do have to trudge through it in the regular old way.*

Through is the act of being present for our fears. Paying attention to them with a keen curiosity and a merciful heart is what takes us beyond the struggling mind. As she said, "But unless you go through it, it won't take you to where you want to be."

134

It takes time and commitment to learn the art of *seeing* fear rather than always being lost in it. If we even had a glimpse of the power of fully being with these feelings, sensations and experiences that take us away from Life, we would have very little hesitation about opening to them. But since we've lived in wanting, disliking and managing our whole lives, most of us don't have a clue about the enormous power of paying attention.

As we slowly and gradually move out of what we think we know and what we think *should be*, and cultivate the art of being with *what is*—especially when fear is up—we begin to reap the benefits. The more we see our fear, the more we can know that centered and alive place that exists beneath the constant conversation in our heads.

THE JOURNEY WITHIN

You know, it's a real decision and your real life when you feel fear and a beckoning at the same time.

David Whyte

In order to meet our fears, we must be willing to look inside ourselves. I once talked to a psychologist who said that most of the people he works with are terrified of closing their eyes—of letting go of the familiarity of an external orientation. We may be afraid of Life, but we are far more afraid of fear. We fervently hope that if we just move fast enough, collect enough material things, and stave off death by the illusion of a perfect body and a perfect life, then fear will leave us alone. But there comes a time when Life will not let us run away any more. For some, this comes on their deathbed. If we are open, Life will move us into meeting and transforming our fears before the last precious days of our human existence.

The amazing thing is that in turning and facing our fears, they are transformed. We discover that in going towards fear, not only are we not engulfed by it, but we feel freer and more peaceful. We actually gain strength and clarity by exploring our fears rather than reacting to them. We realize that we don't need to eliminate our fears or even overcome them. Our freedom comes *when we create a relationship with fear itself*, standing with it rather than always fighting it.

Imagine a mythical land called Separation. Through this land moves the river called Fear. Most of the people live on one side of the river and they stay as far away from it as they can. They go to great lengths to disguise the fact that this powerful and seemingly overwhelming force moves through their land.

When it floods, taking over their lives, they run and hide and then come back to mop up the devastation that is left behind. Between floods, they distract themselves with things and experiences, gathering as many as they can, hoping against hope this will hold back the river of Fear.

This is not a happy land to live in. Everybody is rushing past one another, blindly racing from the fear that runs their lives. Lost in their fear of fear, they distract, numb, judge and struggle, never quite making a true connection with Life. Fear of the river narrows them down to a very small part of the country, and they are unable to use the river for play, transportation or irrigation. Some individuals occasionally emerge from their disconnection and isolation just enough to feel that Life must be more than this. But rather than going to explore the river and tapping into the power that is there, they slip back into distraction, hiding and management.

Most of us live in this land called Separation. At times in our lives, each one of us is brought face to face with the river of Fear. In the beginning, we turn and run away as fast as we can. But each time we are brought to its banks, it becomes more evident that though we have tried to distance ourselves, it controls almost every aspect of our lives. Finally, we realize that it is in getting to know this river and learning how to harness its power for the good of the whole that we become free. So we start spending more and more time at its banks, getting to know our fears and learning how to relate to them, rather than being lost in reaction. We still haven't gotten into the river, but we're getting close.

From this developing relationship, there comes a day for each one of us when, standing beside the river, the weather clears enough that we can see the other side. Not only does its beauty astound us, but we also can see Jesus, Buddha and other Awakened beings living in this place beyond fear. We begin to get inklings that the freedom we so desperately searched for in things, ideas, people and drugs, lies on the other side of the river.

But we don't want to immerse ourselves in the swirling waters. Our fear of fear is so great that we look for every shortcut we can find. We rent helicopters, and build fantastic boats that promise to keep us dry. We do our empowerment exercises, feeling at moments that we are strong enough to slay every fear. We do affirmations, hoping that if we just rise above the river, it will go away. At moments, we do find ourselves on the other side. But there is a little sign on the gateway into this land that says, "Temporary visas granted to all people who transported themselves *over* the river. Permanent visas granted to those who swim."

After many brief visits to this magical land beyond the river of fear (only to find ourselves after a short time back on the other side), we know in the depth of our being that we have to get into the river. We have to dive in and allow Life to support us in this mighty swim. The amazing thing is that the worst time of the journey is standing at the river's edge, ankle deep in water, and feeling afraid. We look longingly back at the land of illusion, hoping against hope that some miracle will rescue us from this daunting task.

When we finally hold our breath and dive into our river of fear, we discover an amazing thing. It feels just fine. From our former home far away and even before we got into the water, we were absolutely certain that what we were looking at was a cold, devouring river of fear. We had been told since the day we were born that fear is something to be afraid of and everybody around us lived as if this was so. As we dive into our fears, meeting them face to face, we discover they are noble adversaries sent from the depths of our being in order to develop within us the skills, the strength and the wisdom that is our birthright.

As we swim, with every stroke we learn more about the gifts of fear, and the terrors that we had resisted our whole lives become our allies. While swimming through the body of fear, there are glorious times when we allow ourselves to be held by these healing waters as they slowly carry us across the vast expanse. There are also times when we struggle, feeling as if the river will engulf us. When we remember to quiet down and allow ourselves to be held by the water, we discover that those who have made it to the other side are with us.

The moment when our feet touch the gravel bottom after our swim is exhilarating. We enter this land dancing and singing, knowing that after a very long journey we have finally arrived home. As we look back at the river we realize that freedom doesn't come from eliminating fear. It comes when we honor and accept its role in our Awakening. Fear is then transformed into an ally that hones our Awareness and opens our heart.

For a moment, we want to believe the illusion that we will never leave this land again. But then we see all the people who are braving the river, the ones that are contemplating the swim and even the ones far away that are doing absolutely everything in their power to ignore it. We know that we cannot stay here as long as there are brothers and sisters still on the journey. Willingly and joyfully we swim back over again, taking on the body of fear. But it is different this time for we see that it is only fear. Even though at moments we get caught, quickly and easily we remember the truth that we carry the land that lies beyond the river of fear with us everywhere we go.

THE DOORWAY OF FEAR

"You gain strength, courage and confidence by every experience in which you really stop to look fear in the face."

Eleanor Roosevelt

Fear is the guardian at the doorway of our true nature. The heroes in the ancient stories had to steal the Golden Fleece from the den of the dragon, gather a whisker from a ferocious lion or carry a treasure through the fires of the underworld. It wasn't that the Gods liked whiskers or fleeces. They gave seemingly insurmountable tasks to all true seekers because it was known that the road to true empowerment is the road of meeting fear.

I was given the great gift in my life of taking on deep terror. When I was young, my mother was convinced my father was trying to make her go insane. She was a student of truth and had incredible insight into Life, but she also was run by paranoia and constantly tried to control every aspect of her life and mine. A Rorschach test done in my late teens described her as "incorporating and devouring."

A number of years ago, I was at one of Stephen Levine's workshops. We were exploring forgiveness and had just closed our eyes to discover who we were willing to forgive. My mother came to mind, but I immediately discounted this. "I have done my forgiveness work with her," I said to myself. Vainly, I searched for someone else to forgive, but she kept popping up. With a sense of resignation, I finally agreed. As I opened to her, rather than feeling the softening in my heart that had been a hallmark of our relationship lately, I felt terror. My heart began to pound, my mind became agitated and upset. I let go of the forgiveness work and attempted to see this terror. It was like riding a bucking bronco, and I kept being thrown off.

At the end of the meditation, I made a dash for the microphone. My fear of revealing this fear in front of 600 people, most of whom I did not know, was nothing compared to this fear of being devoured by my Mother. I was now meeting the terror of being engulfed that had been such a core part of my childhood. In a flurry of fear, I began to describe my experience. Stephen listened in his compassionate and attentive way. My fear seemed to gain more power as I spoke. Coming to the end of my torrent of words, there was a long pause that only increased my terror. Into that space, Stephen said something that changed my life forever. He said, "It is only fear."

I didn't want to hear this in that moment. The fear inside of me was affronted and wanted to be acknowledged. It took me months before I was able to really understand what he meant when he said, "Most of our fear is our

138

fear of fear." It was then that I committed to seeing and moving through the fears that had run my life.

I realize now that one of the greatest gifts I was given is that the river of fear flooded the land of my being very early on and stayed that way for many years. Because I lived constantly in the waters of fear, there was no safe ground, no distraction that could make me ignore the water at my feet. Not even food, drugs or hyperactivity could numb me enough so that I knew moments of surcease from fear.

To be that flooded with fear sent me on a journey down into the underworld of human existence, and that descent was long and terrifying. All along the way were images and experiences that paralyzed and overwhelmed me. I was certain that at the end of the descent, the mother of all demons would devour me. Instead, I discovered solid ground beneath my feet, and from the mouth of every ghoul and from every rock wall, I heard:

> *You have not taken a wrong turn in Life. You are on the journey of Awaken-*
> *ing and are being given the opportunity to meet the fears that not only have run*
> *you but also all of humanity. The doorway out of the underworld is the doorway*
> *of attention. Listen, watch, and be keenly curious. After all, it's only fear.*

Meeting our fear is the work of a lifetime, but the gifts it brings are enormous. This journey is like a spiral. As we awaken, we discover that on each and every rung, we meet the same fears. But the farther up the spiral we go, the circles get smaller. We move through our fears more quickly and our Awareness becomes more spacious and connected. Stephen's words, "It's only fear," gave me the courage to be present for the core fears that had run me my whole life—"I'm not enough." "There is no way out." "I'm doing this all alone." As I have stood with these fears rather than trying to hide from them, I have become more alive, more compassionate, much wiser, and I laugh a lot more. I have come to know a sense of belonging that was inconceivable before.

For most of us, it takes years to get to the river and, once there, we will do anything to avoid getting in and swimming. The writer Parker Palmer, in an article in the IONS Journal, shares a wonderful story from his own life that speaks about our fear of meeting our fear. In his early 40's, feeling that he was in the middle of a mid-life crisis (one that he says started when he was about 17 and persists to this day!) he decided to do an Outward Bound course at a place called Hurricane Island.

> *I should have known from the name what was in store for me. The next time I*
> *will choose the program at Pleasant Valley, or Happy Gardens! It was a week*
> *of sheer terror. It was also a week of amazing growth.*

In the middle of the course he faced the challenge he most feared—rappelling down a 110-foot cliff. After bumping and falling down to the first ledge, the instructor invited him to lean back as far as he could, reminding him that he had to get his feet at right angles to the rock face so there would be pressure on them. Parker *knew* that he was wrong. He knew that the trick was to *hug* the mountain, to stay as close to the rock face as he could. After slamming into the next ledge he finally, with great fear, tried what the instructor suggested and, wonder of wonders, he began moving down the rock face, his eyes on the heavens.

For a while he thought he had it under control, but that illusion was shattered when an instructor called up from below, "Parker, I think you'd better stop and look at what's happening beneath your feet." He goes on to describe what happened next:

> *I lowered my eyes (very, very slowly, so that I wouldn't change my center of gravity), and there beneath my feet a large hole was opening up in the rock— which meant that I was going to have to change directions. I froze. I have never been so paralyzed in my life, so full of physical fear. I knew I could do it if I could just keep going straight, but I could not change directions. I just froze in sheer terror.*
>
> *The teacher let me hang there for what seemed like a very long time. Finally she shouted up, "Parker, is anything wrong?" To this day, I do not know where these words came from (though I have 12 witnesses that I spoke them). But in a high squeaky voice I said, "I don't want to talk about it!" The teacher said, "Then I think it's time you learned the motto of the Outward Bound School." I thought, "Oh keen! I'm about to die, and she's giving me a motto!" But then she yelled up to me words that I will never forget, words that have been genuinely empowering for me ever since. She said, "The motto of the Outward Bound Hurricane Island School is: IF YOU CAN'T GET OUT OF IT, GET INTO IT!"*
>
> *These words were so profoundly true for me at that existential moment that they entered my body, bypassed my mind and moved my legs and feet. It was just so clear that there was no way out of that situation except to get into it. No helicopter was going to come; they weren't going to haul me up on the rope; I wasn't going to float down. I had to get into it and my feet started to move.*

In the willingness to meet his fear, he was empowered.. In our willingness to go *towards* rather than *away*, we discover the doorway to our wholeness. The way we discover this is to go *into* the river. And just as the water will support us if we stop fighting it, our willingness to recognize our fears will take us to the other side.

Whether it is the fear of pain, rejection, homelessness, loneliness or death that runs our lives, it is important to start digesting these fears in small increments.

Just as with the river, we walk slowly out into the swift moving current, becoming familiar with the little fears while our feet can still touch the ground. Spend a day noticing fear: *I won't make this stoplight. I'll gain 10 pounds with just this one bite. I'll be late. I'll say it wrong.* Name it when you see it showing up in your story, "Ah, fear." Every time you name it, you have taken another step out of your fear.

Your meditation time is another good place to get to know your fears. If no fear is present, make a commitment to sit without moving even a finger until the body craves to move. And still don't move. Watch carefully, for under that frustration and anger is fear. As we gain clarity from meeting the more mundane fears, we then have the strength and the courage to meet the core fears (death, pain, rejection) that reside in the center of our story.

IMPERMANENCE AS AN ALLY

Fear is an instructor of great sagacity, and the herald of all revolutions.

Ralph Waldo Emerson

To meet our fear is to allow what we formerly were afraid of to become an ally. There is no place where this is more evident than in our fear of the changeability of Life and especially of death. Even though we can see people growing old and watch the leaves change in the fall, we live as if permanence is possible. But we can see that nothing lasts—not empires, mountain ranges or stars. The initial recognition of the fragility of everything supports our fear. "There is nothing to hold on to," screams the mind. But the impermanence of Life holds the possibility of opening us back into the preciousness of every moment and the safety that comes from opening to Life.

When I was talking to my daughter one day, I had the sudden realization that she had arisen out of Mystery and could return without a moment's notice. My heart contracted. I wanted her to be permanent. For a moment I was completely unwilling to comprehend the possibility that she could be gone in an instant, and yet that is the truth. In the next moment, this fear invited me into the preciousness of our time together. It inspired me to be as fully with her as I possibly could, drinking her in, really listening, loving her as if these were our last moments together. It made that time very real, very alive and vibrant. To live with the Awareness of impermanence is to open to the preciousness of Life's unfolding.

Blinded to impermanence, we think nothing of leaving for work or going to the store still angry at our partner or upset with our children. We assume, expect and believe that they will be there when we return. *Sometimes they're not.* I've heard many stories of people whose loved ones vanished from their lives without any forewarning. There was a family in which the father and children went to the store for ice cream, leaving the mother at home. She never saw them again alive, as they were hit and killed by a drunk driver.

Julie Wester, a wonderful meditation teacher, said that once her fear of impermanence became workable, it turned into an ally, keeping her from getting careless in her relationships. Her husband had lost his father at an early age and Julie was a hospice nurse. Both of them deeply understood the fragility of physical life and this allowed them to cut through a lot of the unconsciousness that we normally live in. She said that when they sit down at the dinner table and look into each others eyes, the stresses and strains fall away as they realize this precious moment has been given to them by Life and that there is no guarantee of any future ones.

Achan Cha, a Buddhist master from Thailand, was asked why he exuded such joy all of the time. He picked up a glass and said, "You see this glass—its beauty, how the light reflects off of it, how wonderfully it holds my drink? It is already broken. I don't have to worry about it breaking, because I've already let it go." In that willingness to lose it, we can deeply appreciate it while it is here. Everything in our lives is "already broken." The only thing that is truly constant is change. That is the way of Life. This is true not only for people and things; it is also true for thoughts, feelings and experiences.

Our attachment to the illusion of permanence makes us victims to life's fragility, and our resistance to impermanence keeps us from being vibrantly alive. To meet impermanence allows Life to flow through us, creating a sense of ease, safety and trust. As Brian Swimme said, "To embrace loss is to achieve eternity." It allows us to not hold on in fear to those things, people and ideas we've become attached to. It also allows us to not fight and resist dark feelings, challenging times and even difficult people. We can then live more and more in the moment that Life appears out of Mystery.

We sometimes need a rude awakening from Life in order to jolt us out of our fear of impermanence. Many people, upon learning of a terminal diagnosis, spin down into the struggle for holding onto their lives. But there are also people who, after the initial horror, discover that it was the greatest gift they have ever been given because they woke up before they died—woke up to the preciousness of every single moment, of every single breath.

When met face to face, our fear of impermanence opens us up to being truly alive. Rather than waiting for a terminal diagnosis, we can meet our fears as they show up in our lives and receive the wondrous benefits of this spacious way of thinking. Imagine what it would be like if everyone realized what a precious gift life in a body is—if everyone could accept that none of us knows when our last breath is going to come.

The benefits of allowing our fear of impermanence to be transformed into deep appreciation for Life are enormous. Some of the ways we can do this in our daily lives are:

- *Wherever you are standing on the Earth, imagine all the feet that have walked on this ground before you and that are now gone: woolly mammoth, Indians, deer.*

- *Find either a book or video tape in the library of someone who had their picture taken every year of their life in the same place, time and position. You can see their whole life unfold before you in a few minutes. Then connect with this moment as a part of the unfolding of your life.*

- *Spend a day seeing everything on a continuum. Find the form or forms that any particular object was before it became what it is now—a field of cotton that turned into a shirt, the board that makes up the stair in your house as it drank the sun in the stillness of the forest, the atoms in your hand that we're once a part of a star. See everything transformed into something else - loved ones, your house, your country, mountain ranges.*

- *Look at your hands. See them getting more age spots, the skin wrinkling, tendons protruding. Then see them in death, and watch as the elements return to Life. Allow the impermanence of Life to invite you into the preciousness of each moment.*

BEYOND FEAR

It is not that you must be free from fear. The moment you try to free yourself from fear, you create resistance against fear. Resistance in any form does not end fear. What is needed, rather than running away or controlling or suppressing or any other resistance, is understanding fear; that means watch it, learn about it, come directly into contact with it. We are to learn about fear, not how to escape from it, not how to resist it.

Krishnamurti

Our fears are the doorway to our wholeness. On some level, every single life is a mythical journey, one in which each of us take on a particular set of fears in order to propel us down the path of Awakening. To go towards our fears is the healing. Rumi, a thirteenth century philosopher and scholar, has a wonderful poem about going through our fears. In the poem he speaks of fire as that which we fear and water as the pleasure we hope will end our fears:

> *If you are a friend of God, fire is your water.*
> *You should wish to have a hundred thousand sets of moth wings,*
> *So you could burn them away, one set a night.*
> *The moth sees light and goes into the fire.*
> *You should see fire and go toward light.*
> *Fire is what of God is world-consuming. Water, world protecting.*
> *Somehow each gives the appearance of the other.*
> *To these eyes you have now,*
> *What looks like water burns.*
> *What looks like fire is a great relief to be inside.*

Whether we know it or not, we are each on the journey through the river of fear back into Life. After having fear be our guiding force for the past two million years, humanity is on the threshold of a new perception, one in which we are transforming our relationship to fear. This transformation holds the possibility that all of the parts of Life—the dark and light, the atoms, molecules and cells; the animals, insects and people; the dark skin, the light skin and the in between; the water, earth and sky; the body, mind and heart—are recognized as a part of a unified whole.

To know this place, we need to examine what stands in the way so we can learn how to use our minds rather than having them use us. We will now explore three other aspects of the struggling mind that keep us caught.

> *May we recognize how deeply fear penetrates our lives.*
>
> *May we have the courage and the commitment to become conscious of our fear, rather than being at the mercy of it.*
>
> *May we discover the place where fear is an ally, supporting us on the journey into becoming fully alive.*

Core Intention: It's okay

Chapter 7
Disarming the Judger

TODAY I HAD TIME

For the first time today I had time…enough time… not too much time.

Time has often been scarce. I've chased it, raced it.

Anxiously wondering all day long if I could get enough of it

to transform myself into acceptable personhood.

Each night going to bed still a failure, not enough hours in the day

to live up to who I should be.

Each night, time turning ironic as hour after hour was laid

at the foot of my bed while I waited for sleep.

So little when I need it, so much when I don't.

And then a rare moment: I would look and behold, time on my hands.

A thrill of pleasure, short-lived, and then a panic.

Seconds were wasting.

"Spare time" becomes wasted time…why am I not doing more?

Oh such suffering and struggle.

Oh blessed path that has led me to this gracious shift.

Today I had time. With a gentle half-smile I saw time.

Today time was a gift, time just was.

Oh tender compassion for the child who was never good enough.

No amount of time, no past redone,

no distant brighter future can ever make you good enough.

You already were made good enough from the Beginning!

Time, now that I have stopped the war with you, will you bring this truth

to my heart?

Teresa Lutterman

PORTRAIT OF THE JUDGER

The greatest barrier to our own healing is not the pain, sorrow or violence inflicted upon us as children. Out greatest hindrance is our ongoing capacity to judge, to criticize, and to bring tremendous harm to ourselves. If we can harden our heart against ourselves and meet our most tender feelings with anger and condemnation, we simultaneously armor our heart against the possibility of gentleness, love and healing.

Wayne Muller

It was early evening and the day had been a disaster. I was 24 years old and for most of my life I had been running scared, disconnected from myself. I had tried to *do it right*—to be an idea of what I thought I *should* be—and I had failed miserably. The resulting self-revulsion had shown up in self-destructive behaviors such as overeating, drugs and alcohol, along with an overall disgust and disregard of my body. After being raped by a stranger, I had packed my things, sold my car and headed off to Europe. The intention was to leave the pain behind. Instead, it traveled with me wherever I went, becoming deeper and broader every day. I ate and drank my way down the road.

For a few days I found myself house-sitting at a beautiful home, high on a hill in Switzerland. The beauty around me totally escaped my attention. All I could see was the liquor cabinet and the challenge of getting enough to drink without the owners knowing I was pilfering their stock. By adding water to the vodka, I set about consuming enough alcohol to numb the pain. Instead, it opened the floodgates of grief and self-hatred. I fell into a whirlpool of despair and hopelessness, only to desperately search for more alcohol to hold back the tide. But that only made it worse.

There was not one iota of my being that felt anything but violent revulsion for myself. All of my anger towards Life was turned towards myself and it was extremely toxic. Standing at the end of a four-poster bed, I raised my arm to hit the bed in rage and struck the end board. Even with all of the pain, it felt good. "You are a worthless human being, and this is your punishment," said the Judger. I raised my arm again and again and again, bringing it down with as much force as I could muster in my inebriated state.

The feelings spent, I crawled exhausted into bed and cried myself to sleep. The next day I woke up to a swollen, throbbing arm and, much to my amazement, was told by the doctor that it was broken.

Even though this is a very sad story, it is not an isolated human experience. Many people on this planet at the exact moment you are reading this book are lost in this level of self-judgment, acting in ways that are destructive towards themselves, their loved ones and society as a whole. But for most of us, our self judgment is more subtle, concealed in a mind that believes we need to be different than we are. Usually subtly, but sometimes quite loudly and obnoxiously, it compares us to some mythical idea of who we should be and then berates us for coming up short of perfection. It comes out of a deep belief at the center of our story that says who we are is not acceptable.

Have you ever been afraid to tell a loved one the truth about a part of yourself because you're certain he or she would leave? That is the *I am not good enough, right enough, perfect enough to be loved* place. The chant goes on to say, "I should be better. I have to, I ought to, I must do or be whatever my arbitrary definition of getting it together is." So we become an ongoing project, struggling to approximate perfection, all the while secretly knowing we've become an idea about ourselves rather than being real.

The *shoulds* and *oughts* within us can grow to monstrous proportions, completely blotting out our beauty, uniqueness and perfection, and freezing us out of Life. Imagine you are sitting in a restaurant with two people in the booth behind you. One is talking to the other exactly the way we talk to ourselves. Most people would have to get up and leave. As Stephen Levine has said, "If we would talk to our friends like we talk to ourselves, we wouldn't have any friends." The mind's cruelty is pervasive and relentless.

THE BIRTH OF THE JUDGING MIND

We are all trying to be cool, very fearful and guarded, hoping we won't say it wrong, or somebody will discover we are a phony.

Patricia Sun

At a gathering of Western Buddhist teachers, a man tried to describe to the Dalai Lama the depth of self-judgment that he felt inside. Because the Dalai Lama had never experienced the level of self-judgment that can warp and cripple a life, he was deeply moved by the feelings this man was expressing. He stopped what the group was doing and asked everyone to share with him if they too experienced this cruelty of the mind. When they all answered "yes," he was amazed.

Every human being, including the Dalai Lama, carries some level of self-judgment. It is called guilt and is a useful tool for functioning within the framework of society. But in the disconnected, industrial societies of the West, this voice has grown to enormous proportions within most human beings, moving from the level of *I've done something wrong* to *I am wrong*. How did this come to be so?

At our birth, we brought with us the gifts of our innocence and our uniqueness. We were also extremely vulnerable. Everything was much bigger than we were and definitely more powerful, and the primal need for survival was nestled in our genes. There was a part of us that knew that these giants we lived with were the ones who could either give or withhold the essentials— food, water and shelter. Our animal nature understood perfectly that to please them meant life. To not please them meant death. Molding and shaping ourselves to the unspoken requirements of our family environment became the order of the day. Ram Dass, author of *Remember Be Here Now, Now Be Here*, calls it *somebody* training—learning the skills to be what we *should be* according to our family system.

We didn't put all of this energy into becoming what our parents needed us to be just to get our basic survival needs met. We also did this to get their attention. Attention is nourishment, and we all thrive in its glow. At its best, it is pure Love, but in whatever form, we needed this as much, if not more, than food and water. In order to fully develop, we needed focused and accepting interactions with other human beings, people who were able to meet us exactly as we were.

Many of the parents of my generation were capable of truly meeting their children only for brief moments before they would disconnect again. The focus of that generation was *acquiring a better life*. They had gone through the Depression and World War II and they were concerned with secular safety and the appearance of things. Two cars in the garage with a washer and dryer, readily available drink and smoke, and life was good. Their focus was so outer-directed that, for the first time since mammals showed up, babies were not nourished by a mother's breast.

Our mothers were also convinced by their doctors that to be anesthetized during the birth experience was the best way to go. And in those first precious days after our birth, when the bonding that is necessary for the mothering experience is generated, our mothers were recovering from the anesthesia, while we lay in a nursery far away. Being this disconnected from their children, these women could accept that bottle feeding every four hours, whether we were awake or not, was appropriate, and that if we cried in between, this was just the child's willfulness which needed to be thwarted.

In my own life, I not only didn't receive the breast, I was not held during feedings. The bottle propper, that invention from hell that hung the bottle above the baby while it lay in its bed, was the rage of the time. There was no heartbeat for me to listen to, no adoring gaze of my mother, no tender playing with my hair. When I tried to give myself some loving connection by sucking my thumb, it was painted with a foul tasting substance. When I sucked my fingers, they were painted too. But the desire to be comforted is primal, and I sucked my fingers, bad tasting gluck and all. My parents were so disconnected that they then splinted my fingers with popsicle sticks. My mother shared with me years later the grief she felt when she listened to me wailing and whimpering in my crib. But the programming and disconnection of her generation was too strong for her to rise above it.

I have been rereading *Gorillas in the Mist*, the story of Diane Fossey's interaction with the gorillas of Rwanda. After years of watching the different families, it was evident to her that if gorilla children had attentive and supportive parents, they were inquisitive and fun loving children, safe in their environment. If their parents were inattentive or unemotional, they often became either very shy and tentative, or irritating and even rebellious.

With no bonding time after birth and with our parents being so outwardly directed and disconnected, most of us got only moments of true connection. This is one of the main reasons we become an idea of what we think we should be rather than what we are. In order to survive, we learned very early on to adapt and become whatever our parents needed us to be to keep the thread of this connection alive.

Children will go to amazing lengths to become the child their parents want, and they are very sensitive and responsive to the unspoken needs of their family. If our parents desired a quiet little girl, we tamed our exuberance. If they demanded a little boy who was brave and strong, we curtailed our tears. If pleasing and molding ourselves to what was expected didn't work, we withdrew or rebelled, both still attention-getting devices.

With every generation since then, we have become more skillful in our parenting, but still, many children don't receive the minimum daily requirement of pure attention that is needed to grow into a healthy and mature adult. We live in a society that is so outer-directed that success is defined by the amount of money we make and the house we live in rather than the quality of our human relationships. *The less we received of the basic requirement of unconditional attention and the more we got the exact opposite is the level to which the self-judging quality of the mind will gain power.*

Given the circumstances, a part of us had to be watching to see if we were doing it okay. The more desperate the situation, the stronger the voice of judgment. It watched every move we made, becoming the architect of the *somebody* we thought Life needed us to be. The Judger listened to the adults in its environment and then internalized their voices, learning how to shame any part inside that felt like it could threaten survival—our rage ("Don't you dare raise your voice to me!"), our selfishness ("You are bad for not wanting to share your toys."), our fear ("Don't be such a fraidy cat!"), our sadness ("Big boys don't cry").

Besides not being seen, there was one other thing operating in our childhood that made the growth of the Judger possible. We felt we were the center of the Universe. Our sense of *other* was not very highly developed, so the conclusion we came to was that if something was not right—if our parents were mad at each other, if they abused us, if they were considering a divorce—it was because we had done something wrong. All we have to do is interview children of all ages whose parents have divorced to discover that every single one believes that they were to blame. Deep in our story, each one of us has beliefs of how bad we were when we were children. Hiding deep inside, they run our lives, lurking as hidden proof of our defectiveness.

Robert Bly, a well-known poet, has a wonderful analogy. He says that we arrive from the far reaches of the Universe as 360-degree balls of radiance, place ourselves at our parent's feet, and say, "Here I am." And they say, "I didn't want you. I wanted a good little girl or boy." That's where the Judger begins. It points out all of the unacceptable parts and shoves them back into what Bly calls the long, dark bag we drag behind us. What we hide composts in the bag, gets wild and builds up a big head of steam while we expend all our energy maintaining a mask by which we purchase love and affection. Whenever these wild parts threaten to break through the mask—our power, stubbornness, exuberance, terror, curiosity, rage—we deny, numb out or project them onto someone else as fast as we can. We relate to these parts exactly as they were met when we were developing the image of ourselves, usually with fear and rejection.

We have become a society motivated by a great yearning for Love, and at the same time permeated by the terror that we won't be good enough to get it. We are performers, moving out of the tragic fear that we are not lovable until we do *it* right. Two of the favorite conversations of the Judger are: *What did I do wrong?* and *What do I need to do in order to stop this?* This keeps us lost in the land of war, always looking for what needs to be different and continually trying a variety of methods to fix, change, get rid of or ignore that which we deem defective.

RECOGNIZING THE JUDGER

If we could read the secret history of our enemies, we should find in each man's life, sorrow and suffering enough to disarm our hostilities.

Longfellow

Ultimately, the Judger is here to open our hearts but in order to move beyond believing what it is saying, it is skillful to see the effects it has in our lives.

The prime detriment is that the Judger cuts us off from our lives. Imagine what it was like very early in your life when you were comfortable with yourself and with your life. You probably don't remember this but you, like all people, lived for a time completely at one with your life. Then you began, in response to people and events around you, to weave a story in your head about who you were and what you needed to be. You became a human *doing* rather than a human *being*.

Now imagine yourself as an adult, sitting in a room, immersed in a novel about your life titled *What I Need To Do To Become Whole*. In order to focus on this story, you have to shut out the experience of Life all around you. For most of the moments of our lives, we are all immersed in this story in our heads rather than being present for the adventure that is our lives.

The Judger also causes us to live in the agonizing land of regret—"if only I hadn't, or why didn't I?" Each of us can feel the dropping sensation in our stomachs as we hear these words. Yes, we all have done things that we shouldn't have. We have all lied, cheated and put ourselves first. We have hurt friends and loved ones deeply, sometimes knowingly, sometimes unknowingly. But if we step back far enough, we can see that each of these mis-takes in our lives taught us something and even, in some deep way beyond our ordinary comprehension, gave to those we hurt essential experiences in the unfolding of their lives.

To be caught in the land of self-judgment also freezes us out of the well of creativity that lies within every one of us. Rather than engaging with the adventure of our lives, we sit on the sidelines, frozen into the belief that we aren't enough. To see how frozen we are, imagine you have just come to this planet and you see somebody whiz by on a mountain bike. You say, "Hey, that looks like fun." So off you go to find a bike. Your first time on it, you pedal a few times and fall over, skinning your elbow. "What did I do wrong?" you say. You get back on the bike and pedal a few more times before falling the other way, skinning your knee. "I can't ride a bike because I didn't get my master's degree. Or maybe it is because my nose is too big," you mumble to yourself. So off you go to have plastic surgery and wonder why it doesn't help. Then you try again, falling over the handlebars this time. You then decide that there must be something so defective inside of you that you stop your engagement with Life and put down the kickstand, trying to look cool. Every once in awhile, you move the bike around so people will think that you have been riding the bike and hope nobody will notice.

Trying to look cool, we cut ourselves off from all that is spontaneous, authentic and creative in us. We close the door to being engaged with the roller coaster of living because the Judger in us believes it isn't safe. The Judger denies, rejects and crushes all that doesn't fit into our idea of what we *should be*. As we get older, it gains momentum and we become tighter and tighter, struggling to make ourselves *better* so we will finally be worthy of the peace and love that we yearn for.

If only becomes our mantra. If only we lose ten pounds or become more loving or understand where our heartaches come from, we will be okay. We become caught in an endless struggle of trying to be perfect and wonder why we feel so empty. There is only one problem. This doesn't work. We have become addicted to the struggle itself—to the idea that we are an ongoing project in need of *getting it together*. But struggle never brings the depth of healing we desire.

One of the most powerful side effects of the Judger is the meanness it generates in the world. It took courage and unflinching honesty to see how much I judged other people. At long meditation retreats I began to notice that if I was in my center, I experienced people at the retreat from either a neutral position or from one of an open heart. If I was struggling, wanting myself and my meditations to be different than what they were, my experience of the others dramatically changed. I would judge them for being too loud, to stiff, too slow, too precise. I would judge them if they were *doing it right* (my version of right), and I would judge them if they were *doing it wrong*. It was astounding and very freeing for me to see that I experienced anybody else's success as a threat to my own. As I began to watch, I could see how much judging operated in my life, usually very subtly, but it was there nonetheless.

There was a vivid moment during a meditation retreat I attended a few years ago when I clearly saw the part of my mind that sees other people's *success* as a judgment upon my own. I was eating a snack during a mid-morning break. My intent for the whole retreat was to be present for my food. I wasn't. My mind was wandering here and there, anywhere except with the eating that was happening in that moment. A woman sat down three tables in front of me and began to eat. Her eyes were closed, her actions were very present, and I hated her because she was doing it *right*. I watched my mind begin to judge her, but very quickly it went into judging myself. My heart completely closed as I beat myself up for my eating and my judging.

Then Awareness kicked in, and I was able to soften and open my heart to how much my mind is always expecting me to be *doing better* than what I am. I let go of my depersonalization of this woman and silently thanked her for the gift she was giving me—just by being herself. I could then rejoice in her moments of Presence, rather than seeing them as a demand that I be better. It became much clearer for the rest of the retreat that when I was accepting exactly who I was, I became deeply accepting of everybody else.

The devastation of comparing and judging shows up strongly in the dance of intimate relationships. When we are judging ourselves, it is practically impossible to see the other person. It took me years after my divorce to acknowledge that my need to focus on the so-called inadequacies of my husband had become the pressure release valve for my own imagined defects. As long as I was trying to change him, I didn't have to see what was asking to be seen in my own life.

The Judger not only keeps us disconnected in one-on-one relationships, but also in groups. One of the places it is easiest to see is within families. Every family has a person who is the repository of its shadow. It is the person who the rest of the family is always talking about, going over their *deficiencies* like a litany. They become the repository for the self-judgment that everybody carries about themselves.

If there is deep insecurity in a family or an organization, a single scapegoat may not be enough. Then the group collectively chooses other groups to put down, to be seen as less than themselves. It happens in the caste system in India and causes great human devastation. It happens among different skin colors all around the world, preventing people from coming together as a whole. It also happens around gays and lesbians. Some of the most gifted people this world has ever known have had to hide their sexual preference or have been deeply persecuted.

There is no place where the cruelty of the judging mind is more apparent than on the playgrounds of our schools. Children taunt, harass and torment any child who is different. This is the activity of the voice inside of each and every child that says, "Stick to the norm (of your family and your society) and then you will be accepted and safe."

I once came across a man speaking on one of the daytime talk shows. I was captured by the quality of this person who was in his mid twenties. He radiated strength, integrity and kindness. Instead of ears, he had little bumps on each side of his head, and he was recalling a time when he was about 8 years old and the other boys on his school bus had ganged up on him. He tried hiding under one of the seats, and when he finally made it to the front of the bus, the driver's response was to put *him* off of the bus. Wandering scared through the city, he finally came across a metropolitan bus stop, but had to search for the courage to get on one of the buses. Thankfully, this driver met him with understanding and compassion and helped him to get to school. The judging voice within children that tries to annihilate anything that is different doesn't disappear when we become an adult. It just becomes more subtle and oftentimes is turned inside towards ourselves.

When we are able to stop judging our judgment, we see that we don't need to judge ourselves, judge others or even judge our own lives. We can see that each and every experience in our lives is a necessary part of the schoolroom of the heart. Each of us got the exact set of parents, the best body, and the most appropriate personality for our soup of Awakening. Each and every one of us has been embarrassed time and time again, sadistically hurt and deeply abandoned. And each of us has fallen short of the mark over and over again.

Having a sexually seductive father with whom I had a very difficult relationship, I carried much blame and a victim mentality in relationship to him. As I met my rage and was able to comprehend myself not as a victim but as an awakening soul, I had a dream. My father was sitting on the floor of the kitchen where I lived during my teenage years, an extremely traumatic time for me. I came into the kitchen and knelt down in front of him. I said, "Do you know that I am the Earth waking up?" And he said, "Yes." I went on to say, "And you were the most perfect father I could have had in order to awaken." Tears began to stream down his face as he received this healing.

Our parents, siblings, teachers and friends were simply acting from the place in the unfolding they found themselves to be. Whatever gifts of pain they gave to us were threads in a tapestry that is being woven from a place that is bigger than we are. As Shakespeare so eloquently said, "All the world's a stage, and the men and women are merely players." There is something going on here that is far beyond our comprehension. Nothing is ever about what it seems to be, and in this unfolding, each of us has particular dance steps we are destined to dance, including pleasure and pain, loss and gain.

154

We can no longer afford to have the judging mind be our predominant view of the world. We need to become honest enough so we can acknowledge that we're all doing the same thing—that we are all caught in the same web of delusion. Sir Thomas More, on the way to his beheading, was supposed to have said, "We're all in the same cart going to execution. How can I hate anyone or wish anyone harm?" If we begin to, with great courage and honesty, watch the judging mind, it will take us to the healing of compassion for ourselves, for our loved ones, for strangers, countries, organizations and humanity as a whole.

Only compassion will heal the eons of fallout from the cruelty of the judging mind. It will allow us to see into all the corners of the human experience and, in deep empathy, connect with the pain we're all in—even if it is a king beheading wives, counselors and Thomas More himself. Compassion can see the pain out of which these actions came, whether it is an individual, a family or a societal group that has judged us as inadequate. With this seeing, the heart swells with a great desire to reach out and tenderly meet and hold this common pain, whether it is inside of us or in the world.

BEYOND SELF-JUDGMENT

The healing is to let yourself in when you find yourself the most unacceptable.

Stephen Levine

There is a way out. And actually it is very simple. It has to be in order not to get caught in the incessant need of the mind to compare and judge our attempts to heal ourselves. We don't need to destroy the judging quality in our mind nor do we need to deny it's there or try to leap over it by becoming *perfect*. This only gives it more power. The healing comes from the ability *to see* the Judger—to begin to *relate to it* rather than being lost in its cruelty.

Our standard approach is to try to understand where these voices came from and how to get rid of them. This can just get us more caught in the struggles of the mind. When various people tried to help me, it was invariably based on the belief that something was wrong with me and I needed to be fixed. This approach got translated by the maze of my mind into proof that I was inherently defective which often just drove me deeper into the maze.

At other times it did help to create better states of mind, and I had moments where I wasn't devastated by the frontal attacks of my judging mind. But the roots of this cruel judger were deeply embedded in my being, and its subtle chant of self-hatred still permeated most of my experiences. I no longer hit or mutilated myself, but I would be driving my car and think of something that I had done *wrong* and would find myself hitting the steering wheel saying "You dumb shit." Or I would be walking up and down the grocery store aisles chanting "bad girl, bad girl" to myself. The Judger still ran me.

It was when I began to be able to step back enough and *see* the Judger that I began to experience a level of spontaneity and freedom in my life that I had never known before. To see the judger allows us moments of not identifying with what it is saying. Through the process of learning how to *relate to it rather that being caught in the middle of it* has come a freedom from the cruelty of my mind that was absolutely unimaginable even 10 years ago.

In order to begin to be able to see and not identify with the Judger, there are four essential things we need to understand about this voice:

The first is that absolutely everybody has it. We're all addicted to self-judgment and we're all very good at hiding it. A good example is John Bradshaw, bestselling author of *Homecoming* and the popular video series *Bradshaw on the Family*. He has done it *right* as far as this society is concerned because he has fame and fortune and has accomplished important things in the field of his expertise. And yet in an interview a few years back he said," If you put me in a room with people with letters after their names like Ph.D. or M.D., my shame voices know these people are going to figure out that I do not know anything!" That is the judging mind we all carry. It is important to notice that no matter what we do, no matter what we become, that voice never completely goes away. It definitely becomes quieter but it can flare up at a moment's notice.

Allow yourself to feel the relief that comes from recognizing that you are not alone. We are all living a lot of the time inside of a mind that demands we be perfect and judges our attempts to be so. It is much like walking down a path with a hand gripping our arm, subtly pushing us along, yanking suddenly to the left, holding us back, insistently turning us to the right. It's constantly saying that we should be farther along the path or even on an entirely different one. We're so busy trying to respond to its signals that we can't see the beauty that surrounds us and are unable to rest in the unfolding of our lives. Often the pressure of self judgment is subtle, but it's usually there.

The Judger loves to decide what it considers to be success. It may be the buff body of a weight lifter, the fancy life-style of a corporate executive or the joyful spontaneity of a free spirit. Then it looks out and sees somebody who appears to have accomplished this and says, "Wow, they did it. They have it together and I don't." Ah, the cruelty of the mind.

We are so occupied in trying to prop up our image that we never take the time to realize that everyone else feels the same way. In my counseling practice, I hear countless stories of people's belief in their imperfection, and all the while, sitting in front of me I see an exquisite facet of the sacred essence of Life!

The second idea that can bring us freedom from the judger is that it was born out of benevolence. If we look closely at its birth, we can see that it was a very skillful tool to have when we were growing up. When it first showed up on the scene, it was trying to stop behaviors that seemed to threaten our survival. No matter how outrageous and unconscious it has become, on some level it has always been trying to take care of us.

Imagine a child in the corner of a room where his parents are fighting. Scared to death, the child is saying to himself, "I was a bad boy. I scattered my blocks all over the floor and made my parents mad. Now they are fighting. If I am neat and tidy, then everything will be okay." To take on responsibility for the messes in our family gave us a feeling of control and safety when we were little children.

The third thing that is important to know about the Judger is that it fails to see that mistakes are an integral part of Life. As a friend of mine once said, if you take a step forward, you move a few feet. If you fall flat on your face, you move at least five or six feet! Rather than allowing for mis-takes, we see them as MISTAKES, proof that we are bad or wrong. We are like an airplane flying on radar from Los Angeles to Hawaii. The plane is continually drifting off course with the radar bringing it back. Our lives are also destined to be lived that way, drifting off course and being brought back over and over again. That is how we learn and grow. And yet most people's navigation system is tuned to the belief that we should never be *off course* and if we are, we are wrong.

We live in the land of duality—male and female, dark and light, up and down. All of these pairs are a given in Life. But the opposites of right/wrong and good/bad are merely creations of the human mind. What one society may deem natural and good may be absolutely abhorrent in another.

Each of us has woven our own code of right/wrong out of the fabric of our family and our society. Rather than using this code as a benevolent radar system for maneuvering through our lives, we use it to bludgeon ourselves. Imagine the pilot in that airplane hating himself every time the radar indicated than an adjustment needed to be made! That is all too often the internal experience of most human beings. The reason we don't use our radar skillfully is that we don't see that moments off course are as integral and important as those moments of being on course. It is our weak points, our failures, our confusions and our mis-takes that define our clarity, wisdom, compassion and healing.

We're all works in progress until the day we die and our freedom comes from allowing ourselves to be human. It is the willingness to embrace our human-ness that takes us home. It's okay to make mistakes. A mistake is just a mis-take. The word sin originally was an archery term that meant "off the mark." Making mistakes is a part of the process of learning. In fact, the fewer mistakes you make, the closer to death you are! One of the main attributes of successful human beings is that they are comfortable with making mistakes. *Our perfection is in our non-perfection*—what a relief!

The last thing to explore about the Judger is that it doesn't take into account all of who you really are. Picture a construction sight in a downtown area that is fenced off with high boards. There are holes so that people walking by can look in and see how the building is progressing. Imagine somebody looking through one tiny hole and what they see is a pile of garbage. The assumption is made that this is a sloppy and messy construction sight. But because the hole does not allow a complete view of the work area or a comprehension of what had transpired during the day, there is no understanding that this garbage was gathered together in one place in order for the dump truck to pick it up that evening. There is not even the willingness to concede that garbage is a necessary by-product of the building project.

That is what the Judger does to us. It looks through a very narrow perspec-tive, focusing on what it considers to be the defective parts, and usually assumes the worst. It doesn't allow that the garbage of our personality composts quite nicely into a wonderful fertilizer for our growth.

An example from my life is that I come from a family of lawyers. My father, grandfather, uncle, sister and some cousins are all lawyers and most of the other people in my family have graduated with some degree. One sister studied at Bryn Mawr and the other at the Sorbonne in France. I, on the other hand, never graduated from college. I was also 18 months younger than a sister whose mode of survival in our family was to become *the accomplished one*. In keeping with that identity, she got straight A's. I got A's and B's and my self-judger said, "Boy, are you dumb." She became a successful lawyer, while I did not discover my destiny until I was almost 40, which proved to me that I was not as intelligent as the rest of my family and that I was a failure.

I believed this deeply for years, and if somebody complimented me on a moment of intelligence, I would think, "I certainly have them fooled." This belief had grown to such enormous proportions that I was defenseless in the face of the Judger's relentless cruelty. When the Judger pointed out to me the million ways that I was stupid, it sounded exactly like an accomplished trial lawyer who had prepared an ironclad brief with footnotes and a bibliography as thick as an encyclopedia.

Being so completely convinced by the Judger that I was inept and stupid, I didn't have a clue about who I really was. As I have discovered how to relate to the Judger, I have learned how to watch it. As I have discovered how not to be seduced by its voice, its ironclad case for my stupidity has dissolved in the light of my attention. And I have discovered that, underneath its conversation, the exact opposite of what I thought myself to be is true—that I have an innate Intelligence that helps me to live a skillful and compassionate life!

SEEING THROUGH THE JUDGER

Our task is not to seek for Love. It is to seek for all of the barriers that we have built that stand in the way.

A Course in Miracles

As we reflect on these four dynamics of the judger—

1) That we all have this judging quality of mind and are not defective for having taken it on;

2) That it was born out the need to have a part of us monitor our behaviors in order to survive and feel safe;

3) That it doesn't accept the value of making mistakes;

4) That it has no idea of who we really are;

there comes a possibility of being able to *see it* rather than being run by it. From this perspective, we don't need to judge the Judger. Our freedom comes when we can relate to these ancient patterns of our story rather than hating or fearing what they are saying. In order to do this we have to get to know these voices. At the beginning it can feel a little like going to confront the fire-breathing dragon in its cave. Much to my amazement, as I journeyed to the dark cave of my self-judgment, instead of finding a destructive monster, I found Puff the magic dragon!

I was given an inkling that maybe the Judger wasn't as all-powerful as I had thought during a retreat Stephen Levine was giving at Breitenbush Retreat Center in Oregon. We were doing small group processes in which my self-cruelty was making itself well-known. A counselor in my group came up to me afterwards and said, "I notice that you have a very highly developed self-critical voice. Would you like to do an experiment with me?"

I was willing to do almost anything to get relief, so I went outside with her and we sat on a swing. She asked me to close my eyes and get a picture of what this voice would look like. I froze. "You never do anything right," said the Judger, "and you aren't going to be able to do this." With her gentle coaxing, I was finally able to see an image of a tall, fierce and very hard old man. He looked like an evil wizard with dark and powerful robes swirling around him. He was standing on top of a mountain, looking down at me with fire pouring out of his eyes. His arm was stretched out in front of him with his index finger pointing out the depth of my imperfection. I cringed when this image developed in my mind. It was so accurate and felt so real.

"Now," she said, "do something funny to him." I froze again. "Do something funny? With him? You've got to be kidding," I thought. I made a feeble attempt. The mountain began to crumble away but he kept his footing, and the finger never stopped pointing at me. Then, in a flash, and from where I do not know, an eagle flew over and pooped in his face! You should have seen his astonished look and felt the laughter bubble up from within me. It was a powerful moment. For my whole life I had believed whatever he said. In that instant, this ancient voice lost its power.

Of course it came back again, but that tiny bit of spaciousness allowed the seed of curiosity to grow, and I began to pay attention, becoming fascinated with what my Judger said about me. I then noticed that as I began to watch, it would hide, becoming very subtle. So I carried around a notebook, and when I became aware of a moment of judging, I would write down what the Judger said.

At the beginning, it was easier to see myself judging other people, but it quickly became evident that all my judgments of others were simply the fallout from my own self-judgment. Whether it was about their looks, actions or thoughts, they were a mirror of my own self-talk. Then I would come home and write these snippets of conversation from the judging mind on a large piece of newsprint tacked to my wall. Over the months I began to be able to see definite patterns in my style of judging and hear more clearly this litany that traveled with me everywhere.

True freedom from the self-cruelty of our minds comes from noticing what the Judger is saying and realizing it is only a belief system that was woven out of our disconnection from Life and an attempt to find safety. To see it, we need to become a *judger sleuth*, with magnifying glass and pen light in hand, exploring and looking for the ways in which our Judger operates.

There are numerous ways to do this. A daily sitting meditation practice is a fertile place to watch the judging mind. When most people begin meditating, their mind is like a puppy dog, wandering here and there, chasing after the mailman and keeping everybody up all night long with its barking. We all assume that a *good meditator* is one whose mind is trained to *heel and behave*. Even though my teachers repeatedly said that this wasn't so, the judging, comparing mind inside of me was so thick and heavy that these words didn't diminish my self-judgment. Every time I found my mind wandering, I would jerk myself back with the judgment, "Bad mind."

Gradually, I moved beyond this mean and painful attitude until I could bring myself back with more mercy. But the roots of the judging mind went so deep that I lived for years comparing one time of meditation over another and berating myself for not being concentrated enough. The way out of this maze of struggle was to see this judgment and bring to it a tender heart.

You can also get to know the Judger as you move throughout your day. It can be helpful in the beginning to write down what you discover. When I was doing this, it was as though I became a reporter doing an article on self-judgment and needing to go out and gather information. This allowed me to be curious about the activity of self-judgment rather than hiding from it or judging the judgment. If this calls to you, carry a small notebook or a voice activated recorder with you, because the Judger shows up at the least expected times. Whenever you notice a moment of self-judgment, make a note of what it says as soon as you can.

It is usually easier in the beginning to notice your judgments of others. It is something that we all do all day long as a safety valve for our own self-judgments. There is no accident whom you judge. The key is to pay attention to who really bugs you. *They carry for you a disowned, disliked part of yourself.* As you pay attention—without judging yourself for how much you judge and without having to figure out what a particular judgment means—these external judgments will reveal to you your own internal self-judgment.

Another very constructive way to see the Judger is to create a gestalt experience, sitting in one chair and placing an empty chair in front of you. When you move to the other chair, become the Judger, looking back at yourself and saying all of the things that disgust you about yourself. Then write down all that it said. You could also use a tape recorder so you can hear the nuances of its litany. Allow it free reign to vent so you can see its story. If dialogue is not your style, you can dance it out, shouting into the space around you these ancient voices.

The key is to do something that allows you to see these voices and get to know how they operate. The old adage, "knowledge is power" is very applicable here. The more I got to know my Judger, the less I bought into what it was saying. When it roared through with one of its favorite voices such as "I can't do this because I am not good enough...or powerful enough...or smart enough," I could now notice, "Ahh, this is the Judger," rather than believing what it was saying.

To bring the Judger to the light of day, it is also skillful to keep a journal in which you actually write to this quality of your mind. You put on paper all of your hopes and fears, your rage and confusion, your desire to heal. Write of the agony these voices have brought into your life and the grief that they leave behind. Let flow out the rage you feel for being constantly watched by the Judger and the fear that you will never be good enough. When there is space around the rage, grief and fear, speak of your longing to come back into the healing of your heart.

It is essential in this journal to allow the Judger to write back to you so you can hear its side of the story. It is a part of you. It was birthed from the need for love and the requirement that you be a particular way in order to get it. You have sent judgment into your Judger. You have sent hatred into that which hates you. You have tried to annihilate it, deny it and destroy it. It has important things to say to you, a perspective on the dance of your life you may never have heard before.

At the beginning it may need to point out again all of your imperfections, but as you give it space to rant and rage, and as you learn how to not believe the content of what it is saying, its inherent wisdom and benevolence will begin to show up. I have learned much about my Judger in this way and I believe that this process was one of the most important steps I took in forgiving this voice that had tortured me for so long.

It can also be helpful to make a list in your journal of all of the things that you like about yourself. When I was first asked to make such a list, I went back to my therapist the next week and said I could not think of one thing to put down. He asked me, "Did you take a shower before you came today?" "Yes," I said. "Did you pick up the bath mat afterwards?" "Yes, I did," I responded. Number one on my list was "I pick up bath mats." That was the level I had to begin at.

This list can help you to be kind to yourself when the Judger takes over again, as it will. In addition, you can make a list on one side of a page of all of the things you most don't like about yourself. And then beside each one, write down what the exact opposite quality would be and begin to contemplate the possibility that this is who you really are.

162

Another useful skill is to work with a mirror. In the beginning you may not be able to even look at yourself without waves of self-judgment. In that phase you can gather much input for your judger journal. I did mirror work quite consistently for a long period of time. I didn't see the depths of the results until one evening, while getting ready to turn off the lights and crawl into bed, I saw my reflection in the window and had an immediate burst of tender-hearted love. What a difference from the first experiences of trying to look at myself in a mirror! Now the mirror has become my ally. If an old pattern of judging has come to roost, all I have to do is look in the mirror and give myself a wink, and the old belief dissolves.

If you have a trusted friend or counselor, it can also be very healing to have a place where you share the conversation that goes on in your head, and, if there is deep trust, parts of your journal as well. It is essential that this person be somebody who just listens rather than trying to fix, judge or rearrange the contents of your mind. It is also important that they have a heart you can basically trust.

Even though it feels risky to name and then share with others what we have hated about ourselves, the pay off is marvelous. There was a woman who shared a secret in one of my Awakening groups. In return, she was received with great heart and understanding. At the closing circle, she cried in relief, but when she called the next morning, lost again in self-judgment, she was certain that the group was just being nice and really wanted to reject her completely. This was not true, but that is the Judger's way.

Exploring how these voices got such a strong foothold in her again, it came down to one person in the group who had been silent the previous night when she was sharing. All of her fears of being worthless got projected onto this woman's silence. Knowing a lot about both of them, I had a strong sense that the silent woman was experiencing fear rather than judgment. Both women had similar fears and the silent one's fears were deeply triggered by the other woman's sharing.

When the woman on the phone could see this, the voice quieted down, and she was able to again feel the love that was there for her. This experience helped her to see that it was safe to share her voices of self judgement. Through this it became easier for her to bring the hidden parts of herself to the light of day in order to discover how off base they are. When the Judger is seen, its power is diminished tremendously.

As you become able—for moments—to see your self-judgment, it is skillful to give this part of your story a name. It makes it easier to relate to it rather than being lost in what it is saying. Before I had any ability to relate to this voice, when I was asked what I experienced when it was there, I said it was like standing on a tiny stage in the middle of a small, dark auditorium. Rising from every single side of this stage were tiers of bleachers, filled with black hooded, faceless beings all screaming their rage at my imperfections. I named these voices the Gallery. This name allowed me moments of not cowering in fear at what they had to say.

The next step was to get to know the various parts of the Gallery. As each of these voices of my litany started to become clear to me, the name turned into the Judger. Every time I was able to say, "Ahh, the Judger," (rather than saying, "I did that wrong, or I will never get it together, or why am I so stupid"), I took another step into freedom from these terrifying voices.

Now, as I have learned to become bigger than this ancient movement of self-hatred and as I have seen that the core intention of the Judger was to make me *good enough* for Love, the name has changed to the Guardian. It still comes through at times, especially when I am tired, but I don't have to identify with it. If I ever do, it is only for a short period of time before there comes welling up from my heart the Awareness that the Guardian is here trying to take care of me.

I can thank the Judger because it carved deep caverns in my heart and eventually cracked it wide open. I would not be who I am today without the fierceness of this voice. In days of old, warriors honored their opponents. They knew they would not come to the fullness of their potential without a great opposing force. I can see now that all of my life the Judger has held the key to the fullness of my potential. It has defined for me what is not Love so that what is Love could become evident. When I say "Thank you," it comes from the depths of my heart.

Once we get to know this ancient voice inside of each one of us, and once we learn how to respect it without buying into its litany, the Judger can return to its original purpose, discernment. We do need to make choices in this journey—sifting, comparing and sorting through myriad options. But we don't need to make ourselves and others right or wrong in the process. Discernment, a necessary tool for survival, is the Judger operating from the heart, allowing us to make skillful choices as we maneuver through our lives.

THE JUDGER AND THE HEART

That I feed the hungry, forgive an insult, and love my enemy...these are great virtues.
But what if I should discover that the poorest of the beggars and the most impudent of offenders are all within me,
and that I stand in need of the alms of my own kindness;
that I myself am the enemy who must be loved?
What then?

Carl Jung

The Judger is the glue that holds together the armor of the heart, and at the same time *it is the doorway into the heart*. Because it is the opposite of an open and present heart, it enables the true nature of the heart to be seen more clearly. We live in the level of duality. If there were no night, there would be nothing called day. Day needs a relationship with night in order to exist. It needs to be in relationship with its opposite. The same is true for the awakening heart. As Stephen Levine has said, "I learned how to be loving by seeing how unloving I am."

All true and lasting healing happens in the realms of inclusion, the place beyond struggle that only the heart knows. Joseph Chilton Pierce said, "The mind creates the abyss, the heart crosses it." After all of the trying and doing and understanding, it is when what has formerly been hated and feared drops into the inclusion of the heart that it is healed. The heart is the only place that can include it all—our strengths and our weaknesses, our clarity and our confusion, our pain and our joy, our dark and our light.

We yearn for this place of mercy, for the ability, at least for moments, to know and accept ourselves for who we truly are so that we then are free to meet our lives in clarity and compassion. We also long in our hearts to remember the sacredness of Life, both for ourselves and for our world.

Because we have traveled so far from our hearts, it is essential to consciously cultivate kindness, compassion, and mercy. We will now explore each of these more fully. If we seed these concepts in our minds so that they can begin to penetrate the thick walls of judgment and expectation that armor our hearts, we will see glimmers of the vast healing capabilities of an open heart.

Kindness

The first and most basic step in cultivating the inclusion of an open heart is the art of loving-kindness. Kindness is the visible activity of the heart. It is the healing of goodwill that says, "I want you to be happy." Underneath the struggling mind that turns people into objects and parts of ourselves into problems, lies a deep well of kindness that carries the capacity to heal the world. As Theodore Isaac Rubin said, "Kindness is more important than wisdom, and the recognition of this is the beginning of wisdom."

The afterglow from an act of kindness for someone else gives us glimpses of what it would be like to be kind to ourselves. Practicing kindness *out there* allows us to cut through our old conversations and gives us the impetus to be kind to the person in our own lives who is most in need of it—ourselves.

To be kind to ourselves is one of the most healing things we can do for all beings. For just like the violence that we do to ourselves ripples out into the world, so too does the kindness. If we can't relate with a heartfelt generosity to the piece of the planet we are sitting in, how can we possibly be kind to the rest? And yet we think this is selfish. Nothing could be further from the truth. To be kind to ourselves fosters kindness in the world.

In Buddhism, there is a wonderful practice called *metta*, the art of loving-kindness. In addition to sending loving kindness to all beings, it includes the phrase, "May I be happy, may I be free from suffering, may I know peace." It is a love song from ourselves to ourselves.

When I first began adding these to my daily practice, it was like peeling layers of an onion. There were days when I could truly wish the best for myself and there were days when all I could feel was my imagined unworthiness. Remembering that Awakening is the art of being with *what is*, I realized that wanting to reject any response of kindness highlighted to me how closed my heart was to myself. I learned that I could be kind to my response of being unable to be kind!

Through cultivating kindness, I am now able to keep my heart open to the formerly unacceptable parts of myself. I have also discovered that I can include in my heart the most heinous of criminals and even the people who have brought the most pain into my life. This doesn't mean that I like or condone their actions. It means that I am able to feel the common pool of pain out of which all of our unskillful actions come. In remembering that we all have known greed, fear, rage and delusion, given the right set of circum-stances, who knows what any of us may do? When I remember this, it then becomes possible to include them in my heart.

The power of a *metta* practice is that we can make it our own. We can listen carefully as to where we need to focus our kindness, whether it is ourselves, a friend or someone we have put out of our heart. Then we can create the words that awaken deep kindness within us. The traditional words—"May I be happy, may I be free from suffering, may I know peace"— can be used as a platform for our own phrases. At one retreat they transformed for me into, "May I be centered no matter what appears. May I know the joy of a loving and spacious heart. May I be vibrantly healthy and alive." At a time when I was meeting great terror, I said to this part of myself over and over again, "May I have the courage to meet you when you appear. May I meet you with a kind and compassionate heart. May I know the peace of remembering that you come from the Divine."

Metta practice is only one possible way of cultivating kindness for ourselves and others. Other ways to add it into our daily lives can be as simple as the willingness to live in the question, "How can I be kind to myself today?" Adding one kind thing we do every day (whether it is something for yourself or for another), paves the road to an open heart. It can also be as basic as imagining your breath moving through your heart every time a phone rings and allowing that breath to remind you to be merciful with yourself.

A powerful act of kindness is to make a commitment for just one day to replace every judging thought we notice with one that comes from tenderness and mercy. Another of my healing practices has become tenderly placing my hand over my heart whenever I find myself caught in judgment. I also rely upon calling to mind somebody with an open heart, imagining what they would do in any given situation. Sometimes it is a wise teacher, sometimes my children and sometimes it is a dear friend.

A phrase that I have learned that allows me to cut through the most contracted of my judgments of others is *just like me*. When I find myself judging another person as wrong and putting them out of my heart, saying "just like me" allows me to remember that we are all in this together. When we are judging, it is so easy to forget that we have also acted from the same unskillful places in our lives.

By far one of the most powerful acts of kindness we can do for ourselves is to receive kindness from others. When we react from our sense of unworthiness that says we aren't good enough to receive what is being offered, we do a great disservice to the person who has come into our lives bearing gifts of kindness. By hiding from or rejecting kindness, we deny them the joy of giving and the depth of healing that can come from these acts.

It is not only people we receive kindness from. It comes from Nature too. We can live because the sun gives of itself every moment of our lives. Rather than recognizing how much it is showering us with its generosity, we either completely ignore this bountiful giving, or else we take it for granted. The wind loves to caress our cheeks and play with our hair. The Earth loves to hold us as we dance through space. We are so loved by Life, but in our failure to receive these gifts, we feel disconnected and alone.

Whatever you choose as a kindness practice, know that cultivating kindness for ourselves and for other is one of the most powerful gifts we can give to the world. Alfred Adler said, "There is a law that man should love his neighbor as himself. In a few hundred years, it should be as natural to mankind as breathing or the upright gait; but if he does not learn it, he must perish." To become kindness itself is a process which often feels exactly like learning how to play a musical instrument. Evoking from the instrument the sweetest music it is capable of takes practice, and some days will be easier than others. But the rewards that come from cultivating an open heart are so well worth it. The healing that is possible for ourselves and for our world—the healing that comes only from an inclusive heart—is beyond our wildest imagination.

The Awakening of Compassion

If kindness is the natural activity of an open heart, then compassion is its fuel. This is the capacity to respond rather than react to the pain that is inherent in living, meeting it from the spaciousness of the heart. Our usual reaction to pain and suffering is to slam closed the door of our heart through judgment, fear and opposition. Oftentimes our favorite chant is, "Oh shit!" Whether we cut our hand, have an auto accident, or meet a sudden death, "Oh shit" characterizes our knee jerk reaction of resistance.

This doesn't just happen in traumatic situations. For many of us "Oh shit" is a core chant of our lives. Pain is seen as something to fear, something to resist, a mistake, an error. Every non-compassionate reaction to pain (our own or others') adds another layer of armoring around our hearts, keeping us locked out of our own lives.

But pain is a part of life in a body. We've all had our hearts broken, our toes stubbed, our hopes disappointed, our trust betrayed. The depth to which we meet pain with contempt and resistance is the depth to which we will be locked out of the healing of our heart. *Compassion is the ability to feel pain—both our own and others'—without falling into it.* It is the art of meeting whatever happens with an open heart and is the great re-weaver of the tattered threads of our lives.

Even though the dictionary defines compassion as the ability to feel another's pain, where it is truly learned is with our own pain. The schoolroom of compassion is our own lives—our own fears, rages and judgments, and our own addiction to acting from the mind rather than responding from the heart.

Compassion is the ability to bring mercy into all those parts of ourselves we haven't yet accepted. It is moving out of a project mentality and into the meeting of ourselves exactly where we are. A wonderful definition of compassion is "nonviolent accompaniment." We do great violence to ourselves by constantly trying to get rid of our pain. Compassion is the willingness to let go of that violence and be present for the ebb and flow of pain in our lives. From that comes the joy of being able to *accompany* ourselves—no matter what is appearing—down the path of our lives.

The quickest way to move beyond pain is not to resist it. In seeing and accepting who we are in this living moment, we begin to have a taste of freedom. By being fully with ourselves no matter what is appearing, the clouds will begin to part and we will discover our own true nature. This is the magical doorway into the mystical union of our most profound teachings, and yet this meeting is so alien to us. We are extremely skilled in bruising ourselves where we are already bruised, in finding the places inside of ourselves that are the most broken, the most painful, the most incomplete and claiming that they are just clear evidence that we are defective. We are also steeped in the illusion that pain is to be feared. It takes courage to see how brutal we are with our own pain. It takes courage to make space for all that we have held in contempt for so long. And it takes courage to allow ourselves into the light of our own hearts.

The phrase we explored in Chapter 5—*this too*—is a powerful awakener of compassion. When I am caught and struggling, lost in the reactionary mind, these two words soften my response, allowing me to make space for whatever is. *This too* says that I don't have to fight this, resist this, war with it. *This too* says yes to even the most painful aspects of my life—that they can be included in the journey of Awakening.

Oprah Winfrey, when describing the gifts Maya Angelou had brought into her life, said one of the most powerful ones came from a moment of great despair. Sitting on her bathroom floor and crying so hard she could barely speak, she called Maya. While Oprah was trying to describe the situation through a torrent of tears, Maya said, "Stop right now, and say thank you!" In other words, include the pain. The willingness to meet whatever comes with an open heart (*thank you* and *this too*) allows whatever *is* to move *through* our lives and keeps us out of the locked prison of resistance.

I once had a vivid experience of the healing that can come from these two statements. I was at a long meditation retreat in the high mountain desert of California. I had called in advance to see if the retreat staff could accommodate my special food needs. They assured me they could. I requested that a good amount of grains and vegetables be made up in advance and put in the retreatants' refrigerator so that I could heat up my own food and not have to bother the kitchen staff at every meal. They agreed that this was a good idea. When I arrived at the center, I put my request in writing and also spoke to one of the cooks.

It took two days and a couple of requests before I got some of the grain that I had requested. And it was not until the 4th night, after numerous requests, that I went to the kitchen in frustration to communicate that I still hadn't received any vegetables, which constituted over half of my diet. Standing in a side hallway, I made my request again. The cook I was talking to pulled me into the kitchen and, in front of a number of the retreatants, proceeded to open the refrigerator and try to make the point with great energy that the veggies had been there all the time and that I was just not paying attention.

There were, of course, no veggies there and I began to argue back, knowing they had never been there. Finally, another one of the cooks, overhearing this rather intense discourse, brought the veggies out from a back refrigerator, one that retreatants had no access to. The veggies had indeed been made up, but they had never been made available to me.

As I walked out of there that night, I felt rage from not being heard and then deep self judgement for having made a scene. Awareness kicked in when I remembered *what is*. As curiosity took over, I was able to feel what was happening in my body and listen to it closely, and I recognized a core pattern of rage and hopelessness.

There could not have been a more perfect scenario for me to meet these core patterns that had been deeply embedded inside of me. I knew I had the opportunity to cut through them and give to myself what was not given when I was young—the ability to be present in a loving, caring and understanding way. My heart began to open. *"This too,"* I said, "I can meet myself here, too." All the resistance to being with the pain fell away, and with my heart I could touch this pain that had been running me my whole life.

Even though I was now meeting myself with compassion, I hadn't yet been able to do this with the other people who were part of this experience. Not only were they completely locked out of my heart, but I also felt great resistance about even being around them. It took a while to recognize that this rage was burning a hole in my own heart.

Asking Life to show me the way back into the healing of compassion, I began to focus more on the gifts that I was receiving rather than on the devastation. I could then see that every single one of these people was an essential player in this necessary but painful awakening of my heart. I couldn't have unearthed this deep core of pain inside of me without their assistance in triggering it.

At times my mind would flip into judgment ("They did it wrong"), justification ("I did it right") and self-judgment ("I handled it wrong, and I can't possibly go into the kitchen tomorrow"). But then I would return to gratitude for their soul willingness to show up in my life this way and the deep heart remembering of how easily we all can act unskillfully in our lives. At the end of the retreat, when we broke silence, I also able to thank the cook who played such a big role in this healing.

It is usually a lot easier in the beginning of Awakening to give compassion to others than it is to give it to ourselves and yet we are the place that most needs it. No matter how great our intention is to be compassionate, we will, over and over again, become unconscious and slip back into the judging, comparing and easily irritated mind. These are the moments where true compassion is forged in the face of its opposite, in the face of how much we still believe in separation and judgment. Cultivating compassion for ourselves and for how all-too-human we can be, allows us to see all beings through benevolent eyes. Through kindness and compassion, prejudice, judgment, comparing and irritation give way to connection, communion and unity.

Mercy

Sometimes when our heart is first awakening or when we come across a place that we have always resisted, it can seem like the armor around our heart will never give way. In times such as these there is nothing more powerful than the healing of mercy—mercy for how closed our hearts can be to ourselves and mercy for how unmerciful we can be to others. Mercy says that for this moment I chose to not send any more pain into my pain. It is the invitation to stop harming or punishing ourselves and others for the places where we all are the most unconscious.

There is no greater power than the merciful heart. Even the word mercy has a healing influence. At a Stephen Levine workshop, a woman at the microphone spoke from the pain in her life, but she shared it from that place of hating it, hating herself and hating the world. The energy in the room began to contract the longer she shared. When Stephen began to gently but repeatedly say,

"Mercy; have mercy; have mercy on yourself," the room transformed from reaction to response. There is not one of our challenges, drawbacks or difficulties that can withstand the power of a merciful heart. And there is not one person in this world who is not deserving of this, too.

A dear friend of mine was in a major transition time. A very important relationship, along with her job and her home were all changing. These are the times where our deepest grief can slip through the cracks of our vulnerability. On the way home from a particularly trying day, she witnessed a family of ducks heading onto the freeway directly in front of a speeding bus. Because there was a fence between her and the freeway, there was nothing she could do. She pulled over to the side of the road and sobbed a river of tears. Instead of being cleansed by this upswelling, she found herself caught in confusion, panic and self-judgment, hating herself for her vulnerability.

Sitting in misery in front of her fireplace later that evening, a memory from her childhood surfaced. She saw herself sitting on a stool in a warm and cozy kitchen, while her favorite aunt made her cocoa and toast. She was filled with the care and tenderness of that act. This remembering moved her into the same level of tenderness and mercy with herself. She said that the transition was so dramatic that it was as if all of the heartache and despair of the past few weeks had been a dream and she was finally awake. The ability to meet herself as if she were a beloved child, even in the most vulnerable of places, transformed her experience.

Again, just as with kindness and compassion, the most powerful place we can learn mercy is with ourselves.

In your mind's eye, see yourself as a baby. Watch yourself learn how to walk and talk, full of curiosity and play. See your beauty and innocence. Feel your core longing to love and be loved.

Now pull into your consciousness an embarrassing situation from those early years—possibly a teacher shaming some work or a failure at sports. Experience for a moment the devastation that comes from the child's perspective— the contraction, horror and self-judgment. Now meet this place from the well of mercy that truly sees how deeply you needed to be comforted and heard.

Move on to your teenage years and the agony and ecstasy of the dating game. Again allow into your mind a time of unease and confusion. Meet it from the place of mercy that recognizes that awkwardness was a natural response to this very powerful (but completely new for you) dance of mating.

Now, come into adulthood and draw forth another experience that you wouldn't want to share with anyone. Feel how it is more difficult to access mercy when the judger keeps a tight fist around the heart—"I should have known better; I never do anything right; I always make wrong choices." Put it all aside for a moment, and breathe through your heart. Suspend all judgment and be merciful.

This is a very long, very challenging and very complicated journey we are all on, and no matter what it looks like, we are all trying to do the best we know how, including you. Raise your hand and place it over your heart, and say, "mercy," a number of times. Be willing for at least this moment to be accepting of this being whom you have held in judgment for so long.

A wonderful tool for accessing mercy is the "As Is, I'm Here" meditation. After discovering the circle of your breath, you say silently to yourself, "As is" (on the in breath). "As is" is the place of merciful spaciousness, the willingness to allow ourselves to be exactly as we are in this moment. It is the art of letting go of struggling with whatever is (our usual mode), and moving into the release that comes from welcoming it. "I'm here" (on the out breath) is the willingness to be keenly curious and attentive to *what is*, in a way that invites us into being present with Life exactly as it is appearing.

This meditation is the gift of meeting ourselves for exactly who we are— the light and the dark, the clear and the confused, the kind and the mean, the acceptable and the unacceptable. It is an invitation beyond the seemingly endless struggle to be what we *think* we should be. This gives us moments, however fleeting, when everything is okay, no matter how it feels. It is the willingness to embrace all of the parts of our being so we can receive the nourishment we are hungry for, from the source that really matters, ourselves.

A forgiveness practice is also a powerful awakener of mercy. Forgiveness is the art of meeting the unhealed—whether it is in ourselves or in another— with mercy. It is not about letting anyone "off the hook"— it's really not about another person at all. It is rather the activity of letting go of what has closed our own heart.

We have all been betrayed by people, by our body and by Life itself, but to hold onto the resentment, pain and bitterness can only cause us further pain. Just the intention to forgive someone or something that has wounded our heart is a tremendous step into our healing. From that intention, we can then let the process bring us to the heart. The roots of reaction and resentment are buried deep in all of our hearts. At times this practice will help us to see how closed our hearts still are and allow us to explore this armoring. At other times it will reawaken us to the spaciousness of an open heart, allowing our ancient pains to float in the healing of mercy.

Much has been written on forgiveness of others and even of ourselves. Very little has been written on forgiving the parts of ourselves that we have hated and feared, keeping us locked out of our own hearts. To forgive a difficulty in our body, a quick temper, and even the Judger itself, mends together the parts that make up the whole of who we are.

After reading this meditation, put down the book and allow into your mind an element of you that you most wish would be gone. It could be a part of your body (small chest, big nose), an emotional pattern (rage, self-pity) or a difficult part of your mind (judgment, lust). In the beginning, start with something that you have touched, for at least moments, with an open heart. If you go straight to that which causes the most contraction, it will only close your heart more if you are then unable to forgive.

When you have chosen something to forgive, either feel it in your body, see a personification in your mind, or imagine it in a chair in front of you. Say to it, "I am here to invite you back into my heart." If this brings up rage or fear, tell this part how you feel. Then go on, "I may fear you and even hate you, but even bigger than that is my desire to heal my heart. You have caused me much pain in my life. I am beginning to realize that you are an essential part of the community of my being, and I forgive you."

As you say these words, breathe this part into your heart. Struggling with it has only generated more pain in your life. "I forgive you for all of the embarrassment, for all of the agony, for all of the upsets you have caused. I now want to allow you back into the healing of my heart. I have grown immensely from your presence in my life, and rather than seeing you as an enemy—as a defect in my being—I realize you come from my soul to awaken my heart. I forgive you."

Into this space see if there is anything you would like to say to this part, trusting your own heart. When this feels complete, let it go, reminding yourself that no matter what your life looks like, your intention is to heal your heart.

It is also important to ask for forgiveness. Every time you have put it out of your heart, it received another load of hatred and fear from you rather than wisdom and compassion. Realizing this, say to it, "I ask you to forgive me for how much I have hated you. Rather than including you as a part of me, knowingly and unknowingly I have sent hatred and violence your way. I ask now that you forgive me for my ignorance, forgetfulness, confusion and rage. I did not see that you were sent from my soul to awaken me. I did not see that it is in letting you back into my heart that we are both healed. I ask that you forgive me for constantly warring with you."

Into this spaciousness allow this part to speak to you. Like all pain, it just wants to be heard. Be not dismayed if it is rage and hurt that you hear. Most of us have sent great violence into these disowned parts, and, as with all relationships, it takes time to heal. Listen carefully, for there is great wisdom there, and it has been waiting for the opportunity to share it with you. When you are done, thank it for whatever it has said, and let it go.

Now include the totality of your being in this forgiveness—the likable and the unlikable, the known and the unknown, the contracted and the spacious, the light and the dark—and say to yourself, "I forgive you," adding your name at the end of that phrase. "For all of the mis-takes in your life, for all of the reactions of a closed heart, I forgive you _____. I see now that you are an awakening being and every single experience of your life was necessary on the journey. I forgive you." Allow yourself back into the merciful heart.

If the mind throws up all of the reasons why you can't be forgiven, watch how unkind the mind can be, and permit this hard edge to be forgiven. Repeat these words numerous times, allowing them to become your own, opening to a tender, caring relationship with yourself.

Now feel this mercy expanding out to all the people of the world. Imagine for a moment that every single person comes to know the power of an open heart. Imagine men, women and children meeting the unmeetable inside of themselves with compassion. Observe violent encounters transformed through the power of mercy. Say to everyone, "May all beings know the power of forgiving themselves. May all beings be free from the judgmental mind. May all of us know that in healing our hearts we heal the world.

There may be times when you say "I forgive you" that your heart slams closed in rage at how much agony this part of you has brought into your life. And there will be times when this part is not sure at all about trusting your new intention to heal. The power is in the intention, the willingness to at least explore forgiveness. And in those times when forgiveness brings up your inability to forgive, you can use them to explore the ancient armoring around your heart. Rather than trying to force your way through, you can then shift into forgiving the part of yourself that doesn't want to forgive!

Cultivating mercy, whether it is through the "As Is" meditation or a forgiveness practice is a ray of light in a cloudy, reactive and judgmental world. Even though the heart can close again in a flash and sometimes stay closed for what seems like an interminable time, do not discount the power of meeting the unmeetable, even for a moment, in the healing of the heart.

THE POWER OF NO

Perhaps those who, trembling most, maintain a dignity in their fate, are the bravest. Resolution on reflection is real courage.

Horace Walpole

There is an important piece we need to touch on to bring this all into balance. To live from the heart is not a passive activity. Too often, because we have lived in resistance for so long, when we look at the heart from a distance, we define it as passive—as occupying the place that is the opposite of force and resistance. This perspective translates kindness into "No matter what is happening, you smile." It changes compassion into the act of condoning unskillful actions. Nothing could be further from the truth. Sometimes the kindest thing we can do is to say "no."

Go back to the river analogy. When we use *not this* to try to fight the current of Life, we are left drained and exhausted. But when we allow the boat to turn around and follow the creative energy of the flowing river, *not this* becomes a tool for riding the rapids and *judgment* turns into *discernment*. It is the paddle that allows for a strong and determined action that keeps us in the main current and out of the backwaters and eddies. *Not this,* coupled with *this too* allows for creative engagement with the river.

There are no hard and fast rules about when the heart needs to be soft and tender and when it needs to be fierce and ferocious. Every single situation will require its own tailor-made response. But it is the heart speaking through the mind that will tell us what is appropriate and will allow for full, creative and compassionate engagement.

IT TAKES COURAGE TO HEAL

I believe that man will not merely endure; he will prevail. He is immortal, not because he alone among the creatures has an inexhaustible voice, but because he has a soul, a spirit capable of kindness and compassion.

William Faulkner

It takes courage to meet the armoring around the heart. And it takes courage to learn the art of navigating from the clear light of compassion and mercy rather than the judging and comparing perspective of the mind. But the rewards are well worth it. After moving through layers upon layers of the armoring around my own heart, I wrote in my journal:

Eons ago, even before remembering,
the doorway to my heart slammed shut—locked, sealed, fettered, bound and
deeply broken.
Slowly, as slowly as a flower appears out of Mystery,
it opened … and my dry and parched soul blooms in pure joy.
The winds of tenderness now cool me when I am hot
and warm me when I am cold.
And for this I am oh so grateful.

Becoming aware of what the Judger is doing and cultivating the heart brings us to the healing in which the mind drops into the heart. It was once said that the longest 18 inches ever measured is the distance from the mind to the heart. This is the healing being called for now on our planet, and it is happening in each one of our lives. Our part in the process is to take loving, healthy and wholesome care of the piece of the planet we are sitting in. We are living in the schoolroom of the heart, and we will be challenged over and over again to respond with the skills of inclusion rather than to react from the contraction of the comparing, judging mind. To be merciful to ourselves is to heal the world for all of the violence and greed we see on this planet comes from people whose hearts are closed to themselves and thus closed to their world. As we claim ourselves beyond struggle we take humanity one more step into the clear and inclusive space of the heart.

May we see beyond our endless need to compare ourselves to
some idea of what we should be.

May we have the courage to meet the unmeetable, in the
healing balm of compassion.

And may we know that each one of us holds within our hearts
the power to heal ourselves and the world.

Core Intention: I'm okay

Chapter 8
The Fertility of the Dark

CLOUD MOUNTAIN

Today my eyes are tired and my back is sore.
The tender morning light evades me
in the refrigerator hum of predawn.
When will my eyes shine and my step be lively?
They used to say it happened in the Promised Land.
But now I say it happens in those moments
when soreness clears a path to a tender heart.
Then behind tired bones a newborn dances
and vanishes like a hologram, like a glint of sunlight…
Like the dawning of a new day.

Dee Endelman

FEAR OF OUR PAIN

Enlightenment consists not only in seeing the luminous, but in making darkness visible. The latter is much more difficult, so it's far less popular.

Carl Jung

In the moment you are sitting here, reading this book, dew drops are reflecting the morning light; a rainbow of colors is appearing out of the heart of flowers; whales are singing their ancient tunes; babies who were just one seed nine months ago are taking their first breath; and wind is caressing ancient bristle cone pines high in the alpine mountains. All around us is a magical realm—earth, air, sun and water being woven over and over again into myriad fantastic forms.

Now notice where your Awareness has been primarily focused for the last 24 hours. Have you been present for this wondrous unfolding? Probably not. As we have been exploring all throughout this book, if you are like most people, your attention has probably been focused on your own individual struggles—big ones, little ones, scary ones and fun ones. If we watch what we are doing all day long, we can begin to see that we are usually *working at Life*. We are oriented towards struggle, lost in the land of always trying to make ourselves and our lives different than they are.

The image I often times use is that we are like little children completely focused on trying to unravel a ball of yarn, and all the while we are standing in paradise. As we have been exploring all throughout this book, we are so busy with our struggles that we are not *here* for Life. Beyond this very narrow focus is a reality—a safe, benevolent, trustable, magical and utterly fascinating reality—that is always with us no matter where we are and no matter what is happening. But we don't notice.

One of the primary reasons we don't notice is that we fear all levels of pain — physical, emotional and mental. In this fear we have become addicted to the endless struggle of trying to get rid of what we don't like in our lives and to go towards what we do. We can see this in our commercials (if you ate too much, just drink this antacid and you'll be able ignore the message in your discomfort and overeat again); it is evident in our religions (salvation is going to the light and leaving the dark behind); in our whole response to the aging process (the dramatic increase in plastic surgery, the billions of dollars spent on potions and lotions); and in our denial of death (the warehousing of the elderly and the sanitation of the dying process).

We want one side of Life (the pleasant) without the other (the unpleasant) and wonder why we are lost in struggle most of the time. "Don't respond to the pain in your life; just go towards the pleasant and the desirable and leave the rest behind" is our litany. If that doesn't work, we deny, blame and manipulate, absolutely certain that if Life is difficult, then something is wrong. This is broadcast from pulpits, the Congress, our therapists and especially ourselves.

In the belief that there is such a thing as a perfect and together human being, we have maimed, brutalized and tried to exorcise the weak and imperfect parts of ourselves. We struggle with what we don't like about our bodies, our minds, our emotions, our relationships, our communities and our world. We are conquerors, addicted to the belief that if we can manage Life by ignoring, denying, fixing or getting rid of what we don't like, then we will know lasting peace.

This approach denies that pain is a thread in the tapestry of Life and has an essential role in the scheme of things. It is as if we decided that the tide coming in is good and the tide going out is bad, completely ignoring the fact that it wouldn't work if the tide always came in. The land would flood, crops would die, and we'd have wet feet all the time! We fail to see that when the tide goes out, it then gathers up wonderful gifts from the sea—beautiful shells, water carved logs, rich communities of sea weed—and on its return, it deposits them on the shore.

If the tide of our physical, emotional and spiritual lives always came in, we would be stagnant creatures. Every single time our spiritual tide goes out, we are renewed and enriched by all the gifts it holds as it flows back in. Because of our refusal to see the essential nature of darkness and all of the gifts that it brings, we are caught off guard, absolutely amazed when the tide has gone out in our lives. We then look desperately for something or someone (often times ourselves) to blame. "Don't trust the ebb and flow of Life; don't listen to the pain and be responsible for what it is feeding back to you; just get rid of it," is the credo we live by.

We need to learn how to work with our pain in new ways, understanding that it is an integral part of Life. We need to learn how to include it rather than exclude it. To awaken our hearts so that we can heal, we need to recognize that each of us is destined to take on challenges in our lives, get lost in them and then finally bring them to the light of compassionate Awareness. As John Lee said in *Writing From The Body*, "Letting the shadow speak its peace is part of the process that leads us to the good stuff. If we can't let ourselves go deeply into the shadow, we may never reach the place in ourselves where tenderness resides."

Freedom comes when we learn to respond rather than react to the difficult in our lives. Whether it is a deeply challenged body, a broken heart, an abusive boss, deep rage, freezing cold, an overdue deadline or a dying friend, we can learn the power of relating to the overwhelming parts of our lives rather than being caught in their web. Pain then becomes an awakener, an ally and even a friend. As Stephen Levine has said, "Pain sucks, but it grabs our attention." The difficult in our lives is here to heal us, and our job is to learn how to pay attention. Let us begin by getting to know how our resistance to the uncomfortable keeps us caught in struggle.

VICTOR/VICTIM CYCLE

Your hand opens and closes and opens and closes.
If it were always a fist or always stretched open, you would be paralyzed.
Your deepest presence is in every small contracting and expanding,
the two as beautifully balanced and coordinated as bird wings.

Rumi

Our addiction to struggling with our pain moves back and forth between two extremes: the victor (powering over) and victim (overpowered). We all swing back and forth on this pendulum, experiencing joy when we feel we *have it all together* and despair when we think our pain will never end.

The victor says that a *successful* life is one in which our relationships are always well-oiled and running smoothly, we never have a compulsive urge, and we are *in control* financially, emotionally, physically and mentally. It is the fixing, changing, manipulating part of us that is irritated in rush hour traffic, believes that our lives would be better if only our mate would change, is hateful of those aging lines, and is absolutely certain that depression is an indication that something is wrong with us.

Its core belief is that difficulty and darkness are signs that we are not doing it "right." This part inside each of us says that if we just think positively, be proactive, take vitamins and exercise, we will not only be able to deal with everything that comes our way, but we will also be able to control what comes. The victor completely ignores the fact that there are forces far greater than itself that influence its life. It is like each one of us is a tiny inlet on the Oregon coast saying that we can control the entire Pacific Ocean. When something goes wrong with our efforts to get everything *in order* (as it is destined to do in the land of duality), the only conclusion we can come to is that we have done something wrong or haven't tried hard enough.

When trying to control doesn't bring us the results we yearn for, we slip into

181

the victim mode —the part that feels overpowered by Life. We so desperately want to feel sorry for ourselves when we are greatly challenged. We also are certain, somewhere deep inside of us, that challenges are here because we have done something wrong. The victim's litany is, "I can't do this; I've always failed before; it's too much; it's not fair; why am I being punished; what did I do to deserve this; I'll never get through this."

The victim mode looks out upon the world and says "they" can do "it," but I can't. It is often times accompanied by blame. If we can't find someone to pin it on (I had bad parents), then we turn it against ourselves, spinning down into a maze of self hate and despair. On the surface it looks like a position of powerlessness but the victim holds great power. It keeps us from dealing with what is uncomfortable (oh, its too much), and it demands that others react to the definition of us as fragile (never confronting, always being kind). *The victim is scrambling for control as much as the victor* is.

The victor is *me against it all*—against my life, my emotions, my body, my mind. The victim is *all of this against me*. The victor comes from the belief that I have to *do it all* and the victim's wail is "I can't." Both are *reactors* to the experience of living rather than *responders*. Both are based on fear—the fear that we are separate and disconnected from the Whole and that the entire responsibility for the unfolding of our lives is ours alone.

This addiction to struggle runs so deep that we never step back and examine whether it works or not. If we look carefully, it becomes evident that this approach to our lives only brings us moments of respite from the struggle of trying to our manage pain. We seem to get our lives together, only to have them dissolve into chaos again. We hide in the deeper realms of our consciousness the parts of our personality that we most hate and fear, only to have them subtly run our lives. We have learned to manipulate the appearance of things while sitting upon an ocean of pain, and we wonder why we are anxious behind the walls of our managing.

It is important to understand that we are talking about *becoming aware of*, not annihilating, the victor/victim mode, for it has a role to play in the Awakening human. Going back and forth between the two extremes is a part of Awakening. Rather than judging and trying to stop the endlessly swinging pendulum, it is far more helpful to begin to notice how we are functioning. In that awareness, the possibility of something new is born. From this noticing, it begins to dawn upon us that not only have we never been able to nail down perfection, but it is exactly this addiction to having everything together—this belief that *the good life* is one that is comfortable all the time—that keeps us caught in struggle.

Jim Henson's movie *The Dark Crystal* beautifully illustrates the integral relationship of dark and light. The movie revolves around a powerful crystal that is the centerpiece of a mythical land. When a shard of the crystal is lost, the crystal becomes dark and the land is divided between good and evil, with the evil forces occupying the castle and using the crystal's power to try to control the land. The forces of light are not the standard saviors, committed to destroying any trace of the dark side. They know the light, but are stuck in concepts and rituals that keep the dark and the light separate. When the shard of the crystal is found, the mystics begin a journey back to the castle. At the moment the shard of the crystal is put back into place, the creatures of both dark and light encircle the crystal and they *merge*. The crystal then becomes radiant and the land is restored. Jim Henson clearly understood the interdependent nature of the dark and the light in our world.

Until we wake up to our need to run away from our pain, we will never truly be free. Peace comes from learning how to ride the pendulum of joy and sorrow, loss and gain, loving and hating, fearing and trusting. So let us explore how we can respond to the challenges of Life in a way that ennobles and energizes rather than depletes and degrades.

There are five basic skills that will shift our relationship to our challenges:

1) The ability to trust that pain is an essential part of our lives.

2) The art of welcoming rather than resisting and fearing.

3) The skill of becoming curious—responding rather than reacting.

4) Naming the parts of ourselves that upset and disturb—in the naming, there is a part of us that is not lost in the experience.

5) Living in relationship with these dark forces—dialoguing, asking questions, listening and learning from them.

All of these skills allow our struggling mind to be touched by the vast healing of our hearts so that we can truly know the peace that we long for. Let us now explore each one in depth.

TRUSTING PAIN

NO OTHER WAY
Could we but see the pattern of our days,
we should discern how devious were the ways,
by which we came to this, the present time,
this place in life; and we should see the climb
our soul has made up through the years.
We should forget the hurts, the wanderings, the fears,
the wastelands of our lives, and know
that we could come no other way or grow
into our good without these steps our feet found hard to take,
our faith found hard to meet.
The road of life winds on and we like travelers go
from turn to turn until we come to know
the truth that life is endless and that we
forever are inhabitants of all eternity.

Martha Smock

What if pain was not a mistake? What if pain didn't mean that we screwed up, *they* screwed up, or God fell asleep on the job? What if each of us received our own measure of pain when we took on a body, not for punishment, but because it would be our teacher of Awareness and compassion? What if there were another way to work with pain, a way that allowed us to open up into a place that was bigger than struggle itself? And what if one of the greatest gifts we could give the world would be to move beyond struggling with our pain into being able to meet it with great compassion.

To open up to this possibility, we have to first explore the very novel idea that pain is not a mistake. Agnus Whistling Elk, a Native American shaman from Manitoba, spoke this truth in a most eloquent way:

If you look at something carefully, you will always be able to see its dark side. And yet we choose never to look into the shadows. Understand that it is what you choose not to observe in your life that controls your life. Everything begins with a circle of motion; without the positive and negative poles there would be no movement, no creation. Without the dark side, your beauty would not exist. Don't be afraid to look at both sides. You need them both. Honor all as part of the Great Spirit.

Everywhere we look, we can see the truth of Agnus's words: "Without positive and negative poles there would be no movement, no creation." This shows up in the atom, which is a combination of positive and negative charges. It is evident in the acid/alkaline balance in our body and in the fact that the opposites of male and female are necessary in the procreation of more complex life forms. It is also noticeable in the violence of Nature. Mountain ranges are born when two tectonic plates collide. New forests are brought forth after lightning fires.

The importance of the negative aspect of Life also shows up inside of ourselves. We need our pain, our imperfections, and our failures. We would not be who we are without them. The author Thomas Moore invites us into this spacious relationship with that which disturbs when he says:

> *This requirement that we have to be perfect, that we have to get ourselves emotionally right, is such a burden. The more we try, the worse it gets! And so we try one type of therapy after another. It's pretty defeating. See, soul really thrives in failure and imperfection. Jung said that soul moves at the weak point, where the personality is thin, where things are not secure and stable. That's where soul has an entry. We need those vulnerable points.*

On every level, in every experience, and in each being's existence, the dance of Life is a dance of dark and light. Darkness is rich and necessary, the place of fertility and creativity. Half of the Earth is always bathed in the dark of night. Out of black, moist dirt comes astounding creativity. Seeds, including us, incubated away from the light, and plants do their growth work in the dead of night. The same is true for our emotional and spiritual life. Each of us was given pairs of opposites, a desire to awaken and great resistance, vast courage and deep fear, raw hatred and an awakening heart. The opposites are our teachers. In a way, the dance of our lives is about cooking the opposites until they blend into the rich soup of our potential.

Brian Swimme, in his video series *Canticle to the Cosmos,* reveals the necessity of the challenges of our lives through the example of a hawk that wants all obstacles to catching its prey removed. When this great hunter demands that the mouse slow down so that it is easy to catch, the hawk's speed is no longer necessary, so it begins to diminish. With further reduction of the mouse's ability to run and hide, the hawk would then not need to fly anymore for it could simply walk after the slow moving mouse, and so its majestic wing feathers drop away. Wishing the mouse to become immobile, the hawk's keen eyesight would not be required, for it could stumble around and bump into its meal. Asking to receive its desires with no obstacles in the way, the hawk's unique beauty would vanish as its razor sharp eyesight, its soaring flight, and its awesome accuracy disipated.

He goes on to say that, embedded deep in the hawk's heart, is the desire for its enemy to flourish, for it knows that *in engagement with the obstacles in its life is the birth of itself.* Brian concludes, "It is only in this engaged life, this marriage with our enemies...that we can discover who we are, what our creativity is and what our destinies are."

To trust the benevolence of Life, especially around the challenges of our lives, is to transform our relationship to Life from one of struggle to one of creative response. Rather than being caught in the victor/victim cycle, we can enter the moment no matter what is appearing with a sense of adventure, a keen curiosity and a compassionate heart. Christopher Reeve, in his first interview after falling from his horse and becoming paralyzed, said,

> *Either the Universe is totally random, and it's just molecules colliding all the time in total chaos, and our job is to make sense of chaos. Or you could say sometimes things happen for a reason, and your job is to discover the reason. But either way, I see meaning and opportunity, and that has made all the difference.*

The healing we yearn for comes from a shift of perspective about the role that challenges have in our lives. Christopher spoke about the terror and despair he felt when he first grasped the enormity of what had happened. He had moments of wanting to die. Meeting something he had no power to stop or change offered the possibility of either ensnaring him in a web of rage and self-pity, or else of transforming his life.

When his son came running into the room yelling "Daddy, Daddy," he realized in that moment that he was much more than his crippled body, and that he was needed. From this perspective, he began to discover the "meaning and the opportunity." His life now has a deeper purpose than before the accident. He has become a spokesperson for spinal cord injuries and is truly making a difference in other people's lives. But he is doing so much more. He is inspiring a society to acknowledge that the challenges in our lives can ennoble, heal and inspire us.

There is another wonderful example of this in *Stories of the Spirit, Stories of the Heart* by Jack Kornfield. A physician speaks about a 24 year-old man who lost his entire leg to bone cancer. At first he was very angry and bitter, caught in a strong sense of injustice and a very deep hatred for all well people. After working with him for awhile, the doctor noticed a profound shift. The young man began coming out of his victim role and out of himself. He started to visit other people who had suffered severe physical loses, being present for them in their grief process as the doctor had been for him and offering a living example of the healing power of accepting *what is.*

A year later, this young man met with the doctor to review their work together. They came across a picture he had drawn right after losing his leg. It was of a vase, and running through it was a deep black crack. This was the image he had of his body right after he had lost his leg. He had perceived himself as an irrevocably broken human being. In response to the picture he said, "Oh, this one isn't finished." He picked up a yellow crayon and putting his finger on the crack he said, "You see here—where it is broken? This is where the light comes through." And with the yellow crayon, he drew light streaming through the crack in the vase, through the crack in his life.

To get a sense of how profound it would be to begin to trust pain rather than always struggling with it, let us go on a journey together:

After you read through this exercise, put down this book, close your eyes, and take a few deep breaths. Begin to notice the living moment of your life—breath rising and falling, pressure from the support you are sitting on, the warmth or coolness of the room. In your mind's eye, see the Earth in all of its beauty—the blues and browns and the swirling white clouds.

Now think of all the suffering that humans have experienced on our planet—terrorist attacks, starving children in Africa, men who have died agonizing deaths alone on a battlefield, people dying of painful diseases in all parts of the world. Feel what happens in your body as you resist this—your body tightens, your mind closes down and your heart aches.

Shift your perspective, and accept for a moment the essential nature of darkness in this land of duality. Trust that it is here not to curse the world or because we are miserable sinners. Know that it comes from the same creativity that molded mountains and birthed stars. Notice what happens in your body as you let go of railing against these dark forces and begin to honor the fertility of the dark.

Now go back to hating and fearing these forces, and see what happens in your body. Feel the outrage and the unwillingness to let go of struggling with these forces, and feel how this energy ricochets around your body, upsetting your inner balance and equilibrium.

Now go back again to the perspective of an awakening world and of trusting the fertility of the dark. When you are ready, come back to your Awareness of the physical world around you and open your eyes. Your life, like the Universe, is made up of great darkness, brilliant light and everything in between. For a moment, just sit in the center of it all.

This is not to condone hurtful acts. There have been many unspeakably cruel things that people have done to other people. The point is that we've tried warring with them, and it doesn't work. We're seeing that fighting them will never solve these problems. We'll just find ourselves addressing them with the same mind that created them in the first place—the mind that perceives light as good and dark as bad. Healing comes in a shift of perspective and takes the radical and courageous step of trusting darkness. In this trust we can then respond to pain—both our own and everybody else's—from a clearer, kinder, more skillful place.

Each of us will have deeply challenging experiences in our lives. By changing our definition of what pain is about and thus, ultimately, our relationship to pain, we can learn how to use these experiences to empower and heal our lives rather than to devastate and destroy. Both Christopher Reeve and the young man who lost a leg were catapulted out of a narrow definition of who they were and what they can give to Life. These challenges eventually brought much more into their lives than they took away. These two men literally became more alive because of their challenges.

The question we are living in is, "How can we change our relationship to pain in our daily lives, both the deep ones and the more ordinary ones? How can we make this shift without having to wait for the big guns of heartbreak, disease and death?" We've already taken the first step by exploring the essential and ultimately benevolent nature of our challenges in our lives. The next step is to actually make room for what we most hate and fear.

INCLUDING OUR PAIN

Pain stayed with me so long I said today,
"I will not have you with me anymore."
I stamped my foot and said, "Be on your way,"
And then paused, startled at the look he wore.
"I who have been your friend" he said to me.
"I who am your teacher—
all you know of understanding Love and sympathy,
And patience, I have taught you. Shall I go?"
He spoke the truth, this strange unwelcome guest.
I watched him leave and knew his words were wise.
He left a heart grown tender in my breast.
He left a far clearer vision in my eyes.
I dried my tears and lifted up a song.
Even for one who tortured me so long.

Author Unknown

None of us have the power to keep pain from our lives, and each of us will continue to be taught by challenges until our last breath. From a limited perspective, walling ourselves off from pain looks like a good idea. We resist, deny and then fight it with all of our might when it breeches our barricades. But a wall is a wall. It may serve to keep our darkness at bay for short periods of time, but it also walls us off from Life. The depth to which we refuse to be aware of our pain is the depth to which we are separate from Life. The radical notion of not fighting our pain is the doorway to freedom.

There is a wonderful story told by Jack Kornfield in his book *Stories of the Spirit Stories of the Heart* about Terry Dobson, a man who was studying Aikido in Japan. Having put in eight hours of training nearly every day for three years, he thought he was tough. He especially liked to throw and grapple. The trouble was, his martial art skills were untested in actual combat, for students of Aikido were not allowed to fight. "Aikido," his teacher had said again and again, "is the art of reconciliation. Whoever has the mind to fight has broken his connection with the Universe. If you try to dominate people, you are already defeated. We study how to resolve conflict, not how to start it."

Even though Terry understood this intellectually, in his heart he wanted an absolutely legitimate opportunity whereby he might "save the innocent by destroying the guilty." One day he found himself on a train, lumbering through the suburbs of Tokyo. The car he was in was relatively empty and quiet, when all of a sudden, as the doors opened at the next station, the quiet was shattered by a man bellowing violent, incomprehensible curses. He staggered into the car, drunk and dirty. Screaming, he swung at a woman holding a baby. The blow sent her spinning into the laps of an elderly couple. Terrified, the couple jumped up and scrambled toward the other end of the car. The laborer aimed a kick at the retreating back of the old woman but missed as she scuttled to safety. The train lurched ahead, the passengers frozen with fear. Terry then goes on to describe what happened next.

I stood up and said to myself, "This is it! People are in danger, and if I don't do something fast, they will probably get hurt." Seeing me stand up, the drunk recognized a chance to focus his rage. "Aha," he roared. "A foreigner! You need a lesson in Japanese manners!" I looked at him with disgust and dismissal. I planned to take this turkey apart, but he had to make the first move. I wanted him mad, so I pursed my lips and blew him an insolent kiss. He gathered himself for a rush at me.

A split second before he could move, someone shouted "Hey!" It was startling. I remember the strangely joyous, lilting quality of it—as though you and a friend had been searching diligently for something and he suddenly stumbled upon it. "Hey!"

I wheeled to my left, the drunk spun to this right. We both stared down at a little old Japanese man. He must have been well into his seventies, this tiny gentleman, sitting there immaculate in his kimono. He took no notice of me, but beamed delightedly at the laborer, as though he had a most important, most welcome secret to share.

"C'mere, and talk with me." He waved his hand lightly. The big man followed as if on a string. He planted his feet belligerently in front of the old gentleman and roared, "Why the hell should I talk to you?" The drunk now had his back to me. If his elbow moved so much as a millimeter, I'd drop him in his socks.

The old man continued to beam at the laborer. "What'cha been drinkin'?" he asked, his eyes sparkling with interest. The drunk barked back, "I been drinkin' sake, and it's none of your business!"

"Oh that is wonderful," the old man said, "absolutely wonderful. You see, I love sake too. Every night, me and my wife (she's 76, you know), we warm up a little bottle of sake and take it out into the garden, and we sit on an old wooden bench. We watch the sun go down and we look to see how our persimmon tree is doing. We worry about whether it will recover from those ice storms we had last winter." He looked up at the laborer, eyes twinkling.

As he struggled to follow the old man's conversation, the drunk's face began to soften. His fists slowly unclenched. "Yeah," he said. "I love persimmons too..." His voice trailed off.

"Yes," said the old man, smiling, "and I'm sure you have a wonderful wife."

"No," replied the laborer. "My wife died." Very gently, swaying with the motion of the train, the big man began to sob. "I don't got no wife, I don't got no home. I don't got no job. I'm so ashamed of myself." Tears rolled down his cheeks; a spasm of despair rippled through his body.

The train arrived at my stop. As the doors opened, I heard the old man cluck sympathetically. "My, my," he said, "that is a difficult predicament. Sit down and tell me about it."

I turned my head for one last look. The laborer was sprawled on the seat, his head in the old man's lap. The old man was softly stroking the filthy, matted hair.

As the train pulled away, I sat down on a bench. What I had wanted to do with muscle had been accomplished with kind words. I had just seen Aikido tried in combat, and the essence of it was Love.

The old man was neither the victor nor the victim. He didn't *react* to the laborer, he *responded*. Without judgment and with great compassion, he welcomed him into his life. In the same exact way, our suffering needs us. The more we fight it, the angrier and louder it gets. As Terry's teacher so eloquently said, "He who fights breaks his connection with the Universe. If you try to dominate people, you are already defeated." The same is true with our internal community. The moment we try to power over the forces that scare and enrage us, we become caught in the endless victor-victim struggle. The way through is to welcome their presence.

Welcoming comes automatically when we begin to move out of the collective delusion that darkness is our enemy into a deep respect for it. Recognizing that what causes havoc and heartache in our lives is a doorway into our healing is to re-engage with Life. The core challenges of our lives are the demons of renewal, and we can only gather the tremendous energy they hold for us by coming into direct relationship with them.

My body has been a great teacher for learning the powerful healing of inclusion. I was born with an extremely sensitive body, and the older I become, the more strongly it reacts to the slightest imbalance. Most of my life, I tried to manage, bargain and plead with Life for a surcease from this discomfort. For varying periods of time this would make a difference, and then the symptoms would come back with a vengeance.

For a time I swung on the pendulum of victor and victim. I would go to doctors and read books on healing techniques. My mind would be in full gear, trying to figure out how to get rid of these unpleasant experiences in my life. I would do affirmations and bargain with God. When this didn't bring about the healing that I wanted, I would fall into the victim mode. Dabbling in the land of despair, I became caught in struggle. I moved back and forth from victor to victim, holding on for dear life, absolutely certain I could nail this pendulum to the wall.

Rarely in that whole process did I stop and listen to my pain. A voice inside of me said that I *must not* feel the depth of what was going on, for it would engulf me in an endless black hole. It was like sliding down a slippery slope, trying to hold onto every branch and rock I could get my hands on. I was lucky enough to be unable to find any hand holds—to be wrenched out of my ability to manage the process anymore. When the depth of discomfort in my body, (along with the terror, rage and despair) got deep enough, I was forced to begin to relate directly to what was happening.

A statement from Stephen Levine helped me immensely when I was learning how to relate to pain rather than being lost in it: "Discomfort is a drill, probing through our armoring and denial, reaching the deep reservoirs of long-held isolations and fears. The tip of the drill is honed by helplessness and hopelessness, the inability to control the uncontrollable."

The moment for me that the drill of helplessness and hopelessness turned into empowerment happened when I got the flu. For most people, the flu is a great inconvenience in their lives. For me, it is like an atom bomb going off inside my body. The depth of terror (it's back forever), rage (this is not fair), despair (I'll never get through this) and self judgment (what did I do wrong?) was immense. My first automatic response was denial. I noticed myself getting very busy, hoping to outrun these feelings. Of course, that only helped to enhance the imbalance. Then when denial didn't work anymore, I dropped into the land of struggle, seduced into trying to figure out where the flu came from and how I was going to get rid of it. It was like riding a slippery bucking bronco in a hurricane. All of the resistance to the uncomfortable aspects of Life arose and almost blocked the light of my Awareness, throwing me again into the land of war.

But I had experienced too many moments of getting off the pendulum and resting in a place beyond the victor or the victim to stay lost in struggle for very long. For moments, I was able to embrace my body from a spacious and curious heart. I was being healed, but not in the way that I had demanded it, since that would have been only a temporary healing. I was being healed of a pain that was far greater than any discomfort in my body. I was being moved beyond fear of Life and beyond the great desire to control it. For moments, when I was at the very center of my experience and beyond the land of struggle, I connected with a deep peace and communion with Life, not on my terms, but exactly as it was appearing.

I was feeling better but the next day I had a speaking engagement I couldn't cancel. On the morning of the talk I didn't feel at all well and my mind freaked out. Closing my eyes to meditate, I found myself tossed back and forth upon a raging sea. I could only rest in the rhythm of my breath for moments before the storms would sweep me away again. Gradually, by persistently returning to the breath, my Awareness began to settle, and I was able to be with the raging storm.

Then what happened was something I had been working towards my whole life. I finally welcomed the actual experience of feeling unwell. It was sur-rounded by a feeling of deep exhaustion, a feeling that had always terrified me. I was able to become curious about what made me label it exhaustion. I followed and explored the feelings as they passed through my body. I began to ask these feelings, "What is your contribution to my Awakening?" It was a moment of inclusion, not exclusion, and a moment of honoring the dark for the great gifts that it brings.

As I ceased fighting the experience, the feelings began to float away like clouds before the warmth of the sun. I discovered that most of the physical upset came from my fear and contraction around these feelings. This was an important speaking engagement and for days I had feared that these feelings of exhaustion would get in the way. As I moved beyond resistance and into actually welcoming these feelings, I began to feel better.

It turned out to be a wonderful, rich day. What I had heard for years—"It doesn't matter what happens to you; what matters is your relationship to it."— began to make sense at the core of my being. To find a balance and then lose it over and over again allowed the very cells of my soul to know that my daily life will always be a roller coaster ride. There is no way I can get all the rubber duckies in a row and get them to stay there. As I have learned how to listen to whatever *is* with a welcoming and curious heart, I gradually opened up into a spacious and supportive place in which I could say "this too," *relating to my pain rather than being lost in it.*

Trusting and including rather than eradicating all that is *wrong* changes our whole lives. The tremendous amount of energy we use to war with *what is* is freed up for curiosity, compassion and clarity. Welcoming is conflict resolution at its best, whether it is done over a negotiation table in Palestine or inside of us. War creates more war. Communication fosters healing, a healing that cannot happen until darkness is allowed a seat and a voice at the table of our being. When I first heard this, I felt such peace, but then I easily lost this perspective again. To the rational, logical mind this sounds like insanity, but to the heart it makes absolute sense.

For myself, at the beginning there were just moments of this healing Awareness, like the flicker of a match in a dark cavern. But each of these flickers of honoring my darkness was a healing balm for my tortured heart. When the match flickers began to become beams of light, I was able to explore the immense cavern of my own darkness. Coming across the bats of terror and the drop-offs of self-hatred, I would again cower in this cavern and cover my head, blocking out the flicker of lights. But it was beginning to seep into my Awareness that darkness wasn't here because I was inherently bad, lazy, stupid or stubborn. It was here to lead me to my wholeness. Eventually, curiosity would get the better of me, and off exploring I would go.

There are two main reasons why we have been reluctant to include pain as a crucial part of ourselves. The first is the belief that going towards it means more darkness. The exact opposite is true. Imagine riding down a road on your bicycle, heading into the setting sun. The details of the landscape around you would be hazy and blurred by the strength of the light. Now imagine turning your bike around and heading into the coming darkness. In a flash, everything would be defined and clear. The same is true for going towards our own darkness. Fear may say otherwise, but it is not true. Meeting our darkness creates more light.

The second reason we resist the dark is that when we go towards that which we have formerly deemed as broken, inappropriate or bad, it is easy to get lost in judgment about ourselves. Coming across the parts of our shadow that we have hidden from our whole lives, it is easy to forget everyone has both dark and light inside of them. Elizabeth Kubler-Ross once joked about writing a book called, "I'm Not Okay, You're Not Okay, and That's Okay." Our perfection is in our imperfection, and each of us carries a part of the human shadow.

WHAT IS IN THE WAY IS THE WAY: THE ART OF CURIOSITY

If there were no confusion, there would be no wisdom....
Chaos is workable...not regressive.
Respect whatever happens, chaos should be regarded as extremely good news.
Respect the upsurge of energy that is emotions, no matter what form. Nothing is rejected as bad or grasped as good.
We grapple only because we feel they will overwhelm the basic posture we have deemed ourselves to be.
Go towards the emotion, then there is no resistance. Let yourself be in the emotion, go through it, give-in to it, experience it. Then there is rhythm. Transmutation involves going through such fear.

Unknown

Imagine a fierce lion, one that represents all we hate and fear. It has been chasing us our whole lives. At moments it gets so close that we can feel its breath on the back of our legs. The closer it gets, the faster we run. If we are lucky, there will be a time when we can't run anymore. We are just too tired. As we fall to the ground, ready to be devoured, the lion screeches to a halt, and we find ourselves face to face with our pain. It opens its mouth (to eat us, we think) and instead, on its tongue is a gift that it has been trying to bring to us for years! *Our pain has waited our whole lives for us to be present for it.*

In order to respond rather than react to our pain so we can gather the gifts concealed within our wounds, we have been exploring two radical shifts in perspective. The first is the novel idea that pain in our lives is essential, trustable and ultimately benevolent. It isn't here because we've done something wrong or because Life is against us. Rumi speaks to the power of trusting pain in the following poem:

194

This Friend, who knows more than you do, will bring difficulties and grief
and sickness,
as medicine, as happiness,
as the essence of the moment when you're beaten,
when you hear, "Checkmate!"
and can finally say, "I trust You to kill me."
                                                              Rumi

If we can trust that our pain is here to "kill" the illusion of being separate from Life, there comes a wondrous feeling of curiosity. If we really knew how much we were missing, if we really could see how much our radiance and our potential has been imprisoned, and if we allowed ourselves to really long for our spiritual vitality, we would be willing to explore our deepest of pains so that we can become free.

The second shift in perspective we've been exploring is the powerful tool of welcoming our pain. To resist gives that which we hate and fear great power. To include, as the old man did on the train, dissipates darkness like the sun meeting the fog. There comes more and more willingness to go towards and invite into our Awareness that which we hate and fear, for we know that this is the way to freedom. The tree that resists the wind is uprooted. The grass that does not fight this powerful force—that in fact dances with it—lives.

The great beings on our planet—the ones whose very Presence awakens something inside of us—are those beings who have met their dark side. Because they have welcomed their shadow, the energy they formerly used to deny, control, obliterate, understand, fix and control their darkness is now available for radiance, compassion, vitality and being fully present.

From this foundation of trust and welcoming, curiosity about our pain is possible. Remember Carl Jung's quote at the first of this chapter: "Enlighten-ment consists not only in seeing the luminous, but in making darkness visible. The latter is much more difficult, so it is far less popular." The key word there is *visible*. Our healing is in *seeing* our darkness, not in fixing it.

Instead of paying attention to our pain, our relationship has been one in which we consider it an uninvited guest within the party of our lives. When we first become aware that pain has shown up at our party, we try to get rid of it. We uninvite pain only to have it show up anyway. We run around locking all the doors and windows, hoping this will keep it away. When that doesn't work, we try to ignore it, standing with our back to it whenever it is in the same room. We feel resentment and rage for its ability to make its way in through locked doors. "Pain is ruining the party," says the victim inside us.

What we are exploring here is the possibility of trusting that this person at the party—this aspect of ourselves that we wish were not there—is no accident. It is an essential part of our dance. The experience of going to the party, after we finally acknowledge that maybe this is not the enemy we thought it was, shifts our whole perspective of the party. We may not relish it showing up, but at least our energy is not spent in resisting. Even a begrudging willingness to include it in our social circle begins to show up. From this foundation comes the wondrous feeling of curiosity. "If pain (this experience that I fear and hate) is an essential part of my life, what is it here for?"

Rather than always turning our back on pain whenever it is in the same room as we are, we begin to become very curious, watching (out of the corner of the eye), noticing and getting to know it from afar. Finally, we walk across the room, introduce ourselves and begin a conversation that ultimately allows us to listen and learn from it.

LISTENING TO THE BODY

The body remembers, the bones remember, the joints remember, even the little finger remembers. Memory is lodged in pictures and feelings in the cells themselves. Like a sponge filled with water, anywhere the flesh is pressed, wrung, even touched lightly, a memory may flow out in a stream.

Clarissa Pinkola Estes

The best place to discover how to become curious about pain—learning how to respond rather than resist—is in our bodies. If we can learn how to pay attention to what our bodies are saying, we will be amazed at the wisdom that we discover there.

Let us explore what it is like to bring our attention into our bodies:

After reading this section, put down the book. Close your eyes and take a few deep breaths, allowing your belly to soften and your jaw to let go. Ride the rhythm of your breath.

Now bring your attention to your right foot and allow it to rest in that experience. There are many sensations moving through your foot right now—warmth and coolness, pressure (against the side of a shoe or the floor) tingles, discomfort. As you allow your attention to settle there, it becomes like a Polaroid picture that is developing.

196

"Ahh, there is an itch. There are tingles in the bottom of my foot. My big toe is comfortable but the rest of my toes feel sore." Find at least 3 different sensations in your right foot.

Now compare the right foot's experience to the left. How are they different? When the mind drifts off, bring it back, to simply being curious about the sensations that are dancing through your feet. When you are done, open your eyes.

This exercise hones our ability to pay attention, and it also shows us that at all moments of our lives there is a symphony of sensations dancing through our bodies. Whenever we are caught in reaction to Life, this resistance manifests in very specific ways in our body. To discover exactly what is going on while still lost in thought is like trying to read a book in the middle of a hurricane. The mind is usually a whirling mass of judgments and fears. But the body is very specific in its expressions. To notice the dance of sensations while you are in a heavy state is the first step in actually creating a relationship with the difficult parts of our lives.

The body has *never forgotten* its connection to the whole. It knows it arises out of, is supported by and is deeply interwoven with absolutely everything. The mind thinks it is the seat of Intelligence; the body recognizes Intelligence everywhere. Because of this, the body *resonates with Life*. It not only carries within itself the memory of all that humanity has experienced and learned, it also knows what is happening in the environment at any given moment. If we walk into a room filled with strangers, the mind will probably be focused on looking cool, telling us exactly what is going on in the room.

It will also inform us about what is going on inside of ourselves. A friend may notice we are upset and asks, "Are you angry?" and we say "No." All the while our stomach is one huge knot. "Are you afraid?" the friend queries. "Absolutely not," we respond. And yet our anal sphincter is held tighter than a drum. The mind runs away from pain; the body does not. This makes it an exquisite biofeedback system. The body will tell us very clearly what we are actually experiencing.

It will also tell us what we have experienced in the past. From the moment of our birth, every single experience has been registered and stored in our cellular memory. The rage we felt when our older sibling taunted us is there. So, too, is the terror of that rage. The agony and helplessness of watching our parents argue is held deep in our bones, along with the despair of losing our first love.

We can find the core places where we get caught in struggle by listening to sensations as they move through our bodies. We may be whirling in a cloud of

197

confusion and reaction, without a clue about what is going on but the body will tell us if we only listen. Every moment of our lives the body is saying, "Listen to me; I carry the wisdom you yearn for."

There is a general language of the body. You can see it in our favorite colloquial phrases. For example, terror is often felt in the lower belly (It scared the shit out of me); anger is often felt in the solar plexus (He was livid; I am going to vent my spleen; that really galls me); judgment is often felt in the neck and shoulder area (She has a chip on her shoulder; He is a pain in the neck); and grief is felt in the throat and chest (I am all choked up; My heart is broken). It is best not to get any more specific than that, for our body has its own special language and as soon as we try to analyze a particular sensation, we are again lost in our heads and gone from the healing power of attention.

To get to know the language of our bodies is not about understanding. There is a phase in our growth when understanding is essential (I feel this feeling because my father beat me when I was young). But understanding keeps us in the mind. Healing happens when we can learn instead how to meet what we are experiencing. *To be fully present for the feelings as they emerge is where healing lies.* And in a very wondrous way, when we meet our pain, the understanding that we've yearned for (the kind of understanding that comes from the actual core of the discomfort rather than from an intellectual idea about it) shows up.

Let's explore what it looks like to be present for our pain.

After reading this section, put down the book, and find a quiet place to be. Close your eyes and begin to breathe long slow breaths. Slowly allow your attention to meet yourself right here, right now. Feel the warmth or coolness of the room; see the light playing on your eyelids; feel the tingles of pressure in the places where your buttocks meet what you are sitting on.

Now scan your body, discovering a place of discomfort. If there is no definite spot of discomfort, go to one of your favorite places of holding on and begin to pay attention—a tight neck; a sore back; a pain in your head. It may be hazy and undefined, but allow your attention to rest there. When the mind drifts off, bring it back again.

Begin to describe the sensations that present themselves to your Awareness. The sensation could be pulsing or aching, sharp or dull. It could have specific boundaries or could be fuzzy and undefined. It could be steady like a tight fist or come and go like clouds dancing with the moon. Does it move around or stay in one place? Is it warm, or is it cool? What is the truth of this experience?

For a few moments, be willing to be present, letting Life be exactly as it is. When you drift away, notice how the body tightens around the experience. As you again merge your attention with this discomfort, soften and open around this pain. Don't push it away. If that is hard to do, enhance the contraction. Physically tighten the muscles surrounding this area, and then slowly, ever so slowly, let go.

Meet this discomfort as if it were an abandoned child asking for the mercy of your Awareness. Know your discomfort wants exactly what you want when you are hurting—loving acceptance and compassionate attention. Imagine your hands radiating loving acceptance, and bring them to the discomfort. Gently and with great care cradle this experience. When you are finished, open your eyes.

By actually meeting an experience as it arises in the body, we are moving into *direct relationship* with whatever we are experiencing. This allows us to be present for that which we have formerly resisted so that we can unlock the valuable energy bound up with it. We are now ready to introduce ourselves.

GIVING IT A NAME

This noting of mental states encourages a deeper recognition of what is happening while it is happening. It allows us to be more fully alive to the present rather than living our lives as an afterthought.

Stephen Levine

The next step in truly healing our pain is to name these mental, emotional and physical states that we have formerly resisted and reacted to. To give these experiences a name allows us to bring them out of the mire of unconsciousness and fosters the ability to relate to them through a process of internal dialogue with them.

When we first arrived here as an infant, everything was a swirling kaleidoscope of colors and sounds with things blending into one another. Slowly we began to see objects and associate sounds. After a time of pure sensual experience came the process of naming things. It was how we were taught to make sense of our world.

We are now embarking on an exciting new adventure of naming. We are beginning to separate out who we really are (Awareness itself) from who we thought we were (the objects of Awareness—thoughts, feelings, and experiences). Our feelings, thoughts and experiences are a swirling, whirling dance that most of the time we are lost in. Naming these states allows us to relate *to* our experiences rather than being caught *by* them.

Let us explore again an exercise from Chapter Three:

Take your finger and move it all about in front of you, following it with your eyes wherever it goes. The finger represents the 60,000 thoughts we have each day. This is what happens when our attention is caught up in identification with all the various sates of mind that pass through us. If the mind says, "I am depressed," we feel depressed. If it says, "I am angry," we believe WE are angry. Now, still moving your finger, keep your eyes straight ahead. You can see the movement of your finger, but your attention is not following it.

This is the difference between being lost in our experiences and the ability to begin to watch them. It is the difference between being in reaction (I am so angry), or response, (Ahh, anger). Naming is the key here. It is an exquisite tool that frees us up from the constant shifting sands of Life. Naming brings the helter skelter movement of our experience into our conscious attention.

At the beginning, this is difficult to do with more intense experiences. Our muscle of attention, being weak, easily gets caught in reaction. But as we learn to respond instead, we will know great freedom. A woman from one of the Awakening groups shared her experience of naming terror. This state of mind had almost completely overtaken her life, making work impossible and causing great heartache.

A wave of terror had been building for days, and she found herself caught like a rabbit trying to outrun a shotgun. She ended up lying on the floor, crying that she couldn't take it anymore, and imploring Life to take it away. Then Awareness kicked in and she named what was happening. "Ahh, this is terror." She began to rate it on a scale of 1 to 10. This is a 7; now it is a 10+. She was relating *to* it rather than being lost *in* it. *For that moment, she was no longer the state-of terror; she was Awareness itself.* As she went towards the terror, in a flash she remembered experiencing this same terror when she was 8 years old, a particularly difficult year in her life. Her heart opened, and she was able to be kind and compassionate with this state of terror and with herself.

The first time I named one of my demons brought a momentous shift in my life. One of the core states that I used to react to is dread. This is a combination of terror (Something horrible is going to happen) and self-hate (What is wrong with me that I caused this?). This was one of the primary feelings of my childhood. By the time I reached adulthood, the years I spent trying to get away from dread had made me contracted and exhausted.

As it began to seep into my consciousness that the healing came through meeting my darkness, I was able to inch my way towards seeing and including irritation, self-judgment and fear, but dread was too big. Numerous times I was asked to teach what I was learning, but dread would say, "No! Absolutely not! I can't do that." I was terrified of even speaking with a group of friends and would often berate myself afterwards for what I had said. My greatest fear was that someone would ask me a question I didn't know the answer to and I would make a fool of myself.

A friend who was teaching a meditation class at a local college finally said, "Please, come, and share with us. You don't have to be in charge of anything. All I am asking you to do is to speak whenever it feels right." The first night I was there turned out to be a transformative experience. The next week he became ill, and with only a half hour notice, I discovered that I was to lead the class *by myself!*

The choice was either to freeze and not do the class or to go in and just let go. I let go and it was wonderful. It was a *do or die* situation, one in which I didn't so much meet and work with dread as I just rose above it temporarily. But it taught me that I could function in a place beyond dread. I was slowly and surely moving towards being present with dread.

Later on, I was invited to spend a weekend with a group of women at a cabin in the Olympic Mountains. I initially resisted, as socializing used to be uncomfortable for me. On the way up, my friend who had organized the weekend asked me if I would lead the evening sharing. Dread ricocheted through my body. "No," I said. When we gathered in the circle, the group was floundering without a leader and so, being a confirmed rescuer, I stepped in. Things began to weave together until a friend of mine lambasted me for what I was sharing and how I was leading the group. To this day I cannot remember what she said, but I can still feel the horror and immediate contraction that took over my whole being. I froze completely.

When we broke for the evening meal, I was caught up in a whirlwind of self-hatred, mainly for freezing. I can still remember the agony of that evening. Some people came to me and criticized her, but that didn't feel right nor did it make me feel any better. If I had driven my own car, I would have made a hasty retreat. Instead I was left in agony and in complete *reaction*.

Most of us were sleeping on the floor of one large room. I grabbed a corner, rolled myself deeply into my sleeping bag, and with my back to the room, covered my head with a pillow. This cocoon brought a modicum of safety, enough for curiosity to show up, and I began to *respond*. "Ahh, *what is* going on here? What part of me is asking to be met?" I became very curious about what was happening. I dropped into my body and felt the sinking feeling of dread, with terror knotting my gut and self-hatred a vise around my heart. A thrill ran through me. "I'm here. I can see dread!!"

I began to talk with it. "I see you. I know you have waited my whole life for me to not hate or fear you, for me to recognize and be present with you." The dread began to dissipate, and I can remember saying, "Don't go. I want to get to know you. I want to be your friend." I slept a half-sleep that night, waking up over and over again into tenderness for this dread and a deep thankfulness that I was present enough to meet it.

Who we are is Awareness itself, not the states of mind that are flowing through us. In the dark of the night in that cabin, I began to free myself from this ancient story of dread, one that had run me for years. There were three key shifts that night. The first came when my foundation of trust and inclusion began to kick in and curiosity took me towards the experience rather than away. The second was when I dropped into my body and began to feel the sensations there. The third occurred when I gave a name to what was going on. When I am in reaction to dread, it feels like I am drowning in my terror. Naming is like a life raft in the middle of a raging sea. It allows me to relate *to* the state of mind rather than *from* it.

Another powerful story of naming came from a woman who was lost in self hatred over how she handled a meeting at work. From the moment she began her preparations, she knew she was not going to be good enough. Much to her horror, the boss who brought up these feelings the most had shown up at the meeting. As a result of her feelings of inadequacy, she led the meeting from a faltering and contracted place and had been lost in a whirlwind of self-judgment ever since.

In our counseling session, I asked her to close her eyes and recreate the experience as vividly as she possibly could—to see it in her mind and to feel the painful feelings in her body. As she did this, I could literally watch her whole being contracting. Asking her to stay curious, I invited her to feel what was present and imagine what this voice would look like if it had a body. She went inside of this feeling, but couldn't get an image. I could tell that the fear of doing this was getting in the way.

"What is there right now?" I asked. "Ahh, self-hatred," she responded. As she saw, rather than reacting to what was present, she told me that she immediately got a picture in her mind of a fire-breathing dragon. "If this is ultimately a benevolent force and not the demon you thought it to be, what would be its name?" I asked. "Puff the Magic Dragon," she said.

In one name, her entire relationship with this cruel judger shifted. We then walked through the entire experience of the meeting from the place of power that comes from relating to the feeling rather than from it. She saw herself naming it whenever she felt the urge to believe what it was saying. As she did so, her body literally began to let go. When she opened her eyes, she was glowing with the understanding that her self-hatred had waited her whole life for her to see it without fear and judgment. She understood that being able to name it, she could see it when it appeared and get to know its many voices, its needs and the gifts that it held for her.

After reading this section, close your eyes, and bring to your mind a particularly painful experience, one that causes you to cringe when you feel the memory. See the experience in as much detail as possible in your imagination and feel the corresponding feelings in your body.

Now begin to ask questions. What is asking to be met? What is going on here? What energy pattern has come for a visit? When you see what it going on, give it a name, a somewhat light, compassionate and even silly name. It could be "here comes da judge," if self-hatred is present or "little one" if fear is there. The key is to allow these names to be created from a light and loving heart. These aren't the horrible demons you thought they were. When you are ready, open your eyes.

We all have many parts of ourselves that are longing to be seen. They have been either partially or completely excluded whenever they have begun to enter our consciousness. Becoming whole is seeing, naming and integrating these parts. Some of the parts that you may meet are:

- Fearful part
- Procrastinating part
- Victim
- Cruel judger
- Pusher (thinks it knows the way)
- Despair (it's too much/too hard)
- Stubborn part (wants what it wants)
- Angry part

- Wise crone
- Needy one
- Perfectionist/controller
- Scared and overwhelmed
- Exuberant & playful child
- Joy addict
- Noble warrior
- Inclusive mother

Allow your life to become an adventure, discovering all of the alienated parts of yourself. See it as a treasure hunt for that which you formerly called *bad* or *wrong.* Know that your daily life is specifically set up in order to bring these disowned parts into your Awareness over and over again until you can meet and greet them. Keep a list in your journal of all of the parts of yourself that you discover. Ask them what their names are, and as you hear them, write them down. As we learn how to approach these forces, they will reveal not only their stories, but also the gifts they have been waiting to give to us.

CREATING A RELATIONSHIP

What we choose to fight is so tiny! What fights with us is so great!

If only we would let ourselves be dominated as things do by some immense storm, we would become strong too, and not need names.

When we win it's with small things and the triumph itself makes us small.

What is extraordinary and eternal does not want to be bent by us.

I mean the angel who appeared to the wrestlers of the Old Testament, when the wrestlers' sinews grew long like metal strings,

He felt them under his fingers like chords of deep music.

Whoever was beaten by this angel (who often simply declined the fight), went away proud and strengthened and great from that harsh hand, that kneaded him as if to change his shape.

Winning does not tempt that man.

This is how he grows: by being defeated, decisively, by constantly greater beings.

Rainier Maria Rilke

Now that we have been introduced to this unwelcome guest—this *stranger across the room*—it is time to begin restoring the relationship. When I believed that healing was about trying to get rid of what I didn't like rather than meeting it, I spent my whole life feeling like a failure. I couldn't seem to rise above my darkness. Stephen Levine taught me to go the other way, to realize that my suffering *needed me.* What a novel concept! I had been resisting it so hard my whole life I had never *listened.*

The healing we seek is not about going *away.* It is about going *toward* what we don't like. As long as we cannot welcome and integrate the darker parts of our lives, we give them enormous power, staying stuck like a fly on flypaper, twisting in the wind. As Robert Bly once said, "The dark forces get pissed because we are not listening to them." In order to heal, besides trusting, welcoming, being curious and naming, we need to learn how to *be with* our pain, allowing these parts of ourselves a voice.

The ability to create a relationship with that which we formerly hated and feared rests upon a foundation that knows you are not alone in your suffering. Stephen Levine tells a story of one of the most miraculous healings he ever witnessed. Rose was a hard-nosed businesswoman, dying of cancer. During her hospitalization, the nurses called her the "bitch on wheels in 42-B." Because of her adversarial, resentful life-style, she found herself dying with no one there to support her. She was estranged from her children and had never even met her grandchildren.

One night, after repeatedly ringing the call bell for more pain medication and not getting an answer, she felt she was going to be engulfed by the unbearable pain in her hip. With no way out, she spontaneously began to go towards her pain and suddenly experienced herself as a young Eskimo woman, dying in a breech childbirth with unbearable pain in her hip. She then became someone who had fallen and was dying alone in a jungle with searing pain in their hip. She experienced many other people, all dying with the same unbearable pain. She realized from the depth of her being that this was not her pain—this was *our* pain—and her heart was torn wide open. In the six weeks before her death, she reconciled with her children, met her grandchildren, and her room became the place that the nurses would come for their breaks.

After you read this section, put down the book. Breathe a few deep breaths, and soften into your body. Find yourself here in the living moment of your life by connecting with the actual sensations of pressure, breath, heart beat.

Now bring into your heart a particular challenge that you have been experiencing in your life. Imagine this experience on a continuum. If you are feeling the loss of a relationship, acknowledge all of the thousands upon thousands of people who are also experiencing the same pain, including someone who just lost their whole family to death. If you are dealing with a muscle injury in your body that is limiting your physical movements, feel all of the people with ALS, the many amputees and the myriad paraplegics and quadriplegics.

If you are experiencing waves of depression, feel people who right now are lost in a seemingly endless tunnel of hopelessness and helplessness. If you are overwhelmed by your life, connect with all of the people who, at that same moment, are in the act of killing themselves. Open your heart to our common pain.

When you are ready, open your eyes.

Every single pain you have ever felt—whether it be deep grief, irritation at the driver before you, cruel self judgment, whirling worry, consuming hatred, a stubbed toe or immobilizing terror—is being experienced right now by millions of human beings. Whenever you are lost in pain, *you are not alone*. The full continuum of that particular pain is being felt by hundreds of thousands of others *in that same moment*.

Besides understanding that our pain is OUR pain, there are other things that we can do to create a healing relationship. When a formerly disowned part is present, like anger or grief, we can allow it to reveal itself through movement. Put appropriate music on and dance it. Encourage it to unfold and express itself. If you find yourself moving again from your head, stop, stand still, and ask your body how it would like to move. It may be one movement repeated over and over again. By allowing the body to share these feelings, we not only become more aware of them but we free up the energy bound within them.

If writing is your way, write letters to it as if this were an old friend with whom you had a falling out. Write of your rage, confusion and despair and of your desire for a lasting friendship. Then allow it to write back to you, telling of its experience of being cast out from the community that is you, of being branded the bad one and of its desire to be respected and heard. These parts of ourselves want a voice, just like you do when you are deeply wounded. They want to share their hurt and their rage and their wisdom.

Ask them questions. Remember that these are ancient forces that come from the depths of our yearning to awaken. Ask open-ended questions in which you do not expect an answer. "Who are you?" "What are you trying to tell me?" If the feeling is not clear, ask, "What is asking to be met?" My favorite question right now is, "What do you need from me today?" I can be in reaction to a challenge in my life, and when I drop into my body, feeling the contraction there, I then ask it how I can be of support. This lessens my resistance and opens my heart. I usually then experience a flood of connection with my own life and a knowing that help is always with me.

We can also perform acts of honoring these forces and the roles they have played in our Awakening. For a while I wore a pouch filled with the Earth. It was not a fancy rock or a beautiful crystal. It was actually the dark, fertile Earth itself. I did this to honor that I come from the Earth and I am the Earth awakening. It reminded me that an essential part of my Awakening is receiving all of the gifts that darkness brings.

I also do rituals with my darkness. When I met my stubbornness, I did a forgiveness meditation with it while holding a stone. Then I went and asked the Earth to hold my stubbornness, to remind me not to war with it. I buried it in a wonderful place high in the mountains where I can visit it from time to time. Another way to honor the dark is to create an altar in your home honoring these forces. It can be as simple as a candle you light every day or as elaborate as a dark velvet cloth on a table that holds the symbols of your grief, rage and terror.

Gratitude can help immensely too. Stephen Levine has spoken many times of people who were truly thankful for all the gifts that life-threatening illnesses have brought them, even if they went on to die. In my own life, self-hatred has taught me all about kindness. Terror has taught me about deep, abiding trust. Despair has birthed me into knowing I am never alone. My darkness wouldn't allow me to stay asleep. It stayed with me, persistently pushing and shoving, sometimes gently and sometimes very forcefully. To express gratitude, you can write it letters of thankfulness, or put a symbol of gratitude on your altar to honor all the gifts that darkness has brought you.

Be willing to be silly. Laughter is music for the soul. We have been struggling with these states so much and for so long that whenever we get close we get very serious. A man in one of the Awakening groups shared one of his dreams. He was standing on a flat plain with a full-blown tornado bearing down on him. He was frozen to the spot, unable to move at all. Right before the tornado was ready to engulf him, out of the ground popped a goddess in full *goddess regalia*. With a twinkle in her eye, she turned to the tornado and waved her magic wand. In a flash it dissolved and there on the ground was a little tiny man with his eyes closed and his body twisting all around, trying to keep the tornado going!

When he shared this dream, he said it reminded him of the perspective of lightness, of not being quite so serious about the ups and downs of his life. To create lightness, you can write silly love notes to yourself or dance like a fool. Be a little kid, and do somersaults and log rolls in the back yard. As Stephen Levine would say, "In order to awaken you have to be willing to be God's fool."

Be patient. Zorba the Greek one day noticed a cocoon in his back yard that was just barely beginning to open. He made a commitment to watch the birth of the butterfly. Soon he became impatient and began to blow his warm breath upon the cocoon to hurry up the process. As the butterfly emerged, it struggled in vain to open its wings. As he held the dying butterfly in his hands, Zorba realized that in his impatience he had forced the butterfly out of the cocoon before its time. Just like him, we blow the hot breath of our own impatience upon our journey and wonder why it gums things up.

Turning towards what disturbs us is the birth canal of our healing. It will take all the courage, cuddling, humor, discipline, vision and compassion we can discover to create a relationship with that which we formerly hated, judged and feared. But the time and commitment is so well worth it. It will take us to the wholeness we long for.

THE RESPONSE OF KINDNESS

To open to Life requires a deep and heartfelt compassion for all that is around and within us. The place where we can most directly open to this mystery of Life is in what we don't do well, in the places of our struggles and vulnerability.

Jack Kornfield

Ultimately the core intent of the five skills is to awaken our heart for it is the place of healing. It is the only part of us that can see, allow and include all of the many parts of ourselves and the many experiences of our lives. It is the chef of Life that knows it is only when we include the sharp and the bitter, the pungent and the sweet, the succulent and the delicious, that we can move into something greater.

Awhile ago I got a visit from the latest *crud*. It was located in the throat and sounded like a bevy of frogs had moved in. The worst part of it was the nighttime coughing. Whenever I would finally drop off to sleep, a coughing fit would awaken me. I finally broke down and took Nyquil, only to wake up with a medicine hangover and a very nasty mood. "This is it. I've had it. This is too much," I chanted. I hated my life; I hated myself; and I definitely hated those frogs. It took all of my discipline to sit and meditate. I just wanted to read, eat, sleep—anything but be with this discomfort.

Instead, I decided to meditate. At the beginning of the meditation, it was like living in a dust bowl during a hurricane. But I know from experience that when the mind is wildly whipping around, it's because there is a feeling it doesn't want to experience. Slowly, I caught the rhythm of my breath and curiosity kicked in. "What am I feeling?" I first noticed the physical sensations—the sore and congested throat, upset intestines from the Nyquil, and a feeling like a Mac truck had hit me.

As I named and acknowledged each one, I began to move under them. It was foggy at first, but slowly I was able to recognize and name despair. "I want to give up," despair said. "I can't take anymore. I'll never feel well again." I stayed with it for awhile. This is never done with great precision. It's like the sun dancing in and out of the clouds. It becomes very clear, and then the mind wanders off into some story about despair. When I bring it back, it takes a few moments to focus again on the feeling.

It felt like I hadn't quite met what was really there. I asked my body, "What do you want to show me?" Almost immediately what began to reveal itself was meanness. It was the ancient self-hatred that believes when something is painful, I am to blame. It was breathtaking, the depth and breadth of it. I approached it in curiosity. In that moment of meeting, something very deep inside of me let go. What came burbling up from the depths of my being was the statement, "Let kindness be your response to pain." My whole being began to soften and glow. I had moved out of struggle into inclusion and compassion.

I then took a walk. One of the great fears of these heavy states is that they will be here forever. Before the meditation, my mind had already claimed that this was going to be a rotten day. Instead, my walk became a time of wonder and mystery. Everywhere I looked, I saw the sacred, creative force of Life spiraling out of the void and manifesting as trees, dogs, people (including myself), houses and grass. When I was caught in struggle, I was lost in separation. It was the world against me and me against the world. Simply by meeting the darkness that was present, I was moved into the experience of connection and interconnection. Did it fade later? Yes. Was there some grief and struggle associated with this? Yes. But I am learning to not blame myself for contraction and to trust the rhythm of Life.

Jack Kornfield tells the story of Maha Gosananda, aCambodian monk who was in the refugee camps where thousands of Cambodians fled the atrocities of the Pol Pot regime. Maha called upon the people to gather for a Buddhist ceremony. The soldiers roamed throughout the encampment and swore that anybody who went would be killed. The next day over ten thousand refugees converged at the tiny temple the monk had built. He chanted the invocations that started the ceremony, and the people began to weep. They had been through so much, lost so much, and now they were risking their lives for this all-important connection with their religion, a religion that had been com-pletely suppressed by Pol Pot. Maha then went on to chant the following verse from the Dhamapada, a sacred Buddhist scripture:

> *Hatred never ceases by hatred; but by Love alone is healed. This is an ancient and eternal law.*

Over and over again these people who had lost everything and had every reason to rage and hate, chanted with him, moving into the knowing that all healing is done in the heart.

All that we have explored has been for the awakening of the heart. We touched on trusting darkness and being willing to include it as a part of our lives. We contacted the wondrous tool of curiosity, the willingness to go towards what disturbs us, along with the ability to actually create a relationship with it *The radical notion we are exploring here is that our pain is longing for our heart.* Our terror is afraid; our aloneness is lonely; and our rage is isolated and alone. The only way they will be safe enough to reveal themselves to us and give us the powerful energy and gifts that they carry, is to meet them with kindness and mercy. Our pain is not only worthy of our attention, it is worthy of our love.

THE DOORWAY TO FREEDOM

Pain, which we cannot forget, falls drop by drop upon the heart, until in our own despair and against our will, comes wisdom...through the awful grace of God.

Escalus

To honor rather than suppress or get lost in our pain is a radical step in our growth. It is *how we view our pain* that either opens us up into the possibility of creative living or condemns us to the status quo of struggle. In the movie *Mindwalk*, the physicist says, "We are destroying rain forests at a rate of one football field per second. Brazil is doing this in order to pay their national debt through money raised from cattle ranches and land speculations. The barren forests are one of the main causes of global warming. We create cattle ranches in order to produce more red meat, which is one of the direct causes of heart attacks and high medical costs. These are examples of interconnectedness. You cannot look at a single one of our global problems in isolation, trying to understand and solve it. You can fix a fragment of a piece but it will deteriorate a second later because what it was connected to has been ignored. We have to change everything at the same time."

The politician then says, "Suppose you are right and everything is connected to everything else. Where do you start?" "By the way we are seeing the world," she responds. "You are still searching for the right piece to fix first. All the problems are fragments of one single crisis, *a crisis of perception.*"

The shift of perception that is being asked of us as a group begins with individuals transforming their relationship with the challenges in their lives. Most people are lost inside their own personal war. So, of course, humanity uses war (trying to get rid of what we don't like) as a solution to its problems. The challenges we face on this planet are too great to meet with war (the victor/victim pendulum) anymore. We are in the no-man's-land between the old and new perception. The old style meets our problems on the same level they were created and only creates more problems.

The new style says that our challenges haven't gotten so complex because we've done something wrong or because Life is out to get us. The very complexity of the crisis is a gift, forcing us out of the old style and into the new. The new style says *pay attention*; trust and work with *what is* rather than always trying to make the circumstances of our lives different, and slowly bring them into the inclusion of the heart. To bring curiosity and compassion to whatever is happening right now is the movement out of separation into immediate connection with Life and into becoming a healing force in the world. Each person who has learned to include rather than war with the opposites of dark and light holds the transformation of life in their heart.

May we know that pain is an essential thread in the tapestry of Life.

May each of us discover the courage and the compassion to meet our pain.

And as more and more people move beyond war, may the world become free.

Core Intention: I'm here

Chapter 9
Beyond Control

I WANT TO DIE

I want to die before I die.
I want to die before I'm dead enough to
get dressed up, perfumed, a smile put on my face,
and tenderly placed in a royal coffin.
I want to give up this life,
surrender this life, before I exhale
the very last breath from this sacred vessel
and fill a space on the *other* side.
I wish to become nothing before I become nothing.
I want to dance before You, lifeless, naked, empty,
and move like that within *this* silence
before the *other* silence.
Who is saying these words?
The One that remembers.
The One who wakes up in the middle
of the night and hears the whisper in the wind.
These words, they are pebbles tossed in a pond;
They disappear, sink to the bottom,
only to find a new home.

Jim Ayala

AN INVITATION TO LET GO

My personal theory is you don't have to make an effort to change or stop a certain behavior you don't like. In fact, effort gets in the way. The important thing is to see it clearly, to observe all its aspects - to just witness it, and every time it arises and you see it, it doesn't catch you by surprise. The change is not a question of will. Will is necessary to cultivate awareness of the problem, defect or hang-up, but it often gets in the way of that kind of subtle profound inner change. That kind of change moves us in a direction of a way that's beyond our understanding and certainly beyond our capacity to consciously will it. It's more of an allowing, an opening - like grace.

Treya Wilber (from "Grace and Grit" by Ken Wilber)

As we begin to see that we are not the stories in our heads—the endless wanting and fearing that we have lived in most of the time—and as we begin to relate to the fear, self judgment and pain that is inherent in the story, the clouds of our mind begin to lift. We can then see there is something waiting for us *here*—the living moment of our lives and all of the joy that it holds. We can also realize that the safest, most healing thing we can do is open to our lives.

One of the places where I have discovered how safe it is to let go is around writing, for letting go is where creativity lives. Even longtime writers speak of that moment when, faced with a blank page, their stomach feels like it's poised at the top of the largest drop in roller coaster history. Up to this point in the book, all I had to do was start writing, without critiquing what was being said, and the process seemed to sort itself out. Over and over again, I was amazed at what was asking to be born through me.

This chapter was different. I knew what I wanted to say. I could feel it, but when I put pen to paper, the words became dry and lifeless. All of the controlling and judging voices in my story took over. "You can't do this," they said. "Besides, it won't be any good." I watched myself slowly move into the consciousness that is the antithesis of creativity—control. "You have to do this," another part of me said, "and you have to do it now." I became tighter and tighter, more fearful and self-judging.

Rather than being able to access simply listening—that creative state of receptive alertness that requires the letting go of expectations, demands and judgments—I found myself relying upon my own will and intellect, feeling that I alone was responsible. The harder I tried, the more contracted and frustrated I became.

The evening of the Oscars, I recorded the Barbara Walter's Special that was scheduled to air right after the awards. As usual, the Academy Awards went longer than expected, so I got on tape the Best Picture award. Sidney Poitier walked up to the podium and without preamble said:

> *Through pathways in the heart and across rivers of the mind......*
> *Instinct guides us to a place...somewhere in human consciousness that has no known address.*
> *There we look inside of ourselves, confront our demons and do battle with a mystery called the creative process.*
> *Sometimes we win; sometimes not. Such battles, such journeys are the stuff of which dreams are spun.*

Sidney reminded me that, in order to allow forth the songs that have been singing themselves inside of us since the day we were born, we need to go through a birth process, with all of the joy, messiness and pain that accompanies birthing. All of a sudden I realized that this contraction phase—the time when I was actually living this chapter by getting lost in the illusion of control—wasn't here because I was doing it wrong. It was here because it was a necessary part of the process. As soon as I could see the self-judgment without believing it, I was able to make space for the contraction. By not holding onto it and by not pushing it away, it could now pass through me like a storm front sweeping across the plains.

Moving beyond expectations, demands and time frames, curiosity kicked in, and I could now relate to the process of struggle that I had become so enmeshed in. In that simple seeing of *what is* rather than being lost in it, I could then bring compassion to the conversation inside of me that is constantly trying to *do* this book. A faint voice from deep within said, "You know, this book is living you, and someday what you are trying to express will become clear. *Let go.*

I stopped writing for awhile and simply lived in the question, "What does Life want to say through this book?" From this spaciousness, the floodgates of creativity opened again. New images began to burble to the surface, coming from a place far more intelligent and creative than my own limited mind. They astounded me with their clarity, and my pen could not move fast enough across the page. As I let go of control, I moved from *writing* a book to allowing it *through me.*

For all of us, the story that flows through our mind loves control. It not only loves it, but it deeply believes in it, courting it at every twist and turn in our lives. There is a very essential truth we fail to recognize while identified with the controlling mind—that there is something far bigger than us in charge of this dance of Life! Whatever it is that creates galaxies, snowflakes and carpets of moss doesn't just exit the scene in the daily dance of human life. In fact, it is orchestrating a perfect unfolding for our Awakening, with everything in our lives necessary for this heroic journey.

Each of us is given the exact set of experiences, the right type of health, the perfect type of relationships in order to awaken. But we don't see the perfection of this. The "I have to *do* my life" conversation keeps us caught in the narrow perspective of the struggling mind.

When we are *working at Life*, we don't see the perfection of the unfolding of our lives. It's all there, but we don't know how to look. So we fail to see that the Intelligence that has brought forth the extravagant abundance of life on Earth is always with us. It is supporting us in every experience of our lives, speaking the clues to our healing through our dreams, through what we overhear at the grocery store, through the symptoms of our body. It is revealing itself in the play of the wind, in the beauty of a tree and in the Breath that is inside our breath.

In having moments when we let go of *doing* and learn how to show up for our lives, *we move from trying to manage Life to engaging with it.* Each of us has had moments such as these. I have known them while racing across fields on my horse with no past, no future, only the pure joy of Life; lying on my back on a mountainside watching meteorites streak across the night sky; glorious moments at dawn in a hot spring where my desire for my life to be different than what it was disappeared and everything became alive and luminous.

In all of these experiences the *me* who was having a conversation about *doing* my life let go, merging back into the experience of the living moment of Life. These moments taught me that there is something available in this moment— in every moment—a Presence that lies behind the controlling, fearing mind. To touch and be touched by Life in this way gave me the fuel, the curiosity and the willingness to unravel the part of my mind that is absolutely certain that everything I truly long for will be found through trying to mold Life into what I think it should be. To open to Life again; to rediscover the ability to *be* is what true healing is all about.

THE FEAR OF LETTING GO

Living is a form of not being sure; not knowing what's next or how. The moment you know how, you begin to die a little. We guess. We may be wrong but we take leap after leap in the dark.

Agnes De Mille

The true art of letting go is quite different than what we imagine. To the mind, it either sounds like an invitation to jump off of a cliff, with the hope that something will break the fall, or else it sounds like getting rid of what we don't like. *True letting go is letting be.*

Take a moment to soften your jaw and let go of your belly. Take a few deep breaths, softening and opening into your own life. Without changing anything, be curious about what is—the space you're sitting in, the sensations in your body, the feelings in your heart. Connect with exactly what is happening, in the moment it is happening. This is a moment of letting go to Life. This is a moment of letting Life be.

Letting be happens when our attention is focused on exactly *what is.* When we are not lost in trying to make ourselves and our lives different than they are, our attention is freed to merge with Life rather than living behind the walls of separation. This is not about being passive. This is an active, alive, conscious engagement with the living process. This is also not about being at the mercy of Life. The challenges of Life are dealt with much more easily and with greater skill when we are *here,* responding rather than reacting.

In order to know full connection, we have to meet our fear of letting go and letting Life be. The stories around this fear feel seductive and real for each one of us, but the safest place we will ever discover is in showing up for our lives. Water is a very powerful metaphor for both the fear of letting go and the safety. In deep water, there is no ground beneath your feet and in its murky depths lurk all sorts of things that can either tickle your leg or devour you whole (depending on your imagination). But water also has very supportive qualities. It heals, cleanses and nourishes every cell of our bodies. And it is very buoyant. Water will literally hold you, if you let go.

A woman from one of my Awakening groups had a water dream about both the terror of letting go and its safety as well. All of her life she has been afraid of being on a boat, afraid of falling over the side into the endless abyss of water. Living in the Puget Sound area where there are lots of ferries, she learned to manage this fear by staying in the middle of the boat. At the time of the dream, she was moving through one of the most challenging phases of parenting—that of letting her child go to his destiny. Her son was now moving into young adulthood and had had a number of difficulties. Most of the time she thought of him with trepidation and felt an urgent need to manage his life. In the middle of this painful letting go process she had the following dream:

She was on a huge ferry, very far from shore. "I am looking out the gaping entrance hole in front of the ferry with a clear view of the water," she said, "but I am well back from the edge. All of a sudden my son dashes by me, sprinting the many yards to the edge and takes a slow, soaring dive into the waves. My initial experience is one of shock at his abrupt appearance, but that quickly turns to panic. Almost as an aside, I notice his soaring into the water is very graceful and athletic, but that is overtaken by desperate fear that he will drown. Just as his body breaks the surface of the water, a stop action occurs. His plunge halts with his upper body under the water but his legs, from the waist to his toes, still visible. He begins to dance in synchronized swimming motions that I recognized from the Olympic Games. Much to my amazement, I see that he is putting on a show just for me. I feel his huge grin of satisfaction at surprising me with this colossal trick. The ferry continues on its way, as I watch the scene pass in front of me.

I am drawn ever closer to the edge of the ferry so I can continue to see him as the distance between us grows ever greater. I still am focused on his comic, absurd, dancing legs but as we move further away, I can see more of what is happening. A whole regatta of fishing and pleasure boats surrounds him. It has the feeling of a party, a celebration with flags and horns and I am awed by the colors. They are fresh and clear and, even in the dream, I name them as Easter egg colors. I now can hear the sounds from this scene, and my son is laughing a wonderful laugh of confidence, assuredness and support."

What a wonderful dream. It speaks of the fear we all carry of letting go and letting Life be. It also shows the support and safety that meet us when we do (a whole regatta of celebration). It is safe to let go, but the controlling mind that stays in the middle of the boat says this is not so. It is able to give us ironclad dissertations on why we have to hold on. And yet there is something niggling deep inside, a part of us that knows that when control becomes the predominant way we move through our lives, it brings contraction, isolation and disconnection rather than safety.

At the threshold of letting go there are two very common fears that we need to meet and pass through. The first is that if we let go of controlling our lives, darkness will take over. We fear the fall into the void of depression, inertia or despair. We've all had times in our lives when we have known these deep wells of darkness. We have stayed caught and struggling because we have been taught that they are wrong. In Awakening, we begin to learn how to gather the gifts that lie nestled in the heart of our darkness rather than being engulfed by it. These parts of ourselves are a necessary facet of human life. Just as the night defines the day, our challenges define our strengths and our darkness reveals our light.

I have been graced for years by an exquisite willow tree outside my bedroom window. One spring evening as I was getting ready for my son's 18th Birthday, a rainstorm moved into the Northwest and I was drawn to look out the window. The willow was in the beginning stages of putting on her summer dress of vibrant green, and the sky framing the willow was black and stormy, as rain danced horizontally past my window.

Suddenly, the clouds opened up on the horizon, allowing the setting sun to bathe this stormy sea with its vibrant light. The myriad rain drops on the willow's branches were immediately transformed into individual prisms of light. It was so breathtakingly beautiful that tears came to my eyes. As I looked out the window on the other side of the house, there was a double rainbow, crystal clear against the dark and forbidding clouds. I knew as I watched this gift from the Universe that it was a metaphor for human life. Without the stormy sky to frame the opening for the setting sun, the beauty of the willow would not have been highlighted, and without both the rain and the sun, the rainbow wouldn't have been born.

Our dark states become much more workable when we learn that they are just like the weather—never static, always changing, coming and going for the rest of our lives. Letting go opens us, allows those seemingly static states to float through like clouds moving across the face of the sun. Stephen Levine, after having watched his own depression dance in and out of his life for years, had a recent visit from this old friend. He said that in three minutes he went through the whole cycle that formerly would have taken weeks or months. With every single part of the depression, he was able to say, "I recognize you." In that recognition he was able to let go of any identification with these feelings and they passed on through. Letting go, even of our darkness, brings great freedom.

A friend of mine teaches white-water kayaking. Dancing down the river, cascading over rapids, navigating around boulders, it is a very real possibility that at some time the students will be tossed into the seething cauldron of a whirlpool (just like the whirlpools of our daily lives). The raging water pulls them down and tumbles them around. Their instinctual reaction is to fight it (exactly how we fight the struggles in our lives), but what he teaches them to do is to let go and allow the water to move them as it will. In that nonresistance, the water will lift them up to the top and they can then make their way to safety. The same is true for our lives, and yet this terrifies us. We fear surrendering into Life. We fear letting go of control. To our minds it feels like someone is asking us to be like a leaf in the wind. And yet that terror is a threshold to a level of creativity, safety and adventure that is beyond what most of us can conceive.

The second fear we meet at the threshold of letting go is that if we stop controlling, nothing will be there—that we will cease to exist. This comes from the deep illusion that we are responsible for creating our own lives. The truth is, however, that rather than nothing being there, everything will be there! In letting go, we will experience the radiant truth of our being and a creativity that is beyond anything we can envision.

Letting go—letting Life *be*—moves us into a new level of consciousness, a level in which grand intuitive leaps and sudden insights flood us, a place in which we can see the whole rather than the parts. It is an expansive space in which new perspectives can rise up spontaneously. These creative leaps can happen because when we let go, we are no longer interested in time frames, end results or even in being right and there is tolerance for paradox, confusion and complexity.

The shift into letting go allows us to see that there is another reality available at all moments of our lives and that it lives everywhere—in every single thing and experience. We truly are a part of something greater. We have lived in the perception of separation for so long that we have forgotten to step back and perceive the whole, to notice how well it works.

I was given some beeswax candles the other day and was transfixed by the intricate order and exquisite beauty that Life expresses through bees. As I looked at them closely, my Awareness opened to the awesome order that is everywhere—in the rhythm of the tides and the seasons of birth and death, in the Earth's precisely choreographed dance around the sun and the exquisite symmetry of the spinal column. Whenever I move beyond my fear of letting go, I automatically come out of my own little separate world and see rhythm and order all around me, with a little chaos thrown in to keep things moving on the journey of Awakening.

After many years of practicing softening around the need to control, I found myself early one morning at the upper meditation hall at Cloud Mountain Retreat Center, a wonderful sanctuary where I have led a number of retreats. The hall is built on the side of a steep hill so that while standing on the porch, I feel as if I am hanging out in the treetops. That morning I was fully connected to Life. My attention, totally present in that moment, didn't need anything to be different than it was. As I listened to the symphony of birds, a group of chickadees trilled off to my right. Then the percussion of the crows underscored their notes. A bevy of unknown birds arrived to add their part of the score. After a few moments of silence, there was the heart opening call of a robin. On and on it went, my awareness fully open to Life as it unfolded moment to moment. With tears trickling down my cheeks, *I realized that I finally belonged to Life.* Rather than trying to control, judge or *do* my life, I was *being* Life.

Ever since that day I have experienced more and more moments when I simply showed up for the adventure. This is what we are hungry for—the experience of belonging to Life and to our own lives—and it is discovered as we cultivate the skills of letting go, letting be.

FROM SEPARATION TO CONNECTION

To see a world in a grain of sand
And a Heaven in a wild flower,
Hold Infinity in the palm of your hand
and Eternity in an hour.

William Blake

In order to know the creativity and the connection available to us when we open to Life again, we need to look at two illusions of the controlling mind. The first is that we are each completely separate individuals, disconnected from the whole. This fosters the belief that we have to rely upon only our own limited intelligence and resources in order to maneuver through our lives. The second is that control will bring us the freedom we long for. Let us first look at the illusion of separation.

Separation has been a phase of human evolution. We are like parts of the tree of Life that have been able to step away from the tree and recognize that it is a tree. This stepping back, even though it caused us to disconnect from truly being one with Life, has allowed us to explore Life in individual parts—from the tops of mountains to the depths of the sea; from mighty galaxies to the heart of the atom.

We are now living in a time when human perception is being called to weave the parts back into a whole. Even the leading edge of science is inviting us back into the understanding that there is no reality to separation. When we entered the atom, we discovered particles dancing into waves and back into particles again in a sea of unpredictable interrelationships. In the film *Mindwalk,* Liv Ullman's character says:

> *Physics is proving that what we call an object, an atom, is only an approximation, a metaphor. At the subatomic level, it dissolves into a series of interconnections. Here, there is a continual exchange of matter and energy, between hand and wood, wood and air. It is a real exchange of photons and electrons. Like it or not, we are all a part of one inseparable web of relationships.*

This happens on all levels of existence. Everything in the Universe is a part of an interconnected dance, dependent upon everything else for its existence. Breath is the place where this can be most readily seen. Every time we breathe we give of ourselves to Life on the out-breath and receive Life on the in-breath.

After you read this section, put the book down and become aware of your breath. Your breath is not an isolated, separate event. It is a part of a river of breath that has moved through you since your first breath. It was there when you made mud pies; it was there during the moment you rode your first bike; and it was there for your first kiss. It is the same river of breath that has been moving through all of Life for billions of years.

Every single breath you breathe contains atoms that have been a part of everything that ever was, from stars to dinosaurs to your next door neighbor. Every single breath you give back to the world is filled with atoms that were once a part of your leg bone, the blood coursing through your veins and the wondrous intricacy of your liver. Every time you breathe in, you breathe in the entire world. Every time you breathe out, you give yourself to the world. Since the moment you were born, the endless river of breath that not only animates all living beings, but also contains the whole Universe, has breathed you.

Nothing has an existence unto itself. We are given the gift of life in a body and are able to sit here and read this book because of the first one-celled organisms that made the atmosphere, because of the first molecules that figured out how to come together to create the minerals that make up our bones, because of our great grandparents attraction to one another, because of the trees from which the paper is made and because of the sun's willingness to give of itself. We are a set of relationships, living in a sea of relationships that are extended through all time and space.

Interconnection is also a truth in our emotional life. We are all doing the same dance of separation. We are all lost in the same fears, hatreds and delusions. The depression that you experience is *our* depression. The fear you get lost in is a common experience. Whatever feeling you are feeling—whether it be irritation, fear, joy, boredom, sleepiness, numbness or love—it is, at this same exact moment, also being experienced by millions of other people and will continue to be for a long, long time.

The illusion of separation seduces us into taking these feelings personally and has allowed us to fall into that trap that *my* fear, *my* depression or *my* rage is special, unique or worse than everybody else's. This is just not true. On one level your feelings are your own. On another level, these feelings are human feelings that come from our collective pool of delusion. This is why we can make such a big difference in the healing of humanity by becoming awake around our own feelings. Every moment that a person can relate to a feeling, rather than from it, is another step towards freedom for all beings.

Interconnection is also evident in the realm of thought. The story that moves through you is the same story that moves through me. You may have more of a particular quality, like fear or anger, and you may couple them together in a different sequence than I do, but we all have the same illusions moving through us.

Interconnection is the truth of who we are. Our journey into separation was a journey into isolation. It is as if we were all hairs on the back of a dog, waving in the wind, absolutely certain that we were each unique and divided from every other hair. We are beginning to notice that our roots are all connected and draw their very life from the same dog!

To see that it is all one energetic event, unfolding in unison from the beginning of time, is to come back into Life, out of the illusion of separation. Life is one Being with every single thing interconnected with everything else throughout all space and time, including us. *Our healing is about becoming aware of the interconnection of Life and discovering ourselves as a part of that flow.* The more we weave ourselves back into the tapestry of Life, the less we become interested in trying to control it and the more fascinated we become with living it.

Once we begin to taste the nectar of interconnectedness, we can see that nothing cuts us off from connection faster than the urge to be in charge. Over and over again, our attention is pulled into trying to manage and manipulate Life rather than being intimately connected with it. In order to move out of separation and back into connection, we need to dismantle the second illusion of the controlling mind—that efforting, trying and doing will bring us freedom. As a wise person once said, "If you want to make God laugh, tell it your plans." This isn't that control is bad. It is a useful tool when used appropriately, *but it will only take us so far.* Letting go will bring us levels of freedom and healing that are far beyond the realm of control.

There is a primal place inside each of our stories that reacts in terror when we even contemplate this because, from the beginning of our species, our safety and survival was dependent upon mastery over our environment. We didn't have warm coats of fur or feathers nor did we have great speed. We also didn't have the strength to muscle our prey to the ground or the claws to open them up. Learning how to manage fire, shelter, farming and tools allowed us to survive. Through archeology we can see the unfolding of humankind as we, step by step, gained mastery over different aspects of our physical lives, and we can observe this with great respect and admiration.

The urge to dominate Life has propelled human history to the point that we have now gained major control over our environment. We live most of the time in artificially controlled buildings, travel in high-speed, climate-controlled vehicles, eat genetically altered food, and rely on an assortment of medications to alleviate pain. And yet we pay a heavy personal price for living in the illusion that we can and must control everything. The price is both incredible stress and great grief. The more we have controlled, the more we have moved into the illusion that we are responsible for holding together the very fabric of our lives, and we now find ourselves caught both in the despair of separation and in the anxiety of trying to control our lives rather than *letting Life live us.*

Remember the story of the little boy holding his finger in the dike? He is all alone with the dike looming above him which holds back the sea. If for a moment he lets go of his vigilance, the water will engulf him and all that he cares about. He perceives himself to be completely responsible, all by himself, for the life or death of himself and his community. He is temporarily in control, but he is clearly not free. That is how most of us live.

Fortunately, the insanity of living in a deep need for control drives us to look for another way. And what waits for us just a step beyond our urge to control is the breathtaking wonder and deep healing of opening to Life again.

LETTING GO 101

We were given freedom of choice so that we have the ability to choose not to use it.

Marlo Morgan (from a talk in Seattle)

The mind may not remember the joy of letting go and allowing Life to be, but the body does. The connection with Life that resides in the memory of every single one of the cells of our body knows the safety of letting go. This is evident in the spontaneous deep breath, accompanied with the sound of *ahhh* that makes up a wonderful sigh. The body naturally expresses this sound of letting go after a particularly satisfying meal or after the mind has finally understood something that has been deeply perplexing (ah ha!). It is also nestled in the heart of a good belly laugh and shows up within almost every word that we use in order to describe the energy that is God—Allah, Buddha, Jehovah, Muhammad, and even the word God itself. Ahhh is the sound of letting go, and letting go is the birthplace of radiance.

One of the most powerful gifts of letting go is that it creates space. We can see this clearly in the medical world where the idea of softening around physical pain is catching on. We know now that most of what keeps pain alive and also what slows down the healing process is that we tighten around it, creating more pain. Imagine a pinched nerve in your neck and someone coming and pressing down upon it—excruciating pain. And yet, this is exactly what we do to our own pain—we tense around it. This is not only true physically, but also mentally and emotionally too. Softening and letting go opens up space so that the creativity of Life can come flooding in.

We can support the joy of opening to Life by cultivating letting go in our bodies. When you are caught and struggling, your body contracts. Softening around our armoring clears a pathway back into the living adventure. The more you see this, the faster your body becomes a wise friend that will tell you, long before your head realizes it, that you are in control mode. You'll find yourself in the middle of an argument with your mate and all of a sudden Awareness will kick in and you will notice your jaw clenched like a vise. Or you'll be fearful of sharing a difficult feeling with a friend and you'll notice that your belly is tighter than a drum.

In those moments when you want to struggle against *what is*—fighting it, denying it—the simple act of physically letting go can dramatically alter your experience. At the beginning, you probably won't notice much difference, as your tendency to hold on will snap back faster than a rubber band. But with repeated invitations into softening your jaw, dropping your shoulders and letting go of your belly, you will begin to emerge from the maze of control.

As I have learned how to let go of the tension in my body, my center of gravity has moved from my head back into my belly. I feel rooted to the Earth and supported by Life. I now experience a safety that I didn't even know existed. I still have many automatic reactions inside of me in which I find myself, in the blink of an eye, armoring against Life, but now contraction is a signal to let go, moving me into the healing of softening, opening and connecting rather than running from *what is*.

Physically softening transforms our lives on many levels. It allows the healing energies of the body to flow easily into injured places. It also softens the armor around our hearts, allowing deep emotions that we've formerly resisted to move through us without our getting caught in them. The act of letting go of the tension in our bodies also invites us to soften around the contractions in our mind, teaching us how to relate to, rather than from, the chaos of our story. Letting go, even for a moment, may look like a very simple act, but it is a golden thread that eventually turns into a strong rope that is finally woven into a bridge between our ideas about Life and the living experience of it.

Letting go through the body happens in little moments. Whether you are sitting at a stop light, standing in line or washing your hands, throughout your day you can allow the body to become a mirror for the holding of your controlling mind. In these moments of pausing and connecting with your body, become very curious about where you are holding. Is your jaw tight, your anal sphincter? Are your arms hanging from your shoulders or are they subtly held? Choose one spot and consciously let it go. If it's hard to access that, tighten the muscles even more, and then slowly, very slowly, let them go. Notice what that feels like. You can choose one favorite area in your life where holding on is easily seen and then notice what the tension level is like throughout your day.

Consciously letting go in tiny increments throughout the day is a doorway back into Life. As our body and mind let go, we open into the living experience of our lives the moment Life appears out of Mystery. We then notice that Life is a constantly changing dance and, just like with a roller coaster, it is the safest and the most fun when we show up for the ride! We don't have to take a flying leap. A moment here and a moment there are powerful transformers of our addiction of trying to control our lives.

A BALANCE BETWEEN CONTROLLING
AND LETTING GO

The strategic mind gets enormously frightened around change because it knows it doesn't belong there.

David Whyte

To see how pervasive control is, we can notice how easy it is to slip into the idea that says, "Letting go is good and control is bad." What we're exploring is not about eliminating control nor is it about controlling our urge to control. Control is a useful tool for maneuvering through Life, but it is a horrible master. Control is very good for producing, scheduling and getting things done, but it also tends to dominate, struggle, fear and resist. Our difficulty lies in how it has taken over our lives, cutting us off from everything we want to experience—the well of creativity and connection that can only be known in letting go into the living moment.

A great place we can see a healthy balance between controlling and letting go is in our bodies. The latticework of our skeletal structure allows for the fluidity of our muscles. Now imagine that our need for control is our bones and letting go is our muscles. Rather than being a helpful internal structure in our lives, control has taken over so much that it has turned into external armoring, making us tight, rigid and fearful. The kind of control we believe in is like having our skeleton on the outside of our bodies. This rigidity makes it very difficult to maneuver through our lives— to bend, to flow—and leaves our bones more vulnerable to breaking.

To honor control but not allow it to take over our lives is very healing. The place where I learned about a healthy balance between controlling and letting go was around public speaking. People had asked me to teach for years before I actually had the courage to do it. I was terrified that I would freeze in front of a group—that I wouldn't speak clearly and people would ask me questions I wouldn't know how to answer. Because I couldn't figure out how to control it all, I stayed frozen and separate from my destiny.

The very first time I spoke in public, I was given the chance to take the place of a speaker who had become sick. I had one and a half hours notice, leaving me with time to get dressed and little else. I had the choice to desperately create a talk and try to remember it or to let go. Awareness said, "Relax. Live in the question, 'What wants to be said?' and watch it appear." When I spoke later that morning, I let go and the words poured through me.

In future speaking engagements, when I had time to plan how it *should be*, fear came up and the judging mind took me out of the experience. Rather than opening to the experience I found myself caught in a conversation about how I should be doing it differently. I would get tighter and tighter, speaking more and more from my head rather than from "what wants to be said." Operating from what I thought I *should be* threw me into being dependent on my intellect and will rather than on the Infinite Intelligence that permeates everything and every moment.

It took me awhile to again let go to that place that I had opened into during the initial speaking engagement—the place where I was *being* Life rather than doing it. In the meantime, I filled notebooks with what I should do or say and set schedules for when things should happen. There were times when I would let go enough that something new and unplanned would come flowing out. But usually, I'd very quickly be back into my agenda, checking to see if I was following it right.

I began to notice, however, that in those moments of letting go, the room would become electrified and we would move into a sense of empowerment together. The deep yearning to know more of those truly creative moments that we enter only when we are fully present finally invited me into letting go. I began to realize that my own limited intelligence wasn't smart enough to figure out what needed to be shared in any given group, but that what was needed would unfold when I showed up in the living moment.

So I stopped creating agendas and didn't take notes with me. Before I spoke, I would live in the question, "What wants to be said that is for the highest good of all beings involved in this situation?" I would then become aware of a feeling, a feeling that opened and brought peace to my being. Along with that feeling would usually come a few major points. I learned to go into public speaking with a sense of this feeling, a remembering of the few main points, and a willingness to watch for what would show up. This was a perfect balance between control and letting go. If I went with too much structure— too many preconceived ideas—magic wouldn't appear. If I went with no structure—not holding to the main ideas—both I and the group as a whole would wander everywhere.

We need a sense of internal structure and we need to ability to open so that the wellspring of creativity within us can flow freely. Balance is the key. A good metaphor for the balance between control and letting go is ice skating. In the beginning, we hold on because of our fear of letting go. We lock our knees, imagine the worst and only reluctantly allow our fingers to be pried away from the railing. There is no possibility of joyous movement or dancing freedom in too much control. When we do venture out onto the ice, we fall a lot because we haven't yet learned the art of controlling the proper muscles.

We need both a sense of internal structure and the ability to be open so that the wellspring of creativity can live us.

Balance is the key, the doorway into the new. As we develop our internal 'muscles', we gain the strength and the support that is needed in order let go to gliding, spinning and dancing. I think one of the reasons we are so fascinated with ice skating events on television is that what we see when a seasoned skater dances across the ice is a perfect balance of control and letting go.

We all want to dance again, opening to Life so we can know the place where true creativity lives. No matter how scary it may seem to the story in our heads, the deepest, wisest parts of ourselves are constantly inviting us to open, let go and allow Life to be. It's safe. It's home.

BEING LIFE

If one does not know that everything has its time and wants to force things, then indeed one will never succeed in becoming concentrated, nor succeed in the art of loving.

Erich Fromm

Fortunately, Life won't allow us to stay under the domination of the controlling mind. We are slowly and surely being drawn back into engagement with Life the moment it appears out of Mystery.

We are like musicians, learning how to play the musical instrument of Life. We are completing the phase in which we've laboriously and painstakingly cultivated control. We've learned the notes, the chords and the positioning of our fingers. With that structure in place, we can now let go, and music that has never been heard before can be born.

This new rung on the ladder of evolution is inviting us into the recognition that, *as long as we are busy creating, we can't be here for Creation.* As long as we are busy planning, we can't listen to *what is.* The spirit of Life passionately wants us to let go to a healing that is beyond our wildest imaginations. It is demanding, cajoling, requiring us to open to the Unknown, to let go of our bastion of control and to reconnect with Life. Even though the ego screams, cries and rages when it hears the invitation to let go, the Unknown whispers in our hearts, "Don't fear me; respect me. Honor me. Do not take me lightly, but be willing to let go. It's safe."

Feel yourself sitting here, holding a book with your breath rising and falling. This is a moment of moving beyond control and joining the river of Life. At the beginning this will happen for a moment here and a moment there and *that is enough*! We have been gone a long time, and we cannot expect a quick transformation from managing to merging. Gradually, by adding a daily sitting practice and cultivating moments throughout our day when we show up for the river—tasting a bite of food, hearing the sound of a lawnmower, connecting with the rhythm of our breath—we discover more and more moments when the boat naturally turns around and we engage with the river of our lives.

Know that one of the most helpful tools for re-engaging with the river of Life is the resistance to doing this! Every single one of us feels fear about allowing our boat to turn around and engage with the river. Our resistance to awakening and engaging with the river serves as a guide, and when it is respected, it is a skillful helmsman for navigating the river. It will tell us when it is time to dance with the river, when it is time to be more cautious, and when it is time to take a break and rest on the bank.

As we bring our urge to control into balance and learn the art of letting go, we will begin to have more and more moments when our Awareness is freed up to reconnect with Life, the awesome Mystery that is unfolding completely new in every moment. Know that every time in our daily meditation when we bring our attention back to our breath, and every moment throughout our day when we allow our senses to reconnect with Life, we are cultivating the ability to skillfully dance with the river. In doing so, we discover all of the support, wisdom and Love that is there.

May we know the safety of letting go, letting Life be.

May we trust our resistance to doing this.

And may we discover the joy of engaging moment to moment with the river of Life..

Core Intention: It's safe

Chapter 10
Rebuilding Trust in the Flow of Life

UNTIE THE KNOT

Untie the knot, leave the front door open,
let the chairs and tables come and go as they please,
like little chickens.

Let whatever you put your weight on roam around outside
beneath the open sky.
Breathe the fresh air and doze beneath the house
in the cool hand of the Earth.

If the dark hooded one passes by and stands around your door,
invite him into your house. He's very, very quiet.
Don't let that worry you, though.
Look for his eyes and you will find the night sky without any stars
and the purest silence.
Sit quietly, have tea and cookies, maybe share some dreams.

Untie the knot,
open the windows wide,
throw the curtains into the yard; turn on some music;
invite the rain in and dance till you're soaked!
Whoever said we had to take this ride so seriously?

Untie the knot.
The stars in the sky are tokens to your heart.
Get up in the middle of the night and harvest as many as you like.
Just like a dream. Sleep in as late as you like

Untie the knot.
Have friends over for tea, hold hands, look in their eyes.
This conversation is ancient...

Jim Ayala

BOATING SKILLS

The chief act of will is not effort but consent. To try to accomplish things by force of will is to reinforce the false self. Receptivity is not inactivity. It is a real activity, but not effort in the ordinary sense of the word. It is simply an attitude of waiting for Ultimate Mystery. You don't know what that is, but as your faith is purified, you don't want to know.

Father Thomas Keating

Now that we have looked at some of the core structures of the mind that believes it is separate from Life, and we have explored the safety and the creativity of opening to Life again, let us explore how we can support this opening. Going back to the river analogy, it reminds us that the mind that we live in most of the time believes it has to paddle upstream, trying to make Life be what it thinks it should be. This kind of mind works at Life, using efforting, trying, acquiring and doing—all skills that come from wanting to manage Life. It is externally oriented, believing that what we hunger for will be found outside of ourselves.

The style of mind that knows how to *be* Life is about connecting and engaging with our lives. This is the place of showing up for the living experience in an attentive and creative way. It is based in trust, the ultimate benevolence of the Universe and the safety of letting go to Life. It is the place where, for more and more moments, we allow the boat of our attention to turn around so we can engage with the river of Life. This turning around not only connects us with the treasures of our inner world, but it also shows us that we are a part of a highly intelligent, exquisitely ordered and ultimately supportive process.

Turning our boat around and engaging with the river doesn't mean being helpless. We can't control the river, but we can learn boating skills—ways to use our minds to skillfully maneuver down the river of Life. Curiosity and compassion are skills that we have already explored. The deep attention of curiosity allows us to notice what is going on and reveals to us how we can learn from each and every part of the river. The inclusion of compassion allows us to drop out of the struggling mind, touching whatever is happening with the healing of our heart. This enables us to work skillfully with whatever the river brings. The more we cultivate these tools, the more the river becomes safe and adventuresome for us, no matter how challenging it may be.

Besides compassion and curiosity, there are other creative ways to engage with the river. The skills we will explore in this chapter all come from the knowing that *Life is for us.* Einstein said that the most important question we can ask is,

"Is the Universe friendly? The answer," he said, "is 'yes'." The key word here is "Universe." Our world is not necessarily a friendly place. Human beings do unspeakable things to one another and to the Earth itself. Greed and fear are evident everywhere. But the Universe is ultimately *friendly* in the sense that it is *for* Life, supporting its unfolding in ways we can't even comprehend, let alone see.

In exploring the ultimate *friendliness* of Life, Stephen Levine once gave the example of getting down on the ground to watch an ant war. It is violence at work—heads and limbs being torn apart, lives destroyed. And yet, if you stand up and step back, you see that baby birds are being fed from the body parts and that a deeply buried seed will now be able to germinate because of the dirt that was moved by the ants. He said that the longer he is alive, the harder it is for him to say what is grace and what is tragedy.

When we stand back far enough, we will see that Life is for life in all of its forms, including humans. In fact, it weaves the opposites of dark and light into a dance that is orchestrated for the emergence of conscious life.

In order to fully engage with the river of Life, we will explore four *boating skills* that will allow us to turn our boat around and engage with the river. We will then explore four ways we can partner with the river of Life so that the fullness of what is asking to be born through human consciousness can be manifested. The four *boating skills* are Welcoming, Don't Know, Gratitude and Generosity.

Welcoming

We were introduced to this skill earlier, but it is such a valuable tool in our partnership with the river of Life that it is important to explore it further. Welcoming understands that every river has rapids, waterfalls and snags, as well as long stretches of flowing water and still clear pools. We need both extremes.

Wherever we look, we see that Life consists of opposites—day/night, winter/spring, male/female, expansion/contraction. Welcoming—accepting both poles of existence—allows us to remain at the center of the opposites. It moves us out of the belief that light is good and shadow is bad. "The problems of our lives are here to awaken us," says Welcoming, "here to break the armoring around our heart and to move us out of the delusion that we are separate, isolated and alone."

Welcoming invites us to listen, to really listen to that which we formerly resisted, hated and feared. The old paradigm of fighting what we don't like says that we have finally gotten it all together when our lives are easy, placid and flowing and that we've done it wrong when they are turbulent, chaotic and scary. Welcoming allows us to see that our lives will always dance between these two poles and that we miss deep understanding and an abiding sense of peace when we try to do away with the difficult and get to the light without listening.

Rather than always contracting around the difficult, unsettling and confusing parts of our lives, Welcoming teaches us to stay open, curious, alert and receptive to *what is*. Have you ever watched a baby for a while? It's like watching the weather dance across the face of the Earth. Anger comes; anger goes. Laughter comes; laughter goes. Babies don't get stuck in any one state. As we become older and are trained to fear and hate that which is deemed inappropriate, incorrect, wrong or bad, the times of ease become shorter and shorter as more of our energy is spent in fixing, resisting, self-hatred and fear.

In the Awakening groups I lead, I continually witness the power of welcoming. The hidden pieces of people's lives that become visible can range from the embarrassment of shoplifting to the experience of someone being irritated with what is happening in the group and being afraid to say so. When these parts that we don't want to see about ourselves (let alone allow other people to see) are spoken into a welcoming space, amazing things happen. I've seen people sob from relief that a part of themselves was finally received without judgment, and I've seen people stunned with the realization that even irritation or resistance to what is happening right now is okay.

Arnie Mindell, author of *The Shaman's Body*, tells a welcoming story from a conference he led in Russia on conflict resolution. Members of the parliament and delegations from groups in conflict from the various regions of the ex-Soviet Republic were there. As they gathered together, it was noted that this was the first time in history that these groups had even agreed to be in the same room. Slowly, one after another, they spoke of the suffering of their people, describing war, poverty and ongoing racial prejudice. They spoke of terrorists invading their localities and of the effects of the imperialist policies of the Soviet leaders.

Arnie, realizing that the victim viewpoint was present but that neither the imperialists nor the terrorists had a voice in the room, invited people to act out the different roles. They got up and stood in places set aside for the three divisions: the imperialist, the terrorist and the victimized community. The tension was thick in the room when suddenly, everything exploded into roars of laughter. Imperialists were demanding that everyone submit to their domination. The terrorists screamed back, "To hell with you!"

In that moment, when the imperialists and the terrorists (those who were formerly hated and feared) were included, the group moved beyond the victim stance and became an alive, connected, functioning whole. Arnie said they were then able to cry and laugh about our world, witnessing together humanity's tendency to dominate, to suffer and to rebel. Nothing was solved immediately, but something shifted. For that time and in that place, they became bigger than war, both the internal war of "I hate me" and the external war of "I hate you."

What was discovered in that room is also true inside each of us. Welcoming knows that each of us is a community. It is not only the benevolent, powerful, clear and strong parts of ourselves that are necessary. Our fears, shadows, hatreds, confusions, and even our sore knees are all essential pieces of the community that we are. As we include the various parts of our being without shame or blame, we then become a human being who knows that terrorists, victims, saints and mad men are a part of the whole (just as they are a part of our inner life, too). Welcoming knows that each person, each relationship, each business and each country *needs to have all sides*. This shift in perspective makes space for ideas and actions that are inconceivable when we separate Life into good and bad parts.

The more we welcome, the quicker whatever we are resisting can move through. The Buddha once told a story about Sahka, the ruler of the Devas.

> *While Sahka was out visiting the far reaches of his land, a sullen, potbellied dwarf came to visit the castle. Finding the King absent, he went up and sat upon the throne. This was an act of supreme sacrilege. Sahka's followers tried to bully, shame, taunt and scare the dwarf away, but to their dismay, he grew bigger and stronger in exact proportion to the resistance to his presence.*

> *At length, the King was called back from his journey in order to get rid of this unwanted guest. Upon entering the throne room, instead of challenging the unwelcome guest, he draped his own robe over the dwarf's shoulders and knelt in respect before him. With every act of welcoming, appreciation and recognition, the dwarf became smaller and smaller until finally he vanished.*

The King understood that resistance feeds the parts of our lives (both internally and externally) which we hate and fear. It is our aversion and judgment that give them power.

Oftentimes, upon hearing about welcoming, our initial response is horror. "If I allow it to be there, it will take over," says the mind. The exact opposite is true. For most of my life I was a compulsive eater. In one year alone I gained 97 pounds. Never in all those years did I stop trying to fight and control this deep hunger that would roar through my best intentions like a wild fire on a windy day.

Then I learned the art of welcoming. I would say to the hunger, "I am choosing to move beyond hating and fearing you. You are a part of me. You can have a voice in the community of my being. I want to hear what you have to say. I want to know you. I want to understand what your contribution is to my Awakening." At first it grabbed its freedom and ran with it. It felt like it had been let of prison and wanted to eat everything that it could lay its hands on. But very quickly when this part of me was met with true inclusion, it had nothing to fight against, and I found myself beginning to celebrate the joy of zucchini (it actually looked delicious to me) rather than always being obsessed by chocolate.

The more I listened, the more I began to appreciate this part of me that I had formerly thought of as a monster. I could see how it was created in my infancy out of a need for survival. I was finally able to say, "Thank you for taking care of me all of my life; you were born out of the desire for safety and connection." The more I showed it respect and acceptance, the less it felt a need to push. The more I made space for the uncontrollable hunger, the more it revealed the deep pain out of which it arose, and slowly and surely my response to these urges moved from control, fear and hatred into deep compassion, respect and inclusion.

We can't fake it. The mind, once it sees the magic of making space for what we formerly resisted, will try to use welcoming to get rid of what it still hates. It won't work. Just as we know deep in our gut when someone isn't quite being honest with us, our shadow has a highly tuned radar system for what is true welcoming and what is not. True welcoming says that it is okay for whatever is here to be here. It is willing to stand with our pain, our fear, our rage because it knows they are a part of the community of our being.

Welcoming is not about indulging in unhealthy feelings, nor is it about justifying unhealthy actions. It's about creating enough space around our feelings so that we can *see* them, learn about them and figure out how to work *with* them, rather than always being *against* them. It is also not about standing in front of a tidal wave of emotion and saying, "I want to listen to you." There is a time for welcoming and a time for boundaries. In my own life, as I've found a greater sense welcoming, not only are my boundaries much clearer, but they are also more easily and compassionately declared.

The most powerful gift of welcoming is that it opens the field of our being. As we practice the fluidity of welcoming, the energy we formerly used for struggle is available for our natural state of radiance and reverence—a glowing, alive, grateful and present state of being. It is pure joy to watch the transformation point when one shifts from resistance to welcoming.

Don't Know

At this point in evolution, Life is giving us a gift of great importance—the gift of uncertainty. Experts say one year that salt is bad for us, and we then find on the market shelves a variety of salt substitutes. The next year they say their research has now discovered that it isn't as bad as they thought. Political commercials manipulate the facts so much that there can be two completely opposing viewpoints coming from the same set of statistics. And terrorists are causing havoc all over the world. This uncertainty is permeating the very core of our collective mind set and it causes a deep sense of unease. We want a place to stand, a place that is solid and unchanging. So we search for the truth, the absolute truth. The fact is, there is none. All truth is relative.

Our need for control rages when it hears this. It wants absolutes that say this is the right way and that is the wrong way. And yet the transformation that Life is about right now is much too serious to hold onto the old style of thinking that demands certainty. Truth always includes both sides. The ability to not know, not position and not seek absolutes is the place in which the parts can come together as a whole.

There are two little words that can shift us out of our addiction to being in control—*don't know*. These words can engender great confusion and fear, or they can open us back into Life. In the struggling mind, we operate from "have to know." We have to know what to do, how to do it, when to do it and where. And we've been caught in this box of control to such a level that we truly believe that our minds can understand and control it all.

It was Plato who said that what is real could never be comprehended by the thinking mind. Yet we live as if this were so. If we say we don't know, in our society this is equal to admitting confusion, stupidity or resignation. So we keep ourselves away from this sense of failure by staying contracted in the need to know. This cuts us off from so much. To live in the known is to live in the old. It separates us from what is new, magical, mysterious and adventuresome.

I saw this clearly at a long meditation retreat. We were relieved of the normal demands of daily lives. We didn't have to cook, talk, do errands, run a business or be social. And yet, as my awareness sharpened and centered, I could see that most of what my mind was doing throughout the day was planning what was going to happen next and, at the same time, trying to figure it all out. It felt like I was living in constant circles of busyness inside of my head.

At moments I would be present, resting in the breath, connecting with the newness of Life, and then the clouds of confusion would arise. The mind would struggle with the confusion, trying to figure out what was happening so it would go away. I could also watch the mind planning the whole day. "If I do this now, then that will come next and then I will be able to do that, and then..." If something caught my eye—a beautiful cactus or a hummingbird dancing its song—my mind would say, "I can't stop and explore this now, I have to_____."

Upon seeing this relentless demand to have it all ordered, orchestrated, figured out and timed, I began to play with *don't know*, saying to myself, "I don't know what is going to happen next, and I don't need to know." As I did this, bubbles of joy would arise from the core of my being. "Knowing is not the way," Awareness would say. The mind would calm down, and the living experience of Life, formerly blocked by the struggle to control and understand, became evident. I also began to say to the planning mind, "We don't need to know what is going to happen. Just for these few days, let's allow Life to unfold and see what appears."

I was willing, at least for moments, to let go to something bigger than my own ideas about Life. These moments would bring great connection with the perfection of it all and a deep trust in the unfolding. At other moments, not planning would bring up waves of terror, and I would need to go back to allowing the mind to be in charge. Slowly, as I worked with this over a number of days, I began to move into more and more of what is called *body time*. We usually live in *thought time*—planning for the future and trying to understand the past. To live in *body time* asks us to be present NOW and to allow whatever understanding and planning that is needed to arise out of direct connection with the living moment. *Body time* moves us into the place of being truly connected with our own lives.

Don't know is not about getting rid of planning. It is a useful tool for maneuvering through our lives. We need to make lists, keep schedules and figure out directions. But rather than *using* the ability to plan and orchestrate our lives, we have become *lost in* planning and organizing. When someone is speaking, we're usually focusing on what we're going to say in response rather than really listening. When someone requests a moment of our time, we often can't give it fully because we feel caught in what we've already planned. We don't stop for the beauty of a sunset or a child's eyes because we're already on to the next thing in our schedule. The biggest downside of the planning mind is that it keeps us lost in the illusion that we have to do it all. In order to use the planning mind effectively, we need to become aware of when it is appropriate and when it is not.

We also need understanding. We may fear something—a person's behavior, a feeling in our bodies—and as soon as it is explained to us (it's just a gas pain and not trouble with my heart), we soften into it. Our shoulders drop, the furrow in our brow eases. But this can only take us so far. When we come to the edge of our limited understanding, the urge to know can flip us into struggle, heightening our fear and birthing more self-judgment and confusion. So much in Life cannot be understood. On many levels, Life is an unfathomable mystery, and we are too narrowly focused to really see what is going on.

To stay constantly in the mindset of having to know and plan is to miss one of the true joys of Life—the freedom and creativity that come from experiencing times of letting go to the process and letting something bigger than our ordinary mind be in charge. When we come to the edge of our understanding and our best laid plans dissolve in front of our eyes, and when the mind flails, whirls and spins, this is the time to cultivate *don't know*. Whenever we are at this edge, saying "I don't know" can move us beyond our attempts to control, bringing forth waves of joy and relief.

Learning the art of *don't know* takes time, but as we are willing to live on this edge, something real, authentic, alive and healing can show up. *True knowing is something that is experienced, not figured out.*

These two powerful words allow us to be fully present to Life over and over again throughout the day. To cultivate *don't know*, you can add to your daily practice a wonderful Zen meditation.

On the in-breath say to yourself, "Clear mind, clear mind, clear mind." On the out-breath, chant in one long breath, "Don't know." Be willing to play with don't know. *As you meet different choices, challenges and uncertainties in your day, say, "Don't know. Don't need to know. Don't have to know. Don't got to know." Watch the moments that this brings up fear, and watch the moments when it opens you to the spaciousness where creativity lives.*

Gratitude

The Buddha says that to be given the gift of Life is as rare as if there were one turtle living in the seven seas of the Earth with one golden hoop that floats on these same seas, and only once every hundred years does the turtle surface, and only once in every hundred times does it surface through the golden hoop. Not only has each of us been given this precious gift of Life, we've also been blessed to be born into a land of mind-boggling magic and awe-inspiring beauty. Flowers appear out of nowhere. Babies evolve out of one tiny cell. Spring arises out of winter without fail. We find ourselves in a land of rainbows and butterflies, orchids cascading over trees, the songs of frogs, the softness of cotton, the playfulness of clouds.

We have so much to be grateful for. It took every single being that has gone before us to make this beauty possible. Everything that lives is beholden to absolutely everything else. Our sun would not be able to bestow its many blessing if its parent star hadn't become a supernova and spewed forth into the creative void of space the necessary elements for its birth. Plants would not exist if the algae in the primal seas hadn't ventured out into the foreign world of dry land, and we would not exist without all of the vast experimentation of Life that has preceded us.

Gratefulness is the consciousness of how much we are given by Life. We live in the middle of a bountiful feast of giving. Take a moment to feel your next breath—in and out. Do you experience it as a given, something you are entitled to, or as a precious gift from the generosity of Life? It is truly much more a gift than a given. Because we are not always aware of how much we are given, we find ourselves living in the narrow world of more—I need more, I must be more, I have to do more. The grief of *more* is that it is never enough, narrowing us down to an arid and endless treadmill of consuming, becoming and struggling.

Most things that we take for granted are harder to come by in the rest of the world. Our experience is one of available food, comparatively safe neighborhoods, basic survival needs readily available to most people without a life and death struggle, and a relatively high standard of health care. We have lost sight of the sacred thread of gratitude, that upwelling of deep appreciation for all we've been given and that heartfelt recognition of the preciousness and impermanence of everything.

I heard a story from a friend who was traveling in the Far East. The process of making one glass of ice tea took 14 hours—gathering the water, making the ice, preparing the drink. And she was truly grateful for that glass of tea—something she had drunk many times in her life with no sense of appreciation. In that priceless moment of gratefulness, even for something as basic as a glass of tea, there was no wanting. In the absence of wanting, we find ourselves connected with Life, filled with the heart-healing consciousness of enough. *This moment, this bite, this breath is enough.* In gratitude there is no past, and there is no future. The struggle of *more* ceases, and we are left with wonder and connection to Life the moment it appears out of Mystery.

After reading this paragraph lift your eyes from the book. This moment is possible because of the labors of countless beings, human and nonhuman. Take a moment and recognize all of the food that the Earth has given to you so that you could live. Now become aware that without the sun there would be no life on Earth. Without earthworms, the soil would be too compacted to grow anything. Without bees, butterflies, hummingbirds and wind, there would be no pollination of our fruits and vegetables. All of this was necessary in order to create the food you need to live. On and on it goes, everything connected in a web of being.

It is not only nature that gives to us without us recognizing it. It is also countless human beings. Albert Einstein once wrote:

A hundred times every day I remind myself that my inner and outer life are based on the labors of other men, living and dead, and that I must exert myself in order to give in the same measure as I have received and am still receiving."

To cultivate the all-encompassing consciousness of gratitude, we sometimes need a rude awakening from Life itself. I was quite ill a few years back, unable to take in much food and wracked with so much pain at times it was hard to walk, lift an arm or even sit up for an extended period of time. When my health returned and I could walk more easily and eat a limited number of foods, I was stunned at how precious the gift of life is and how much I had taken for granted.

I watched TV commercials of people eating cheesecake and pizza and wondered if any of them recognized the amazingly intricate Intelligence that repeatedly and endlessly practices the magic of turning cheeseburgers into fingernails, heart muscles and bone. And sometimes when I walked, I would be flooded with awareness of all that Life had to do in order to create the legs that allow me to walk. I was filled with gratitude that I am the beneficiary of all of this vast experimentation. I would also become aware of all of the people who can't walk. I may not have been able to run and dance, but I could move around, and that is an incredible gift.

Gratitude can make a carrot into a feast, a painful lesson into a respected teacher and a most basic skill into a precious gift. It can turn a narrow perspective of Life into one of mind-boggling appreciation and thankfulness. It also makes everything workable, connecting us again to our own lives. The more I cultivate the awareness of thankfulness, in those moments of struggle where I am caught in the consciousness of *more*, gratitude opens me up out of that tight ball of contraction and births me into spacious connection.

- For a day say "thank you" to everything that comes—that pain, the difficult co-worker, the sound of a bird, the gift of a hug.

- To cultivate gratitude, write a list of 3 things you are grateful for upon arising and upon going to bed at night. Don't leave the basics out like sight, taste, breath.

- Imagine a day without one of your most basic functions—hearing, walking, touching.

Generosity

There is a very strange belief deep within our everyday consciousness that *getting* will make us happy and successful. It is broadcast from every commercial, spoon fed to our children from the beginning. Craving, hoarding, clinging, wanting and getting are emphasized in our culture, along with the struggle to keep what we have accumulated. And yet, if we really notice how Life works, one of its core principles is generosity. Life shouts this from every tree that makes millions of seeds, from every flower that radiates its Presence and from the great generosity of the sun as it gives endlessly, day in and day out. We live in a generous Universe. Think of how much it gives of itself so you can live—wheat, water, fish, sunlight, apples, oxygen. Your very existence is dependent upon the generosity of Life.

Life is a wondrously rhythmic cycle of giving and receiving. Think of plant life giving off oxygen and receiving carbon dioxide in return, and leaves dying in order to make rich soil for the mother plant. We are a part of this giving and receiving river of Life, and yet most of us live in the unbalanced state of getting more than we give. Because we have not given back, the Earth is struggling. Think of the salmon that are dying and the streams that are clogged and the species that are becoming extinct because of our voracious hunger for trees.

When we live in this continuous land of getting, not only does the Earth become just an object in our minds, but people do too. When we are in the presence of another person, rather than bearing witness to the wondrous expression of the Mystery of Life that is before us, we often narrow our perception to what they can give us—how they can fulfill our needs, wants and desires. This can be very subtle and unrecognized by our normal everyday consciousness.

Living in the mindset of trying to acquire what we want cuts us off from abundance (from the Latin *abundare* which means "to flow"). As a wise proverb says, "If my hands are fully occupied in holding onto something, I can neither give nor receive." Generosity is the opposite of holding on. It is letting go into the flow of abundance. Anything freely given is a recognition of the generosity of Life, a recognition of how much is given to us.

Generosity is found at the core of all the great religions—"It is more blessed to give than receive." (Christianity); "Bounteous is he who gives to the beggar who comes to him." (Hinduism); "Blessed is he that considers the poor; the Lord will deliver him in time of trouble." (Judaism); "If we knew the power of giving, we wouldn't let a single meal pass without sharing some of it." (Buddha); "The poor, the orphan, the captive, feed them for the love of God alone, desiring no reward, nor even thanks." (Islam) Generosity is a law of Nature, and since we are a part of Nature, then it follows that our natural state is one of generosity.

Hoarding is so painful. When I was deeply compulsive around food, I was willing to lie, manipulate and deceive in order to get what I felt I desperately needed. This grasping also showed up around money. For most of the time my children were growing up, I was a single parent with an extremely limited income. Once I was able to save $200 out of our meager funds. I took the money and hid it in my sock drawer, and it was absolutely fascinating to watch the controlling mind protect this hoard, fear its discovery, plan and lie so it wouldn't be spent. Very rarely are we aware of the grief that comes from this mind set, the grief of being isolated from the continual feast of giving and receiving that is Life.

One of the core keys to being able to extract oneself from the addiction of *getting* is the understanding that giving not only gives to the receiver but to the giver. Remember a time of doing something special for a loved one. There was the joy of planning the surprise, the exhilaration in watching him or her be surprised and the warm glow that comes from remembering the experience. Generosity brings peace, joy and contentment. The more generous we become the more our whole view of ourselves shifts. It brings more respect, appreciation and kindness.

Generosity can also take an ordinary moment, one easily forgotten in the millions of moments of our lives, and turn it into something precious. James Barez, a Vipassana meditation teacher, tells a story about a long retreat he attended at the Insight Meditation Society in Barre, Massachusetts. The meals were very basic—rice, vegetables, tofu, etc. A piece of buttered toast was a treat. One day while he was washing dishes, a friend left him a foil-wrapped package. Upon opening it, he discovered a piece of cheesecake. What a gift! Instead of eating it himself, however, he cut it up into little pieces and put them in a the dinner bowls of a number of his fellow meditators. When they came into the dining hall, he watched as they discovered the treasures in their bowls. One person even cut his piece up, giving part of it to another. If James had just eaten the cheesecake himself, this experience would eventually have been lost in the endless procession of life experiences. Because of his generosity, it touched many people.

In a very basic way, the best way to *get* what we most wan' grandmother would say:

It is in loving, not in being loved, the heart is blessed.
It is in giving, not in seeking gifts, that we find our quest.
Whatever be thy longing or thy need, that do thou give.
So thy soul shall be fed, and thou shall indeed surely live.

I once heard a wonderful phrase—that giving is a selfish thing. It is an actual law of physics that every action has an equal and opposite reaction. You can't give without receiving. As an old saying goes, "You can't help someone up the hill without getting closer to the top yourself."

There is also another wonderful paradox about giving. One of the most generous things we can do is to allow someone to give to us—to allow them the joy of generosity. In some ways this can even be more challenging than giving itself. All sorts of conversations can come up in our head: "I am asking too much"; "I'm a bother"; "They will resent me." A few years ago, I broke my leg and I was in bed for ten straight days. I had to ask for absolutely everything. Over and over again I came to that wall of wanting to do it myself because I didn't want to be a bother. And over and over again, I saw first hand the joy that came into people's lives because of my needs.

Of all of the possible things we can give to the world, the gift of ourselves is one of the most precious things we can give. Giving of ourselves comes not only from the things we do. It comes from our Presence. It is the willingness to be fully here with whoever is in front of us. Great counselors, ministers and speakers have this ability. "Behold I do not give lectures or a little charity. When I give, I give myself," said Walt Whitman. That to me is the most profound and healing gift we can give.

Giving also teaches us that we can truly make a difference in the world. We don't need to go to Africa to help the starving (although if that calls to you, by all means do it). We can make a difference in our world with little acts of generosity—a smile, a kind word, heartfelt listening. They all have a ripple effect. If we smile and take a few moments of quality time with the grocery store clerk, people following in line after us may very well benefit from the fruits of our giving.

Be willing to live in the question, "How can I give today?"

PARTNERSHIP

There was suddenly a very deep gut feeling that something was different. It occurred when looking at Earth and seeing this blue and white planet floating there, and knowing it was orbiting the sun. Seeing that sun and seeing it set in the background of the very deep black and velvety cosmos—seeing that there was a purposefulness of flow, of energy, of time, of space in the cosmos and that it was beyond man's rational ability to understand—suddenly there was a non-rational way of understanding that had been beyond my previous experience. There seemed to be more to the Universe than random, chaotic, purposeless movement of a collection of molecular particles. On the return trip home, gazing through 240,000 miles of space toward the planet from which I had come, I suddenly experienced the Universe as intelligent, loving and harmonious.

Edgar Mitchell, U.S. Astronaut

All of the skills we have been exploring—curiosity, compassion, welcoming, don't know, gratitude and generosity—are bringing us back into intimate and immediate connection with Life. Once we're here, it becomes evident that we are truly a creative aspect of Life. Rocks don't create and the newness that comes through trees happens very, very slowly. We have discovered that apes do live in the world of creativity but compare that to what humanity has done and you will get a glimpse of the depth to which creativity wants to move through us. Up until this point in our evolution, we have created from a very limited part of ourselves—the part that thinks it is separate from Life. It is now time to become partners with the Intelligence that permeates and penetrates absolutely everything.

Rather than feeling that we are responsible for it all—whether it is our finances, the health of our relationships, or even the challenge of terrorists all over the world, it is now time to become doorways for the creativity at the heart of Life. *We don't need to create our lives as much as we need to open to them.*

The gift that we are being given at this time in evolution is that the challenges of our times are too great for us to figure out all by ourselves. In a way, that is why they are here—so that our only option is to go to the source of wisdom within us and to listen to what wants to happen through us. In this kind of partnership we don't have to figure out what wants to happen, nor do we have to figure out how to do it. That is all being orchestrated by forces much smarter than us. All we need to do is learn how to ask questions, listen, feel what feels right within us and then allow whatever is calling to us to move us from within.

In this listening, we are ready to feel within us the highest possible vision for ourselves, for our loved ones and for our planet too. We are ready to feel this in the very cells of our being, knowing that this is the most powerfully creative thing we can do. We don't need to create the healing that is calling to us. We need to feel it. We need to generate it on a physical level within our body, mind and heart.

Then we need to get out of the way. Rather than going back into the mind that feels it has to *do* Life, the most powerful thing we can do is show up for Life, allowing through us what wants to be born. That is true partnership with Life.

There are four skills of Partnership that will allow us to open into this creative way of living. The first skill we will explore is that of *Living in Questions*. Questions are a doorway into the living Intelligence of Life. The second skill is *Allowing*. It is the knowing that we don't need so much to create our destiny as we need to allow it, for it is already here. From this place of non-struggle, we can explore the third skill of *Holding a Space* for what is calling to us, vibrating it in the very cells of our being. We can then explore the fourth skill of Intention which, as Deepak Chopra says, is the organizing power of the Universe.

As it is beginning to dawn on our collective mind that Life truly is a sea of energy—a dance of vibration that shows up as sound, color, light and objects—we can begin to cultivate the curiosity and the commitment to create as the world creates, through vibration.

Living In Questions

Most of us have moments, usually when things are going well, when we trust and feel connected to something beyond our own limited awareness. But give us the simplest of challenges in our lives, and rather than going into spaciousness, we often go into contraction, isolation, struggle and a sense that we have to do it ourselves.

To ask questions of the process is to break free from the struggle mode, tapping us into the Intelligence at the heart of Life. It is one of the most skillful ways I know of partnering with That which resides beyond our own limited human comprehension.

In order to learn how to ask questions in a way that truly empowers us, we first need to see how we have been using questions in our lives. We have two standard ways of asking questions. The first is from the *power-over* mode: "What can I do to get rid of this problem in my life?" "What's wrong here?"

"How can I control it or fix it?" If the intent of our question is only to get rid of a nuisance we will not be able to access the creativity of the Unknown. The answers we get will be based only upon what has been done before. While these kinds of answers are appropriate at moments in our lives, *how do I fix it?* is an endless game, keeping us stuck on the level of managing the problem.

The other way we usually ask questions is from the victim mode: "Why do bad things always happen to me?" "Why do I always do it wrong?" "Why do I have to do this?" "What is wrong with me?" Both styles of asking questions, being closed-ended loops, do not access the creative Intelligence of the Universe.

There is another way to ask questions, a way that truly engages us in the process, and allows us to receive answers from a place that is way beyond our ordinary mind. It comes from the knowing that *true power lies in questions rather than in answers.*

There are two keys to learning how to access the power of questions. The first is *to not look for answers.* The beauty of asking questions without looking for answers is that it doesn't seduce us into struggle. The whirling, spinning, grasping mind that is always trying to figure things out puts up a barrier between us and the Intelligence that is trying to give us an answer. When we ask a question without looking for an answer, it creates a vacuum that has to be filled. It is a law of physics. The Intelligence of the Universe rushes into the vacuum of a question, and the answer automatically, in its own time, condenses out of the Unknown and into our lives.

The second key is to *expect* answers. The art of trusting that the Intelligence of the Universe will answer our questions comes to each of us in its own time and in its own way. It helps to notice that we do live in a sea of Intelligence. Everywhere we look we see its handiwork, whether it is the exquisite balance of the web of Life or the amazing healing that happens in a body if we suffer a paper cut or are in a severe automobile accident. The more we pay attention to Life, the more we see that this Intelligence permeates and penetrates absolutely everything, including the challenges in our lives. It also becomes evident that the resolution to every problem we have ever had or ever will have is nestled in the heart of the challenge. *Life waits for the question.* Moments of pure questions always signal the Universe that we are willing to listen.

We can address our questions to whatever we conceive of as the Intelligence which runs this show—God, Divine, Goddess, Wizard, Higher Self, Christ Spirit, Soul, the Quantum Void. I call it Creative Intelligence. We don't even need to believe that there is an Intelligence waiting for the opening of our question, for open ended questions will work whether we believe in an Intelligence or not.

I just got off of the phone with a person who was very angry and asking for help. My response only fueled the person's rage and they hung up in the middle of the conversation. My old mind would have gone into either judgment of the other person or judgment of myself and then chewed over the experience like a cow chews her cud. Instead I closed my eyes, centered on my breath and asked, "What is the most skillful thing I can do now?" I also asked, "What am I to learn from this experience?" I then went on with my day without the desire to fix anything or to figure it out. A few hours later, with the clarity of a crystal bell, I suddenly knew exactly what was needed to be said and done. When I shared it with this person, it brought healing and closure in this situation.

Answers reveal themselves in the most wondrous of ways. I've received them while reading a spy novel when one sentence stands out from the rest, almost as if I was reading the whole book to just to receive these few words. I've also overheard conversations in the grocery store in which a few words woke me up out of my dream and answered my question. Sometimes while I am taking a shower or cooking dinner, an answer comes burbling up from within, stunning me with its simplicity. It can come with blinding clarity or it can come as an inner knowing that reveals itself gradually like the sun's warmth dissipating a blanket of fog.

The power of asking simple and direct questions of Life is absolutely enormous. Jesus referred to it when he said, "Ask, and it shall be given you; seek and you shall find; knock and it shall be opened unto you. Everyone that asks, receives; and he that seeks finds." Life is waiting for the opening that questions create. We can ask the wisdom at the heart of Life for purification, for guidance, for compassion, for the courage to follow the path of Awakening, for understanding about the suffering in our lives and for an awakening heart. The important thing is to ask and know that, in the right time and the right way, we will live our answers.

There are some standard questions we can use for this new way of working with questions. My favorite question, and the one that I feel has made the unfolding of my life immeasurably easier and clearer is "What can I say or do in this situation that is for the highest good of every person involved?" Whether I am meeting an angry child, counseling someone or getting ready to speak in front of hundreds of people, this question steadies my mind and opens me into listening.

There are other questions that we can use that tap us into the creativity at the heart of Life:

- How can I serve?
- Who am I?
- How can I make a difference today?
- What is a skillful focus today?
- What is Love?
- What was I given the gift of Life for?

We can also use questions to see clearly what stands in the way of living at this level of creativity. Remember, we don't need to get rid of what is keeping us lost in struggle; we only need to see it. I call the questions that clear the clouds from around our head clarifying questions. One of my favorites is "What am I experiencing right now?" Another is, "How can I see this differently?" When I am caught and struggling in an old pattern, I signal the Universe that I am ready and willing to shift my perspective when I use these questions. I also like, "What am I resisting?" It is evident that whenever I am in whirling and spinning mind, there is something I don't want to see. By asking to see what it is that I am resisting, the mind settles, willing to connect with the parts of myself I have formerly resisted. Some other powerful questions are:

- What is the piece of my own puzzle I am ready to see?
- What is my intention?
- Where is my attention?
- What is asking to be seen?
- What is the doorway through this challenge?
- What do I need to see, love or accept?
- How can this be healed?
- What is the shift in perspective that I am ready for?
- What is the lighter side of this challenge?
- How can I see this through the eyes of the heart?

Truly powerful questions come from a bigger place, a place that trusts the unfolding and wants to engage with Life more than it wants to get rid of problems. You may not even know what questions to ask. Go back to the list of questions and listen carefully to the ones that resonate with you. Be willing to ask at least one question every morning. Put it on the dash of your car, in your wallet, on your phone at work. If none of the questions resonates, be willing to live in the question, "What are my questions?" Remember that questions create a vacuum, that has to be filled.

Questions are about curiosity and willingness to receive answers from something far bigger and far more intelligent than we are. As we learn to pay attention with questions, we see that everything and everybody and every situation is our teacher. We don't need to figure out what anything means; understanding will come automatically on its own. It's more the willingness to become completely fascinated by how the journey is showing up.

The art of asking questions is exactly that—an art. As we cultivate it, it will slowly ripen in our consciousness. You didn't play Mozart after a few piano lessons. Be willing to simply ask questions without expecting anything in return. Know that you are signaling the process that brought you forth that you are ready to listen—to be receptive rather than always relying on only your own intelligence.

Allowing

We've been so busy trying to *create* our lives that we've completely lost sight of *allowing* our lives. Allowing is about moving from the grasping of control into making space for our destiny to come to us. *We don't need to create our lives as much as we need to open to them.* We realize the truth of this when we recognize that Life longs to express the fullness of itself through each and every being. It waits for the open door of allowing so that it can flood us with its Presence.

The power of allowing, along with the inefficiency of efforting, has been clearly shown through biofeedback. In Elmer Green's pioneering work, he built a device that would allow people to receive immediate feedback about the temperature in their fingers. When they used conscious willpower to warm their hands, usually the opposite occurred. When they were invited to visualize the change and then simply *let it happen*, many experienced their hands warming, over and over again.

Allowing things to happen brings far more powerful results, not only in warm fingers but also in Life itself. The most profound intelligence of Life is not in the ordinary thinking mind. As David Whyte says,

What we can plan is too small for us to live.

Below the realm of our everyday consciousness lies a sea of astounding creativity that is full of ideas, solutions and evolutionary shifts that are waiting to be recognized. Allowing *what is*—no matter what is—can drop us into those regions of vast, untapped potential, a pool of creativity that is awaiting the spaciousness of allowing so that it can communicate with our ordinary mind.

Tony Schwartz, in his book *What Really Matters*, speaks about one of his biofeedback experiences that shows clearly the depth to which efforting and grasping keep us isolated and away from peace, creativity and innovation. The intention of this particular weekend was to access the alpha brain state, the more focused and peaceful brain waves lying just below our everyday clutter. He actually felt a bit cocky as he began. Having meditated every day for the previous two years, he felt he could easily *do* this. Instead he found that his most reliable meditation techniques only increased his alpha by a modest amount and frustration set in.

Before long he found himself stuck, unable to increase alpha no matter what he tried. A sense of failure took over. This only made him feel more frustrated and more self-critical. In describing his experience, he said, "The issue was control. In the face of feelings of helplessness or inadequacy, I fought harder to succeed at relaxing. But the harder I tried, the tenser and more exasperated I became, and the more my alpha dropped. It was a vicious cycle and the only plausible way out was to let go of my need to control the outcome. The problem, I realized, was that I found doing so oddly frightening."

The next day, mired in the emotion of hopelessness, he became aware that he was in familiar territory, caught in his negative internal dialogue. As a wave of sadness washed over him, his alpha levels immediately increased. "Aha," said his mind. "All I have to do is feel rather than think, and I'll create more alpha." But no sooner did he consciously try to create feelings than his scores plummeted once again. He realized that actively seeking anything required analyzing, labeling, rating and conceptualizing, all wonderful skills of the ordinary mind that allow us to maneuver through daily life, but skills that keep us out of the sea of creativity.

He realized that dropping out of the often chaotic ordinary mind could not be done through the skills of the ordinary mind (trying, efforting, figuring out). It could only be done when he was able to authentically be with whatever was happening in any given moment, even if what was happening was chaos itself. In that willingness to be authentically present and to allow the alpha to come rather than trying to capture it, the ordinary mind calmed down, and the peace and creativity of alpha was able to be experienced.

This is one of the best descriptions I've ever heard of the power of turning our boat around and engaging with the river of Life. When Tony was able to be with exactly what was happening in that moment, not trying to get any-where (to the alpha) or be anything (a good meditator) he immediately tapped into the more peaceful and creative alpha state.

Life wants to fill us with its creativity. Notice that if we denude a hillside, into that void will rush Life. First will come small plants and, if left for a long enough time, it will progress through stages until it blooms into a full-grown forest. The same is true of individual human beings and the Earth community as a whole. There are whole worlds of creativity that are waiting to be expressed through us. It's time we become the fertile field of allowing so that the seeds can be planted and bloom.

Holding a Space

Allowing, coupled with the ability to hold the highest vision possible in the cells of our being, is true partnership with Life. Holding a space is about checking into what hums— what is calling to us—and generating in our body what it would feel like if it was already here. As we allow ourselves to feel, to actually radiate what is calling to us, focusing our attention on vision rather than on trying to make something happen, we draw it into our lives like a magnet.

A good example of holding a space is the community of Greenfield, Iowa. Their economic base, along with the viability and quality of their town, had been declining for years. When they had exhausted all of the old paradigm skills of trying to find results, creating committees and searching for seemingly nonexistent resources, they hired Stan Berkowitz, a community animator. By the time they called him in, the whole community was in a state of discouragement. He helped them to see that they were holding a space of what was wrong and had bought into the belief that struggle was the only way to right it.

As they began to hold the space for possibility, things began to happen, and Stan reminded them to think big and act small. The grocery store printed on their bags the question, "Is there anything you can think of to strengthen this community, using the resources we have right here. If so, call this number." These bags didn't come out of a committee that created lists of what people needed to do or city officials who vetoed all of the dreams because of lack of finances. They came out of the space of claiming what was right about their community right now.

The people held a vision for the community and then *allowed* the steps of their healing to appear. A father and daughter planted marigolds throughout the community. Someone else started up the farmer's market again, which brought people into town. The antique airplane collection became a museum. There was now enough activity to support refurbishing the old hotel. This all came out of a generative field of possibility and *allowing* the pieces to come to them instead of trying to create them.

The three aspects of partnership that we have explored so far are evident in this story: living in questions, allowing the process to unfold, and holding a space. When they focused on what was right within their city, the citizens of Greenfield could then feel in their minds, bodies and hearts the possibility for their community. ·

This is what I call a *feeling picture*. The Universe is vibration, and when we vibrate what is calling to us, we attract it to us like a magnet attracts iron fillings. A *feeling picture* is worth a thousand to-do lists and a million moments of efforting. Rather than trying to plot and plan and figure out how to bring something into our lives, we become an energy magnet, drawing to us the people, experiences and things that support this vision. Holding a space opens us, and into this space comes rushing the Intelligence of Life.

It is very important in cultivating the art of holding a space to trust our desires. We are given them, not because they are the sole purpose of our lives, but because they are the avenues of our Awakening. If your desire is to be a race car driver, do not question this desire. *The fulfillment of the desire is not the goal. The goal is to show up for the process.* Your journey to becoming a race car driver will lead you through the steps of your Awakening.

If it isn't evident what is calling to you at this time in your life, live in "big picture" questions—"What is asking to be manifested through my life right now? What is the next step in my destiny? What is the most skillful thing I can do in my life right now that is for the highest good of all beings?" "How can I serve the Awakening of humanity?" Then allow these questions to germinate, and watch what calls to you.

If you observe closely, you will begin to see what has been calling to you for as long as you can remember. It may be buried under layers of self-judgment, of discounting your capabilities and of mistrust of yourself. But nonetheless it is still there. In order to claim it again and to consciously follow where it is taking you, it is important to think big. Explore beyond even your wildest imagining. The actual manifestation of the vision is not nearly as important as generating the feeling.

In working with *feeling pictures* we oftentimes need to begin on the level of our own needs. If you are interested in a comfortable income, feel abundance as a free flow of energy throughout your body. If it is health, generate the feeling, even if only for a moment, of vibrant health. The key is not just to conceive of it, but to experience it in the feeling realm. Use image and movement to enhance this feeling. Become it, for at least moments, in the level of vibration.

A good example of how this works is following the yearning to be in relation-ship. In the old style we made lists of what we wanted—tall or short, young or old, funny or serious. We would then get very busy trying to make this happen. We put ads in the paper, elicit the help of family and friends to hunt for the right person and then go through the ups and downs of waiting, hoping and looking.

Holding a space is a far more effective way. It is about allowing ourselves to *feel* what it would be like to be in a relationship with the kind of person that calls to us, generating the experience in our body. The details—when, where, and what (size, career, skills)—are not our concern. In fact, we only gum up the process by focusing on the details. Holding a space sets the attracting power of the Universe in motion, causing doors to open that we didn't even know were there, and experiences to happen that will take us beyond our limited dream of a fulfilling relationship.

The power of holding a space and then allowing the process to move through us is evident in the movie Apollo 13. After a major explosion on the space ship, the chances of the three astronauts returning to Earth were practically nonexistent. With the odds against them, the people in Mission Control were bordering on resignation and frantic inefficiency. But Gene Krantz, the Flight Director at Mission Control in Houston, was not going to give up. He *felt* that they were going to return. With great passion he announced, "We've never lost an American in space and we're sure as hell not going to lose one on my watch. Failure is not an option."

This core feeling that he generated infused the consciousness of everyone close to him, and into that space came flooding ideas and solutions that nobody had thought of before. These ideas and solutions resulted from holding a vision and *feeling* the possibility rather than trying to *solve* a seemingly impossible problem.

Holding a space is not about exerting force. As we have seen, force cuts us off from the very creativity we are trying to access. Holding a space frees this creativity to be manifested in a way that is for our highest good and the highest good of all people concerned.

An important key to holding a space is to let go of the outcome. We have been so trained to go for the goal that it almost seems like insanity to suggest that the outcome is not the important thing here. If we keep on looking for results, this only throws us back into the contraction of struggle and control, cutting us off from the creative Intelligence of Life. It is important to leave the details and the outcome to the process. We don't know what is best for us. We just think we do. It is important to recognize what it is that is calling to us (a career, health, abundance) and vibrate it in our being. But then we need to *show up for the process exactly as it is appearing.*

End results are just an illusion anyway. The process is the goal. It is our addiction to results that has kept us cut off from our own lives. True richness comes not from attaining something. It comes from being awake and alive in the process itself. That is why people, upon reaching a goal, often are left with a sense of emptiness rather than fulfillment. As tennis pro Jerry Alleyne said, "You must always play to win, but you can never make winning important. To set winning as a goal provides structure and focus, but to worry about the result only induces tension and distraction."

The power of holding a space and at the same time being spacious around the outcome was shown clearly in a study that was done at the Omni Institute in Oregon. They seeded a number of plants and gave them all good quality soil, nutrients and light. The only difference was that half of them were held in the prayer consciousness of a local prayer group. And to no one's surprise, the prayed-over plants grew faster and stronger than the others. They then took it one step further. After creating a number of new flats of seedlings, they again divided them into two groups. Half were prayed over by asking for specifics—that they grow strong and tall and healthy. The other half were held in the spaciousness that the highest be manifested through them. And to everyone's amazement, the latter plants grew dramatically better.

Imagine yourself being able to eavesdrop on your own funeral. Friends and loved ones get up to speak about you, your life and how you touched the world. Imagine that you had lived the life you really wanted to live. As you take in what they say, allow your body to feel what it would be like if your life was like that right now.

Whether it is the joy of being a great artist, the nourishment of being a kind and loving person, the gift of being a funny and adventuresome friend, the healing of showing up as a wise and inspiring mentor or maybe a combination of all of the above, turn up the amps. Generate this feeling.

Go put on some clothes that evoke this life. Listen to music that reminds you. Walk and talk today as if it were already here. There is no accident what you overheard at your funeral. You were listening to the longing of your soul.

Working with holding a space for our own needs and wants is an important step. But at the core of universal law is the truth that what we give, so shall we receive. Our belief that we only get through getting narrows the stream of support from universal consciousness down to a trickle. It is far more powerful to co-create for others and for the Earth itself. Holding the space for the highest to be manifested through a friend, a stranger, a country or humanity itself not only deeply touches the receiver, but the giving also makes space inside of ourselves that will be filled with what is for our highest good.

This is not to say that we can't work on fulfilling our own desires. They are the seedpods of our Awakening, and as we follow them, they will lead us into healings that may have little or nothing to do with the original desire. But to desire for only ourselves is to stay in a closed loop. To focus on our own separate needs keeps us locked into the prison of wanting. Shantideva once said, "Whatever joy there is in this world, all comes from desiring others to be happy. And whatever suffering there is in this world, all comes from desiring myself to be happy."

Know that holding a space for another truly works. I am alive today because my mother held the highest for me during a very dark time in my twenties. The night before I ran off to Europe in an effort to escape from my mental and emotional hell, my mother and I had dinner at a local restaurant. Walking back to the car, we came across a picture in the window of an art gallery that touched both of us. It was of a young woman standing tall and strong on top of a hill of wild flowers. The sun was shining and the wind was blowing through her hair. When I came back a year later, the picture was above my mother's mantel. She said she bought it because that was how she saw me, even though she knew I was on the brink of self-destruction. Every day during her prayer time, she would look at the picture and hold me in that space of healing and joy, feeling me discovering it for myself.

As I move through my life, I am constantly wishing the highest for people I meet. I do this with everyone from strangers on the street, to my children and my closest of friends. Some of my favorite blessings are "May you know who you truly are; may your heart be open; may you know peace." Not only am I touching the other person with the vibration of Love, but also I am generating these feelings in my own body, giving to myself the gift that I am giving to them. This simple activity also reminds me that there is no separation. The "other people out there" that I am holding a space for are a part of me, as I am a part of them. As I hold this space, not only are we both being healed, but the world is, too.

We can't fake this. We can't say that we will wish this for all beings while hoping it will bring us what we want. It doesn't work that way. We have to feel it from the core of our being. Don't push it. We all progress in stages from the narrowness of our own needs to a feeling of deep and tender care for all beings.

Going back to the example of feeling a desire for a healthy relationship, we may begin by holding a space for what it would feel like to be in a good and healthy coupling. As we mature, we may begin to hold the space that all of our relationships are healthy, nurturing and nourishing. Then as we realize we are a part of a web of Life, we begin to feel the possibility of all of humanity knowing the fullness of clear, supportive and loving relationships. The chances of our own relationships becoming truly healthy are greater when we hold that space for all beings because in some very deep way, our desire for a good relationship **is** humanity's desire to be in a healthy relationship with its totality.

Imagine yourself sitting on the moon, with the beauty of the Universe surrounding you. Now look upon the Earth and recognize the depth of creativity unfolding on our planet. Amidst all of majesty and mystery see human beings, most of them walking around with the clouds of the struggling mind surrounding their heads. Now see a few people break free of the clouds and recognize the preciousness of Life.

See them recognize that we are all in this together, floating on one tiny planet in the middle of vast oceans of space. See them turn to someone else, recognizing the beauty of what is before them and see this person's clouds lift too. Then see more and more people coming out from behind their clouds See their minds be moved in awe and reverence at the wonder of Life. See their hearts filled with Love for every particle, for every person, for every piece of the planet. See their minds be filled with joy, knowing that they have finally come home.

Now feel this possibility in the core of your being, throughout every nook and cranny of your body. Know that if you can feel this possibility so too can others. And as this moves through the minds and hearts of more and more human beings, we will be healed

---

Intention

An essential ingredient in holding a space is the *reason* that we are holding it. Intention is the purpose for doing something, and it resides in every single action of our lives—from the reason we are walking across a room to the reason we are holding a space for a particular vision. Imagine a surgeon wielding a sharp scalpel as he opens a man's chest for heart surgery. Now imagine a murderer also plunging a sharp knife into the chest of his victim. In both cases the actions are very similar. But the intentions – the purpose for each of the actions – are exactly the opposite. The intention of the doctor is to save a life and the murderer's is to take a life. The intention for any action is where the power of that action lives, shaping the outcome.

Take the activity of running errands for example. When I have forgotten that the entire dance of my life—including something as basic as running errands—is a dance of Awakening, I get into my car for the purpose of *getting things done*. With that intention in mind, I visit the first store, but in my mind I am already on to the second and third stop. My consciousness narrows down, and people become objects that can either enhance or detract from my list of things to do. The further I get into my errands the more harried I become. Stoplights are too long, clerks are inefficient and a woman in a wheel chair cart that is blocking the aisle becomes an irritant.

The exact opposite experience unfolds when I remind myself that, rather than doing, acquiring and accomplishing, the intention of any activity in my life is to stay awake. Rather than living from the list, I live in the experience. Whether it is standing in line, driving my car or handing money to the clerk, my intention becomes the willingness to be present. The joy of being alive and the nourishment of connecting with people far outweighs that temporary feeling of crossing things off of my list. Not only is it a much more pleasant way to run errands, but also everything flows more rhythmically and things get done more easily when my intention is bigger than the narrow desire to get things done.

The intention behind any action permeates the entire activity. Jonathan Goldman in his book *Healing Sounds* speaks of how deeply the intention of the person creating music affects the listener. He used muscle testing to record how his body responded to a particular symphony. In describing the experience, he said,

> *I listened to a classical piece performed by an orchestra with a well-known conductor. While I listened to this piece of music, I had my muscles tested for strength or weakness. (And I was strong.) I was also asked to observe my respiration and my heart beat; both of these were slow; I was breathing deeply and regularly. Then I listened to the same piece of classical music performed by the same orchestra with a different conductor. Before I was muscle tested, I was again asked to observe my heartbeat and respiration. Much to my amazement, I found my breathing was shallow and my pulse was fast. When I was muscle tested, I tested weakly. What was different? It was the same piece of music with the same orchestra!*
>
> *How could such a dramatic change have taken place within my body? The answer lay with the conductor. The first conductor was a man who was loved and revered by the classical community. He really seemed to be in touch with the flow of the music that was being created and acted as a conduit for it. His music made me*

strong. The second conductor was a very strict and regimented man who created
fear in those with whom he worked. His music always had to be perfect. His
reputation and his ego were committed every time he picked up the baton. His
music made me weak. Here was a perfect example of intention creating the
difference in the effect of the music. The sound had been the same and yet the
influence it had had upon me was very different."

The intention of any action is carried on the wave of that action. The second conductor was creating music to make himself feel better about himself, and thus it had to be a particular way. Control took over and generated fear and resistance that were literally transferred along the waves of sound. The first conductor was there for the love of music and for the joy of giving it to the world. His intention flowed out of him and touched the orchestra. Then the music flowed out of the orchestra, along the waves of sound and empowered the listener.

We can even see the power of intention in the timbre of our voice. Take for example the phrase, "I like you." When the intention is to let a person know of our warm feelings, there is a certain texture to our voice. Now imagine how the quality of our voice would change if these words carried a sexual connotation. The vibration of our voice carries the intention of our words. Now imagine saying them to someone whom we truly dislike. When we are conscious, we can feel the flatness of our voice as it carries the feeling tone that lies underneath the words.

To check into the reason why we are doing or saying any particular thing in our lives can clean up our lives immensely. Take for example the simple act of reaching for a bite of food. The intention makes all the difference in the outcome. If your purpose for eating a cookie is to numb out, it causes upset in your body that ripples out throughout your life. If the intention is to nourish your body, the body will receive it in a way that promotes health and love.

Checking out our intention also helps immensely in the art of communication. Let us say you are having some difficulty with a friend and have asked to talk with them. If the intention behind your words is to make them see what they are doing wrong, you will find yourself caught in war. If your intention is to bring forth good communication and a healing resolution, holding this intention can heal even the most daunting situations.

We take back deep regions of our own power as we learn the art of pausing before an action or communication and asking ourselves why we are doing it. Play with this today. As you embark upon an activity, ask yourself what it is that you wish to accomplish through these actions or words. Once you see why you are doing or saying any particular thing, it becomes much easier to either let go of unskillful actions or transform them into skillful ones.

THE POSSIBILITY

The peaks were the recognition that it is a harmonious, purposeful, creating Universe. The valleys came in recognizing that humanity wasn't behaving in accordance with that knowledge.

Edgar Mitchell, US Astronaut

As we become comfortable with the power of engaging with the river of our lives and then learn how to partner with Life through living in questions, allowing, and holding a space with the highest of intentions, it becomes evident that we are learning to dance with Life in this way not just to fulfill our own desires. We are learning it so that we can hold the space of healing for our loved ones, for people we've never met and for the Earth as a whole.

That is the first step. The second step, and the most creative thing a human being can do is to show up for our own lives—to cultivate more and more moments where we open to Life—right *here*, right *now*. There is a process that has been going on since the beginning of the Universe and we are a part of it. The place that we discover it; the place where we connect with it; the place where we partner with it is *now*. Our lives have been given to us so that we can *be* this Awakening and then evoke it in all that we see. In this we become healers in the world.

There is unbelievable power in one human being who can be present for Life and at the same time hold and vibrate in the very cells of his or her being the fullness of the healing that is awaiting all of us. Vibrating the possibility of Love and then living in the question, "What can I do that is for the healing of all beings?" allows our lives to become an opening in the field of contraction. Into this space the next step in evolution—the next shift in the consciousness of this planet—can be made known. Into that spaciousness Life will flood us with its highest—with clarity, with compassion and with wisdom—for our own healing and for the healing of all beings.

May we discover the safety and joy of engaging with the river of Life rather than trying to manage it.

May we learn the art of holding to the highest while at the same time showing up for the living process.

May we know the safety of letting go and may we trust the resistance to doing this.

Core Intention: It's safe to let go into the flow

Chapter 11
Healing for All Beings

You Are the Universe

You are a child of Eternity—
A child of light, a child of joy.
Cradled in love's enfolding harmony,
Child of destiny you are.

You are the mother of Mystery—
Sister of dawn, lover of night.
Weaver of all possibility—
Deep tranquility you are.

Rise and dance among the stars;
Feel the passion in your heart.
Know the wonder of infinity—
Life's divinity you are.

You are the Universe unfolding—
A million years, a billion stars
Expanding into all things wonderful—
All things beautiful you are.

Rise and dance among the stars;
Feel the passion in your heart.
Know the wonder of infinity—
Life's divinity you are.

—A Song by
Mary Sue Phillips

THE GIFT OF DEEP ATTENTION

We don't see what is before us. That is our difficulty. We don't see what is before us. Our trouble as a species is that we don't know where we are. We don't know what surrounds us. We don't know what's about us. The task is to initiate ourselves into the Universe, into this enveloping mystery - a region of delight and excitement.

Brian Swimme

We were all mingling after a wonderful seminar on acupuncture. It was a crisp fall day in 1976 at the School of Natural Healing in Santa Cruz, where I was a part of the staff. The instructor, Al Drucker, was standing in the center of the room. He was a tall man and I found myself gazing up as I asked him a question. He was so fully present with me that the moment became alive. It was as if my life had been black and white, and all of a sudden it turned into Technicolor. I drank in the nectar of his full attention. He wasn't waiting for something to happen or desiring that I be any different than I was. I can't even remember what we were talking about. What was happening was way beyond words. His undivided Presence pried open the door of my struggling mind and I connected fully with my own life. I knew then that what we have all been searching for is right *here*, right under our very noses, and that we discover it when we stop looking somewhere else and pay attention.

The intention of this book has been to awaken within you the awesome power of being present for Life. The healing that comes from deep, focused attention is beyond our wildest imaginations. We not only transform our own experience, but we also have the ability to draw the rest of the world into engaging with the living moment of Life. The power of a moment of full human Presence is awesome. My experience with Al, in his willingness to be fully *here*, ignited me. The richness, the fullness of that moment reordered the whole intention of my life, and I became committed to being that fully present.

As more and more people have moments throughout the day when they are fully present for Life, something wonderful happens because everything exists to be known. Everything longs to be seen and heard for its part in the magical and mysterious unfolding called Life. Human awareness is the place in which this can happen. Human awareness *is* Life finally being able to see itself.

This doesn't mean that humanity is special in the universal scheme of things. Everything is essential and everything has a purpose. This is simply recognition of the role we are here to play. The human being is the part of Life that can bear witness to it all. We carry the capability of recognizing everybody else's story—the rock's story, the star's story, the eagle's story, the tree's story, the microbe's story—and of linking it all together as one undivided whole through deep attention.

In the past, we perceived Life in separate parts—each object and being waving the flag of separateness. In the act of giving undivided attention, we discover that we are all in this together. Unity is our fundamental nature. More and more moments of full attention shift our perception of Life from one in which we are separate, isolated and alone into the comprehension that we—along with everything else on Earth and in the Universe—are a part of a greater process.

Let us take a journey together to sharpen our alertness and hone our curiosity about the living moment, making it easier to give our full attention to Life. Either put this meditation on tape or else have a friend read it to you. If neither of these is possible, read it to the end and then close your eyes, and find your breath.

Be here for the rising and falling of this ancient rhythm. From this grounded place of simply opening to your breath, expand your awareness to receive the space you are in—a bathtub, a bus, a park, a prison cell. Really see it, allowing your awareness to fill the area.

Now expand your awareness so that you can look down and see the surrounding territory. Notice the movement of animals, people and cars. Observe the variety of colors, the dance of nature, the quality of light. See yourself there, sitting in the center of it all.

Expand your awareness farther, noticing landmarks, bodies of water, and towns. Slowly keep on expanding until you can see the surrounding states or countries, then the continent you live on, and finally the curve of the Earth.

Keep on expanding your awareness until you become big enough to see the entirety of the blue-green Earth as she rolls silently through space. Take in her stunning beauty. As your awareness continues to open so that the area around the Earth becomes larger than the planet itself, see that everywhere you look there is limitless space filled with billions of glittering stars.

But you are only seeing a small part of one galaxy. Expand your awareness one step further, beyond the edges of our galaxy to the realization that you are seeing millions of galaxies, each with billions of stars, dancing through space.

Now bring your awareness slowly back until the Earth is before you. This is home. Allow your heart to be moved by her beauty and her creativity. She is a living, growing being. She, too, has gone through phases—a birth, a childhood, an adolescence, and now she is approaching her adulthood. It took 4 billion years for her to reach this point, 4 billion years of imaginative creativity that transformed primordial particles into butterflies, sunsets, rainbows and you. All of the vast experimentation that has gone before has allowed you to be woven out of the Earth, coming out of its longing to know itself.

Now move towards the Earth until the planet is all that fills up your vision. As her curves go out of view, focus your attention on your continent, the town you are residing in and then the exact spot where you are. As you gaze upon yourself, move beyond the idea that you are a man, a woman or even a human being. You are a part of the Earth evolving into the fullness of its potential.

You are being gifted with a jewel from the heart of the Universe—the gift of Life. See your breath rising and falling, and see the oceans of the world coursing through your veins as the rhythm of the Universe beats your heart. You are alive because you have a part to play in the unfolding of evolution. And one of the greatest gifts you can give in return is to see Life—to really see it.

Now come back into the place where you are right now. Nothing is ordinary in this space. Whatever you are sitting on, the paper in this book, and even the light in the room are all made up of atoms that were once a part of a star! And it took the Earth a very long time to figure out how to create the eyes that you are seeing with, the air that you are breathing and even the cells of your body. Everything has been woven out of the primordial energy that was present at the unfolding of the Universe, and everything is permeated and penetrated by the sacred Intelligence of Life. Be stunned by the creative imagination of Life that could weave such a variety of things out of primordial dust!

This is it. *All of the billions of years of evolution have led to this moment. All of the millions of hours, minutes and seconds of your life have brought you to this place. Simply receive it. For a few moments, suspend all judgment and from this state of receptive alertness, be with what is. You are bearing witness to the moment that Life appears out of Mystery—the only moment when everything is brand new..*

The mind will resist, of course, creating conversations about Life rather than being with the real thing. Whenever you become aware that this is happening, just return and stand in awe of the miraculous process you are a part of.

Know that in these moments of being fully present for the living moment, you are making a difference. By being here, present to the sacred mystery of Life unfolding as your life, you are weaving the separate parts back into the whole for all beings.

IGNITING OTHER MINDS

Are you looking for me? I am in the next seat.
My shoulder is against yours.
You will not find me in stupas, not in Indian shrine rooms,
nor in synagogues, nor in cathedrals;
not in masses, nor kirtans, not in legs winding around your own neck,
nor in eating nothing but vegetables.
When you really look for me, you will see me instantly -
You will find me in the tiniest house of time.
Kabir says: Student, tell me, what is God?
It is the breath inside the breath.

Kabir

What happened on the journey we just took together is that your attention
became free from the confines of struggle so that it could bear witness to Life.
In these moments you became who you truly are. You are Awareness itself.
You are the ability to see what is happening rather than the happenings themselves.

The ability to be awake for moments throughout our day is the doorway to the
healing that Life longs for. Every time we are present, we move beyond the
struggling mind, taking all of humanity another step beyond war. All of the
wars, all of the greed and all of the violence on our planet come from human
minds that are lost in the illusion of separation. In a moment of being
present, we shift this illusion. It may feel like just a drop of Awakening in a
huge sea, but the power of a moment of being present is awesome. As more
and more people awaken, these drops become a rivulet, then a river and finally
a tidal wave of transformation that will ignite the collective mind.

As we learn how to cultivate deep attention throughout our day, some of the
most important moments we can be present for are those with our fellow
human beings. Most people don't have a clue about their beauty, their uniqueness and their interconnectedness with Life. Because of this, they stay caught
in the struggling mind, acting in ways that divide rather than unite and disconnect rather than connect. In being fully present with another, we open a door
and the sweet fragrance of *remembering* can touch their souls. It doesn't matter
if it is a belligerent attendant smoking a cigarette as he takes our money at the
gas station. What is before us comes from the heart of the Sacred. He may
not know who he is, but we can remember for him.

In the movie *Powder*, Jeremy is an albino who has been severely rejected by
society. But in his isolation, he has connected to his heart and to the possibilities for humanity. In one part of the movie, he is sitting in a park with a friend

of his who recognizes his wisdom and his sensitivity.

She asks him, "What are people like on the inside?"

He replies, "Inside of most people there's a feeling of being separate, separated from everything. And they're not. They are a part of absolutely everyone and everything."

"Everything?" she responds. "I am a part of this tree? You are telling me I am a part of some fisherman in Italy and some ocean that I've never even heard of and some guy sitting on death row? I am a part of him, too?"

"You don't believe me?" he queries.

"It's hard to believe that...all of that," she answers.

Pointing to her forehead he says, "It's because you have this spot that you can't see past. My Grams and Gramps had it—the spot where they were taught they were disconnected from everything."

"So that's what they would see if they could, that they're connected?" she asks.

He looks at her with that deep knowing and then says, "And how beautiful they really are. And that there's no need to hide and lie, and that it's possible to talk with someone without any lies, with no sarcasm, no deceptions, no exaggerations or any of the things that people use to confuse the truth."

"I don't know a single person who does that," she says.

We all long to be seen, fully seen. As I discovered that everyone is a facet of the Sacred and that the greatest gift I can give is my undivided attention, I began cultivating the willingness to be present throughout my day. After years of this, I am still filled with deep joy at how people respond to another human being who is fully with them.

One of my daily meditations is to truly *see* whomever I hand money to. It can be the cashier at the restaurant, the receptionist at the doctor's office or the gas station attendant. We're all so used to rushing and being rushed, and yet we are all so deeply hungry for non-judgmental, undivided attention. To watch what these few moments of connecting with another person can do for both of our lives is astounding. Even though most people won't consciously recognize what is happening, their whole being will respond.

Think about how good it feels to encounter someone who meets your eyes with a smile. When we greet someone with a warm smile, we draw them into the activity of Love that is the basis of the Universe. That is why it is so wonderful to be in the Presence of a great master. They're *here*! We are reminded who we really are simply by their Presence.

I have heard many stories from people about how moments of true connection transformed their lives. Sharon Salzberg, author of *Loving-Kindness*, tells a wonderful story of a young man who was a child in Cambodia when his country was at war. His village was occupied, and all of the children were imprisoned in a barbed-wire encampment. Four times a day people were brought within view of the children to be killed. The little ones were forced to watch and warned that if any of them cried, they would be next.

Every day the young man went through this agonizing experience. To feel would have been deadly, so he disconnected. When he was finally adopted by an American family, a part of him knew that in order to survive in this new environment, he had to open his heart again. He said he learned this by looking into the gaze of love given to him by his foster father. Over and over again he received those moments of deep attention, and those moments dissolved his armoring, opening him back into Life.

In my retreats, one of the most transforming exercises we do is to fully receive another person. We begin with two people sitting and facing one another. Initially, both people keep their eyes closed, taking a few minutes to ground in the breath. Then one person opens his or her eyes and takes time to really see the other. Staying focused on colors, lines, circles, and the dance of shadow and light, the seeing person keeps on bringing his or her attention back to the person who is before them, allowing the heart to open. After awhile the partners shift roles so that each of them can see and be seen. When people are given the opportunity to gift a person with their undivided attention, afterwards they often speak with awe of the beauty they see in the other person's face and form. And when people tell about being seen, what usually shows up is the recognition of the deep hunger that is fed when someone takes the time to be fully present with them.

The transformative power of deep attention happens not only with people, but also with experiences. Grocery stores are a great place of Awakening for me. I often wake up while standing in the checkout line and remember that what is happening is so much more than just people shopping. It is a moment in which the Earth is unfolding to itself. In being fully present, I experience myself as the unfolding becoming conscious of itself. Great caring for and recognition of all the beings and things around me floods my being, and I feel connected with Life.

I know also that I am inviting everybody else into that joy of belonging. Having moments such as these when we recognize the wholeness of Life at the same time we are immersed in the actual experience of Life—whether it be in grocery stores, movie theaters, sports stadiums or while driving down the freeway—touches every person there, whether they are aware of it or not, and contributes to the Awakening of humanity.

We must not forget to include ourselves among the people who yearn for our undivided attention. For most of us it's been a very long time since we experienced this. We are not only disconnected, living in a struggling mind a good deal of the time, but we've also become an ongoing project to ourselves, never quite discovering that moment when we simply can be with ourselves for exactly who we are.

After you read this section, put down the book and close your eyes. Take a few deep breaths and turn your attention to the experience of your life in this moment. Let go of the past and the future and become curious about what is happening right now. Who is sitting here? Of all of the millions of possible human experiences, what are you experiencing right now?

Allow your awareness to be like a finger, exploring first your physical experience (hungry stomach, tight neck, tingling in your feet). Then explore your emotional nature. What feelings are here— contentment, agitation, curiosity, resistance? And what is your mind doing? Is it focused, curious about what's happening, or is it easily distracted? No judgment. Just deep curiosity about what is appearing right now. Allow whatever is here to be. Allow it to be enough.

When you notice you've again drifted off into your story, bring your attention back to curiosity, to giving yourself what you deeply long for—your own undivided attention. When you are ready, open your eyes, and before you begin to read again, take a few moments to really see the space you are sitting in. For this moment, belong to your own life.

No matter where we are or what we are doing, attention heals by transforming how energy manifests and flows. When caught in the middle of an argument, in stepping back and really seeing the other person—seeing through their reactions into the place of commonality—something changes. When we pay attention to disturbances in our bodies and truly listen, the energy of contraction is freed. When we take a moment to truly see a tree, the whole energy field of the forest is shifted. This transformation can happen with ourselves, our loved ones, pets, children on the street and even with our food. Really seeing anything and recognizing its connection to everything transforms the field of energy.

These moments may happen only sporadically at first and may feel like just a drop of water in a lake, but a lake is made up of drops of water. Shifting our awareness, at least for moments, out of the constant struggle of the wanting and fearing mind touches everybody on the planet.

The way this works is illustrated by the *Hundredth Monkey Principle* which is based on a documented experience with the monkeys on the Japanese Island of Koshima between 1952 and 1958. The monkeys had been observed in the wild for over 30 years. In 1952, scientists were providing the monkeys with sweet potatoes, dropped in the sand. The monkeys liked the taste of the raw sweet potatoes, but they found the dirt unpleasant. An 18 month-old female named Imo found she could solve the problem by washing the potatoes in a nearby stream. She taught this trick to her mother. Her playmates also learned this new way, and they taught their mothers, too. Over the next six years, all the young monkeys learned to wash their sweet potatoes before eating them, but only the adults who imitated their children learned this skill. Then something startling took place. One night in the autumn of 1958, every single monkey in the tribe was observed to be washing their potatoes. This was pretty amazing, but the most amazing thing was that, without any inter-island contact, this habit spontaneously showed up on the surrounding islands.

We make a difference with our lives. As we wash our daily experiences in the water of deep attention, we invite people whom we may never even meet back into the spaciousness of a focused mind and an available heart.

IGNITING LOVE IN THE WORLD

The first peace, which is the most important, is that which comes within the soul of people when they realize their relationship, their oneness, with the Universe and all its powers, and when they realize that at the center of the Universe dwells the Great Spirit, and that this center is really everywhere. It is within each of us.

Black Elk

Why are moments of deep attention so powerful? Whenever we are fully present with whatever is before us, we ignite the truth of its interior world, which is Love. At the beginning of my Awakening, I had an experience that brought me face to face with that Love. After fasting for two weeks, I was sitting beside a quiet lagoon on the lake where I lived. It was a vibrant, sunny autumn day, with all of the foliage colors blessing me with their beauty. I was fully and completely *here*. In a flash, my whole field of perception changed and I saw Love radiating from everything, including myself. Tears of joy and relief welled up from deep inside.

Love is the ground of the Universe. It is the activity of attraction that resides inside every atom, in the call of the bull elk in the crisp fall air, in the gravity that keeps the Earth dancing around the sun, and in humankind's longing to know the Sacred. It is the unifying, electrifying, radiant energy that brought it all forth and that permeates and penetrates everything. To express moments of undivided, non-judgmental receptivity to Life ignites the Presence of Love. These moments are the time when the activity of Love (full attention) meets the expression of Love (Life).

The experience with Al Drucker that I spoke of at the beginning of the chapter was so powerful because it was Love in expression. By Love I don't mean the feelings of wanting and holding which we usually call love. This is far beyond that. It is undivided attention to the immediacy of Life. It includes fascination, care, curiosity, respect and recognition that what is before us is a unique part of a great unfolding. It contains no desire to hold onto or change anything. It is simply receptive, non-judgmental alertness focused on *what is.*

If you've ever fallen in love, you may remember that at first, before the struggling mind took over, there were moments when you had no expectations or fears—just pure connection. Everything that happened was included in this field of joy. This is Love in action, but it is the kind of love that requires an external stimulus (a lover) and demands that things stay in a certain way.

The Love evoked by deep attention is unfiltered, free to be with whatever is. It doesn't matter whether your life at that moment is terrible or wonderful, whether you've been feeling good or bad, whether what is in front of you is likable or unlikable, human or vegetable, black or white, young or old. It simply receives Life exactly as it is. All presumed boundaries dissolve, and the core illusions of separation—struggle, fear, isolation and despair—fall away to be replaced by a sense of connection, safety, belonging and a cellular awe of the preciousness and interconnectedness of Life.

Patricia Sun had a vision once when she asked what the purpose of her life was. Her inner knowing responded by saying, "To end all wars." After she moved beyond her disbelieving laughter, she asked what that meant. She saw in her mind's eye the Earth from space, breathtakingly beautiful, gloriously creative. She also saw that approaching the Earth from space were beams of light. As Patricia looked more closely, she could see that the leading edge of each of the beams was a countenance, neither male nor female, but a face of someone who had learned how to totally love themselves while still in a body.

As she watched in wonder, these beams of light came to the Earth and found people whom they could look straight in their eyes, giving them the gift of pure Love. This ignited these people into true and lasting Love. They would then turn to other people and ignite them. This wave of Love spread across the face of the planet in a heartbeat, and written in the sky above the Earth was "20 years". She had this vision in the 70's, and if we look closely, we can now see evidence of this Awakening of the heart everywhere.

We not only cultivate deep attention so that we can ignite Love in the world, but also so that we ourselves can be filled and healed by the Presence of Love. The Dalai Lama was asked why we should cultivate awareness of the present moment. His answer was that this is the only place where Love exists. The rest of it is just an idea about Love.

We are all so deeply hungry for the nourishment of Love. When we are focused on the living moment, we are then available to the depth of Love that is always being given to us, radiating from absolutely everything and penetrating every breath we breathe. This is our destiny, our birthright, to merge with the living moment, with the sea of Love that is Life.

THE POWER OF DEEP ATTENTION

(An astronaut speaking to himself about his spacewalk) "Do you deserve this, this fantastic experience? Have you earned this in some way? Are you separated out to be touched by God, to have some special experience that others cannot have? And you know that answer to that is "No." There's nothing you've done to deserve this, to earn this; it's not a special thing for you.

You know very well at that moment and it comes through to you so powerfully, that you're the sensing element for man. You look down and see the surface of that globe that you've lived on all this time and you know all those people down there, and they are like you, they are you and somehow you represent them. You are up here as the sensing element—that point out on the end—and that's a humbling feeling.

It's a feeling that says you have a responsibility. It's not for yourself. The eye that doesn't see doesn't do justice to the body. That's why it's there; that's why you are out there. And somehow you recognize that you're a piece of this total Life. And you're out there on that forefront and you have to bring it back somehow. And that becomes a rather special responsibility, and it tells you something about your relationship with this thing we call Life.

So that's a change. That's something new. And when you come back there's a difference in that world now. There's a difference in that relationship between you and that planet and you and all those other forms of life on that planet because you've had that kind of experience. It's a difference and it's so precious."

Russell Schweickart, US Astronaut

You and I are the sensing element for humankind. We are being brought—step by step, turn by turn—back into immediate connection with Life. We are also beginning to realize how powerfully transforming a moment of full attention is. It not only ignites Love in the world but it also gives us many other gifts:

Attention is one of the most powerful tools for healing physical difficulties. In fact, if the art of true attention could be bottled, pharmaceutical companies would have a bidding war to buy the rights. Luckily it is something within the reach of whoever has the commitment to learn how to do it. Jeanne Achterberg, in an interview on healing with Jeffrey Mishlove, said, "In looking at other systems of medicine, when you sort out the doctrinal ideas that have evolved for particular reasons and for particular places, you have one ingredient left. That is to take the mind and move it to the problem, giving attention to that place where there is discomfort or disharmony. And some of those systems say nothing more is needed." Nothing more is needed! The power of attention is powerful beyond our wildest imagination.

The best self-defense courses are those that also teach the art of being present. If we are truly present for Life, we can more easily sense ourselves in situations that would become a threat to our physical being. We could feel the energy in a room or down a street before we ever even entered them and thus have the information with which to make skillful choices. And if we are ever in a dangerous situation, focused attention allows us to make quick and clean decisions.

Deep attention also connects us with the sea of Intelligence that is always speaking to us below the busy everyday mind. It opens the door to our natural inclination towards reverence, awe and trust. We live in the middle of, and are each an integral part of, an absolutely fantastic unfolding. Think of all that has appeared out of stardust—huge glaciers, tiny mountain wild flowers, bats, blue lagoons, diamonds, elephants and snowflakes. Awe is a wonderful thing. It is our destiny, our birthright and our way back home. As the Buddha said, "Rapture is the gateway to Nirvana." When the power of awe and reverence flood our being and we begin to vibrate at higher levels, we discover that this is the greatest way to create.

The greatest power of deep attention is that it can bring us to the ultimate healing—that of merging with Life. For most of us, there is still a *me* listening to something happening *out there*. We may recognize that we are a part of it. But the next step is to recognize that we *are* it. When we were asleep, we were not conscious about Life at all. It is as if we lived beside a very beautiful sea, and we never even noticed it. As we awaken, we see it and become very curious. We explore the edges, the color of the water, and watch the ever-changing dance of the waves. At moments, we even dive into it. At those times our awareness is freed from becoming, and we simply relate with the sea. But there is still a sense of separation, a sense that we are swimming in the sea but we are not a part of it. The final step is when our awareness merges into Life and we realize we *are* the sea. We don't exactly experience this place because in those moments there is no one there to experience it. But to be this, even for a moment at this time in evolution, is to become irrevocably and powerfully changed forever.

THE VISION FROM THE MOUNTAIN

The basis of the new world order must be universal respect for human rights, but it will mean nothing as long as this imperative does not derive from the respect of the miracle of Being, the miracle of the Universe, the miracle of Nature, the miracle of our own existence. Only someone who submits to the authority of the universal order and of creation, who values the right to be a part of it and a participant in it, can genuinely value himself and his neighbors and thus honor their rights as well.

Vaclav Havel, President of the Czech Republic

As we learn how to be present for our lives for moments throughout our day, the world is healed. A story that I have used in my work speaks clearly of the journey we've been exploring and of where we are heading. It begins with a child standing at the end of a great valley. This child is you and represents the innocence you experienced when you were young. You were awake, but you weren't aware. As you stand at the end of this great valley, you can see at the other end a regal and mighty Mountain, breathtaking in its beauty. You know someplace deep inside that your life is a journey to the Mountain, a journey to the curiosity and compassion of an awakened mind. Onto your back goes your pack, and you start down the trail into the valley of the mind that believes it is separate from Life.

While making the descent in the first few years of your life, you can still see the Mountain, still stay in touch with your connection with Life. But the older you get, the deeper you penetrate the valley until the time comes when you can no longer see even glimpses of the snow capped peak. The trees of everyday life block your view, and you lose sight of the destination. But it is spellbinding down here in the valley of daily life. For awhile you are fascinated, intent on gathering as many objects, dollars and experiences as you can, forgetting that this is not the purpose of your life.

When you were young, your resilience in dealing with all of the challenges of Life was still strong. But as you went into the valley, it became more challenging. There were lions and tigers and bears. The raging river of fear that you had to cross over and over again had hidden along its banks pools filled with the quicksand of self-judgment. At times you found yourself lost in the seemingly endless bogs of desire. Your body was full of bruises that came from the hidden drop-offs of disappointment. And during the firestorms of rage that passed through you, consuming all of the available oxygen, you knew the terror of being unable to breathe.

Eventually you came to know the mind-numbing confusion of losing a sense of direction in the deep forest of the separate self. After one too many times of having to cross the treacherous river, and after forgetting that your life is a journey to the Mountain of your own true nature, something inside of you closed down and you began to view Life from the very narrow perspective of struggle, control and fear.

At this point in the journey, you came to a fort built deep in the woods. This is the prison of the mind. There was the illusion of warmth, nourishment and safety, but it was not the warmth of the heart nor the nourishing food of communion with Life. You noticed that many people lived here, so you assumed it must be the destination of your journey, and you stayed for awhile. If you were lucky, however, something spurred you on, pulling you back into the cold and the wild, back into facing the challenges of your life.

A short while after leaving the fort, and without you even noticing it, the valley begins a gradual ascent. One day, while treed by a lion, you glimpse a patch of white through the forest. You have no idea what it is, but a thrill runs through your body. There is renewed determination to continue on, even though you're not sure of where you are going, your food supply is low and your energy drained. Trees begin to thin and you get more glimpses of white. Penetrating through the thick fog of the judging, fearing mind comes the wonderful idea that maybe, just maybe you haven't done your journey *wrong*, and it wasn't just the random wanderings of a confused mind. Possibly, just possibly, every step brought you to this place of being pulled and touched by a simple patch of white.

Then one day the trail takes a turn and there before you, in all of its splendor, is the Mountain. Memories from the first few years of your life when you stood at the end of the valley and then began the journey come flooding back to you, and you know your destiny is to climb the Mountain. With renewed vigor, you begin your ascent.

The higher you go, the broader the view. It isn't that the Mountain is a place of ease and bliss. It is full of challenges. But whenever one of your core life lessons threatens to overwhelm you, you secure your ice ax, rope off and turn around. There before you is the panorama of Life and you discover yourself as a part of a greater process. Everywhere you look you see the natural wisdom of Life unfolding before you in the dance of the seasons, in the rhythm of the tides and in the heart beat of Life that permeates every atom, rock, leaf, cell and even you. In a flash, you move out of disconnection, discovering yourself as a part of this great, rhythmic dance.

You understand that your life has never been lived in isolation. You look at your hands and see all of your ancestors present right there, back through your own family tree and on to the mighty incubator of the oceans. As you look out across the broad expanse of the Universe, you recognize that your very existence is dependent upon everything that has ever been. With deep gratitude you acknowledge all you have been given along the way. You were showered with the energy of the sun, quenched with precious sweet water, nourished with the very essence of the Earth, loved by the trees, the ground, the wind and the sky, and animated by the breath within the breath of Life. This spacious view sees no objects, only the Universe unfolding in a web of interconnected Being. As this awareness penetrates every nook and cranny of your consciousness, you come to recognize that everything is sacred—every moment, being and thing—every atom molecule and cell— every breath. You realize that your destiny is to see this, live this, breathe this. In this moment, you belong to Life.

You see the valley you traversed and understand the absolute perfection of every single experience on your journey—every single one. All of the joy and sorrow were essential and prepared you for the vision of connection and compassion that comes after scaling this mighty peak. Your whole perception of your daily life shifts. Rather than being a series of random events that need to be controlled and feared, you see it as the dance of the Universe awakening. You soften and open completely into the living adventure that is your life, knowing that it will include pleasure and pain, loss and gain. The urge to manage it dissolves into your willingness to show up and merge with Life as it unfolds out of Mystery. In each moment of willingness you belong to your own life.

As you look down into the valley you see how many people still live alienated lives, many of them caught in immense suffering, cut off from the greater process, cut off from the knowing that Life is *for* them in every single experience. And your heart opens to the deepest of suffering, to the littlest of children and to even the most heinous of criminals and the most despicable of rulers. The tattered threads of human life are being woven back together in the spaciousness of your heart. You now know that you have made it to the Mountain not only for your own healing, but also for the healing of all beings.

Your struggles were the struggles of the whole; the heartaches you have faced and the pain you have met are common threads in the web of delusion that ensnares all beings.

The Mountain has another truth to reveal. When you saw the Mountain from the trail in the valley, you thought the summit was your final destination. But as you climb, the summit is obscured from view and all you can see is the terrain you are climbing through. The higher up and the more challenging it becomes, the more you need to pay close attention to each step. As your attention becomes totally focused on each step, you suddenly realize that the destination is this step—this moment—and that every step is the destination. You comprehend that you make a difference by showing up for your own life, step by step, owning, belonging to and working with the process Life has given you, while recognizing that your life is part of a greater process.

As you descend again into the valley of the mind that believes it is separate from Life, you bring the perspective of the Mountain with you wherever you go. You willingly go back to the valley because now you have the ability to live surrounded by the narrowness of the illusion of separation and not be seduced. You are able to use your mind to unite rather than divide and to connect rather than disconnect. In the marrow of your bones you have a deeper understanding of what is happening—the threads of Life are being woven together in your heart.

THE VIEW FROM THE HEART

...if the truth appears once, in one single mind, that is enough to ensure that nothing can ever prevent it from spreading to everything and setting it ablaze.

Fr. Pierre Teilhard de Chardin

You and I are living in an extraordinary time. Not only are individuals making it to the Mountain, but humanity itself is approaching its base. More and more people are remembering their wholeness in the middle of the ups and downs of daily life, no matter how challenging they seem. More and more of us are living from the spacious view from the Mountain that is the view from the heart. The heart knows that only one thing is happening here—humanity is waking up and weaving Life back into its heart.

Because of our technology and our curiosity, we've discovered that we are living on a fairly small, exquisitely beautiful and extremely fragile planet, somewhere in the arm of a spiral galaxy that is dancing in space with myriad other galaxies. And it's finally beginning to dawn on us that we're all in this together! As Sultan Bin Salman al-Saud of Saudi Arabia said about his space flight, "The first day or so we all pointed to our countries. The third or fourth day we were pointing to our continents. By the fifth day we were aware of only one Earth."

We can no longer live from the view of separation and disconnection. Through all of the crises we are now facing, we are being pushed, prodded and pulled into the next step of the unfolding of Life. This step lies in humanity's ability to perceive all of the parts of Life as interconnected pieces of an astounding whole.

Everything is our kin throughout all time and space. In our bones are the minerals of mountains. In our blood is the water from the sea. The cells in our bodies are made up of atoms from everything that has ever been. Our roots and the roots of everything we see reach back through the birth pangs of our planet and even back to the stars. This shift of perception also recognizes that the river of breath that moves through us is the same river of breath that moves through all beings. We are part of an interconnected web of being.

What is happening in human minds and hearts is as big as when Life came out of the sea and onto the land. After a long journey into the farthest reaches of separation, humanity is now reconnecting, weaving the parts back into the whole that it is. This transformation is a radical and often disruptive process. Because we are in transition, we find ourselves in a time of great environmental and cultural disruption. This crisis includes the individual, the environment and human society as a whole. And at the same time, we stand on a threshold of great possibility. The word thresh means "to thrash or beat apart." We are literally being cracked wide open—opened back into Life.

The way we respond may make the difference between survival and extinction, between the continuation of songbirds and mountain waterfalls and the end of life as we know it. In order to move from destruction to creation, we need to remember the power of vision—to remember the view from the Mountain. Chogyam Trungpa, author of *Cutting Through Spiritual Materialism* said, "We can trade our small minded struggle for security for a much vaster vision, one of fearlessness, openness and genuine heroism." Life is asking nothing less of us than to stand on the Mountain, lifting ourselves out of ordinary consciousness into a vision of possibility and interconnection.

Sister Miram MacGillis, speaking about how powerful vision is in this time of birth, gives an analogy of planting a date tree in the Middle East. She says that it takes commitment to a greater process to plant a date tree because we will probably never eat any of its fruit. It takes 80 years for the tree to grow roots deep enough to tap into the scarce water that is needed in order to bear fruit.

And during those 80 years, the tree is so buffeted by the forces of nature in that region that for most of the time the tree looks like it's dying. If we didn't understand the process it would be easy to come in and make a judgment about the severity of its condition and cut it down. *If we understand the process, we can make the commitment.* We are being asked to plant the *date tree* of vision for the Earth and for all generations to come.

The date tree story reminds us of an essential piece of the puzzle we need to understand in order to hold vision—that challenges are an integral part of the unfolding of Life. Carl Jung spoke of the necessity of challenges when he said, "The serious problems in Life....are never fully solved. *If ever they should appear to be so, it is a sure sign that something has been lost.* The meaning and purpose of a problem seems to lie not in its solution but in our working at it incessantly." Problems are here as midwives for our shift of perception. When we can lift our awareness out of the mind that sees itself as separate, we tap into a creative field which brings a depth of healing that was formerly inconceivable.

The view from the Mountain—the view of the heart that goes beyond good and bad, right and wrong—can hold it all and create a space that the creativity of the Universe can fill with wisdom and intelligence. Whether this is with our own challenges, those of our loved ones, or the crisis that the Earth is now facing, know that holding the space of possibility makes a difference. Poet and author Wendell Berry wrote a poem that touches me to my core:

> *In the dark of the moon...*
> *in the dead of night.....*
> *in the dead of winter......in flying snow,*
> *the world in danger,*
> *families dying.......wars spreading,*
> *I walk the rocky hillside*
> *sowing clover.*

We have been living on the rocky hillside of the separate human mind, the hillside of struggle and war. And yet we can choose to plant clover. To be able to remember the truth of our wholeness in the midst of chaos and to be able to hold this for all beings is powerful beyond our wildest imaginations.

See the Earth in your mind's eye and feel the possibility of Life awakening to the fullness of its potential. Begin with yourself. Be willing to suspend all judgment and pessimism for just a moment and dream big. Dream way beyond your ordinary ideas of your future. As you open to possibility, feel the softening in your mind and the soaring of your heart. Feel the joy, the radiance, the exuberance and the energy rising in you as you claim the truth of what is calling to you.

Be willing to live for just this day as if the fullness of your possibility is true. Feel it in your body, explore it in your mind. Claim yourself and live the reason why you have been born.

Now dream big again. Dream a dream of healing for the world. Imagine what it will be like as more and more people show up for the living moment, bearing witness to the astounding creativity and breathtaking beauty that permeates everything. Contemplate the choices that people would make if they recognized the sacred dimension that resides at the heart of absolutely everything. In this moment, hold the space for this to happen all over the Earth.

Be willing to live for just this day in the knowing that everything in your life is sacred—every person, thing and experience. And in this recognition, give your full attention to as much of your life as possible. Know that this makes a difference for yourself and for the world.

WE MAKE A DIFFERENCE

Men are capable not only of fear and hate, but also of hope and benevolence. If the populations of the world can be brought to see and to realize, in imagination, the hell to which hate and fear must condemn them on the one hand and, on the other, the comparative heaven which hope and benevolence can create by means of new skills, the choice should not be difficult, and our self-tormented species should allow itself a life of joy such as the past has never known.

Bertrand Russell

One of the most important things to know is that as individuals, we make a difference in the healing of the Earth through our own Awakening. The yearning of Life to come together in its wholeness is at work in our own lives right now—no matter what is happening! Our lives are not ours alone. Our experiences, thoughts, feelings are not separate, isolated events. They are the Earth fulfilling its destiny. Our existence is a part of a vast unfolding and comes out of the longing of Life to know itself.

Rumi said,

It is as if a king has sent you to a country to carry out one special, specific task. You go to the country and you perform a hundred other tasks, but if you have not performed the task you were sent for, it is as if you have performed nothing at all.

So man has come into the world for a particular task and that is his purpose. If he doesn't perform it, he will have done nothing.

The task for each one of us as individual parts of the planet is to show up for our own lives! The journey up the Mountain reminds us that the path is beneath our feet — the destination is this moment with all of the joys and sorrows inherent in it. We don't need to figure it out or try to find the part we are here to play; it will reveal itself as we pay attention. As we show up for our lives, the Creative Intelligence that brought us forth out of Mystery will flood us with its Presence.

Showing up for Life happens in the willingness to pay attention to the living moment. It happens in the commitment to sit quietly every day and invite our restless mind out of *becoming* and into paying attention to *what is*. It happens in the willingness to ground in the actual experience of our daily lives, using our senses to make contact.

Showing up for Life happens in the ability to notice that there is a conversation that over and over again captures us back into a dream about Life, a dream that is filled with wanting, fearing and struggle. It happens in the courage to realize this conversation is not who we are. To be able to relate to this conversation rather than being pushed and pulled by it all day long opens up the possibility of making direct, immediate contact with Life. This contact not only allows access to an Intelligence that is beyond the ordinary mind's perception—an Intelligence that holds the answers to all of the challenges that we are now facing—but it also illuminates whatever it is paying attention to, weaving it back into the fabric of the whole.

Showing up for Life also happens in the journey back into our own hearts. There is no one on the planet who is more deserving of mercy than we are. And yet, like most people, we compare ourselves over and over again to a mythical idea of perfection and usually find ourselves coming up short. Because vast regions of ourselves are deemed unacceptable, we live in war, never accepting ourselves for all of who we are. And because we live in war, the planet lives in war.

A few years ago, my Awakening groups lived in the question, "Why are we gathered together?" Not why *do* we gather together, but why *are* we gathered together every week to explore the healing of awareness and mercy? One morning, in the middle of a meditation, the following answers came to me:

- ♦ To belong to Life, to belong to our own life, to trust the activity of Love.
- ♦ To belong to Life, to belong to our own life, to know the activity of Love.

- To belong to Life, to belong to our own life, to become the activity of Love.

To belong to Life means that, even though we have been living in the land of contraction and separation, we deeply and intimately belong to this process. Our very bodies are woven out of stars, and our essence is connected to everything throughout all time and space.

To belong to our own lives means that even though we may have lost trust in the journey that we are on, it is a trustable one. It's not always an easy one, but it is always *for* us. As we begin to show up, we begin to *trust* the activity of Love. As we begin to trust, we learn to *know* the activity of Love. And as we begin to *know*, we *become* the activity of Love.

PATIENCE

The enlightened being is infinitely grateful to those who have gone before, infinitely compassionate to those who are now present and infinitely responsible for those who are to come.

Unknown

When we know we are making a difference for all of Life simply by our willingness to be present for Life and to touch it as much as we can with our hearts, it becomes easier for us to make a daily commitment to remember the Mountain and to be present in the valley. There is great joy in seeing ourselves as a part of a greater process, committing our lives to making a difference to the whole. George Bernard Shaw speaks about this in a most inspiring way:

This is the true joy in life, the being used for a purpose recognized by yourself as a mighty one, the being a force of nature instead of a feverish selfish little clod of ailments and grievances, complaining that the world will not devote itself to making you happy.

I am of the opinion that my life belongs to the whole community and as long as I live, it is my privilege to do for it whatever I can.

I want to be thoroughly used up when I die, for the harder I work, the more I live. I rejoice in life for its own sake. Life is no "brief candle" to me. It is a sort of splendid torch which I have got hold of for the moment, and I want to make it burn as brightly as possible before handing it on to future generations.

Is it easy to move out of struggle and into connection, out of pessimism and into possibility? No. There is so much we need to digest—thousands of years of believing in separation and all of the dragons that this belief has birthed. Just as the tide needs to go out in order to come in again, our journey into separation was a necessary part of the unfolding of Life.

But something new is now showing up. As the thrill of possibility moves through us, we need to ground ourselves over and over again in the understanding that we can neither force this process to go faster nor can we slow it down. Just like the marigold, a network of forces that are far greater than our individual powers orchestrates our blossoming.

Besides courage, commitment and compassion, it takes a great deal of patience to mature into the ability to show up for Life. I have kept a passage from Brian Swimme's book *The Universe Is A Green Dragon* close to my heart as I have made the trek from valley to Mountain and from contraction to connection:

> *We emerge through the creativity of all that has gone before us. Give thanks. Struggle to become one with this enchanting mystery so that you can contribute, too. Suffer the withering pains of life so that you too can enter the adventure. The desire to make us over into Love permeates the whole Universe. We are initiated into Love when lured into the intense pursuit of the enchanted lover and if the initiation is long and filled with doubt and suffering, the learning takes hold deeply. The slow learner has so many more opportunities to see how shrewd Love can be as it penetrates all his character armor. Such stubborn human beings are the world's greatest lovers for they have been through an initiation that demanded many resources of Love. They make themselves just as irresistible and intelligent as Love in drawing others into the joy of living.*

For just this moment, stand on the Mountain and look down into the valley of your life. Move back through time and watch your progression from babyhood to childhood to adulthood. See all of the twists and turns, the clear times and the confusing times, the skillful times and the unskillful (even the really unskillful), and know the perfection of it all.

You could have come no other way. Move beyond any judgment of yourself, any desire that your life be different and any fear of what is to come, and recognize with great awe—and perhaps some relief—that this is a trustable process. It may not always be what you think you want, but it is trustable.

Feel the easing of your mind and the opening of your heart. This is a grand journey you are on. From this view and for just this moment *let go*. Hear the sounds around you. Feel the rising and falling of your breath. Show up for the living moment of your life. And know, that in showing up, not only are you healed, but so too is the world.

282

I leave you with the words from one of my favorite songs. It comes from the Moody Blues album, *A Question of Balance*.

After he had journeyed and his feet were sore and he was tired, he came upon an orange grove. And he rested. And he lay in the cool, and while he rested, he took to himself an orange and tasted it. And it was good. And he felt the Earth to his spine. And he asked and he saw the tree above him and the stars and the veins in the leaf and the light and the balance, and he saw magnificent perfection whereon he thought of himself in balance and he knew who he was.

Chorus: Just open your eyes, and realize the way it's always been. Just open your mind, and you will find the way it's always been. Just open your heart and that's a start..

He thought of those he angered, for he was not a violent man. And he thought of those he hurt, for he was not a cruel man. And he thought of those he frightened, for he was not an evil man. And he understood. He understood himself. Upon this he saw that when he was in anger or knew hurt or felt fear, it was because he was not understanding. And he learned compassion and with this eye of compassion he saw his enemies like unto himself. And he learned Love. Then he was answered.

Chorus: Just open your eyes and realize the way it's always been. Just open your mind and you will find the way it's always been. Just open your heart and that's a start.

May we all come to know that we are on the journey to the curiosity and compassion of an open heart.

May we, for more and more moments, show up for the living adventure that is our lives.

And may we know that a life committed to this Awakening, no matter what is appearing, *is a life that clears the pathway for all of the generations to come.*

Core Intention: Namaste

REFERENCES

The quotes in this books were collected over a span of many years, some from books, some from workshops I attended, some from tapes of workshops, some from interviews I watched on TV, and some from commercially produced audio and video tapes. And some of the quotes from books were received secondhand from audio tapes or talks I attended.

Since I took down these quotes originally for my own personal inspiration, I did not make notes of where most of them are from other than the name of the person to whom the quote is attributed. My intention in sharing these quotes is to inspire my readers with the footsteps of those who have gone before. I therefore hope that this acknowledgment will be sufficient. More information on the individuals quoted is available through the Web and through library catalogs.

In addition, I would like to personally acknowledge the major contributors to my own awakening as shared in this book—my teachers Stephen Levine, Jack Kornfield and Brian Swimme—by giving a list of their publications so that readers may access their wisdom directly.

Stephen Levine is a teacher of consciousness who teaches through his very being. Through his work with people in crisis and facing death, he has gained profound wisdom about living. And his life journey with his wife and soul partner Ondrea has deepened that wisdom. His books are published by Doubleday and include *A Gradual Awakening; Healing Into Life and Death; Who Dies?; Guided Meditations, Explorations and Healings; Embracing the Beloved: Relationship As a Path of Awakening;* and *A Year to Live: How to Live This Year As If It Were Your Last.* He also has many wonderful audio tapes, which can be accessed through the public library and various web sites that sell books and tapes such as amazon.com and barnesandnoble.com.

Jack Kornfield is a wonderful vipassana meditation teacher , cofounder of Insight Meditation Society and founder of Spirit Rock Meditation Center who has also been very influential in my awakening. His books include *After Ecstasy the Laundry: How the Heart Grows on the Spiritual Path* (2000, Bantam Books); *Soul Food: Stories to Nourish the Spirit and the Heart* (with Christina Feldman -- 1996, Harper Collins); *Living Dharma: Teachings of Twelve Buddhist Masters* (1996, Shambhala Publications); *Buddha's Little Instruction Book* (1994, Bantam Books); and *A Path With Heart* (1993, Bantam Books). His tapes are available through the Dharma Seed Tape Library (www.dharmaseed.org)

Brian Swimme is an inspired gravitational physicist who is the founder of the California Institute of Integral Studies. His video series *Canticle to the Cosmos* is, in my opinion, on of the great contributions to our collective awakening. He is also the author of *The Universe Is a Green Dragon* (1984, Bear, Santa Fe), *The Universe Story* (with Thomas Berry—1992, Harper San Francisco), and *The Hidden Heart of the Cosmos* (1996, Orbis Books). His books and tapes are available through the Center for the Story of the Universe at www.brianswimme.org.

I would also like to acknowledge the work of David Whyte, a Northwest poet and author whom I have quoted in several places. You can find out more about him, his beautiful poetry and his incredible work with bringing consciousness into corporate environments at www.davidwhyte.com

And special thanks to Jim Ayala, Northwest poet and sculptor, for his many beautiful poems on the title pages of this book. His web site is ayalasculptures.com. You may contact Jim at jayala@gte.net or PO Box 16096, Seattle, WA 98116.

MARY'S NEXT BOOK

due out in the Fall of 2002

To some degree we are all compulsive, with our compulsions ranging all the way from over-worrying and overworking to overeating and drugs. When we realize we are compulsive, our only option up to now has been control, but in trying to control our compulsions, they control us. If we do manage to stop one, another seems to take its place.

This book explores a new way to work with our compulsions, one that not only heals our need to be compulsive in the first place, but also allows our compulsions to guide us into the joy and peace that is our birthright.

Mary O'Malley

Author

Mary O'Malley is a speaker, author, group facilitator and counselor in private practice in Kirkland, Washington. For over 30 years she has explored and practiced the art of being truly present for Life, and out of this has evolved a system for awakening into the living moment of our lives which she calls *Awareness Meditation.* Through her organization, *Awakening,,* she invites others into a center of clarity, compassion and trust that can be accessed no matter what is happening in their lives. She offers an invitation to live from the place in which the impossible becomes possible and our hearts soar with the joy of being alive.

Mary is available for speaking engagements, retreats, workshops, phone and in-person counseling. To contact Mary:

email: awaken@maryomalley.com   web site: www.maryomalley.com

phone: 425-889-5937

Diane Solomon

Cover Artist

In 1979 my life turned an abrupt, jagged corner as I faced the accidental death of my 10 year old son. I sat in the stillness of my grief for a very long time. I became ill with a chronic disease. Four years later my cousin gave me a well-worn copy of *What Is Zen* by Alan Watts. I began to heal. As I grew in awareness, I returned to my childhood love of painting. It has been both the source and the end result of the spiritual journey I am on. Each of my paintings is a reminder that here – in this moment – is all the beauty and love we will ever need for awakening and healing.

email: dsolomon@snovalley.com   Web Site: www.inspiredmedicine.com